MY SISTER'S FATHER

Reclaiming Andre

DEBBY FRICKE SMITH

Copyright ©2019 Debby Fricke Smith

ISBN: 978-1-945190-67-4

All rights reserved. No part of this book may be reproduced in any form or by any electronic, mechanical, or other means now known or hereafter invented, including photocopying or recording, or stored in any information storage or retrieval systems without the express written permission of the publisher, except for newspaper, magazine, or other reviewers who wish to quote brief passages in connection with a review.

Please respect Author's Rights.

V-16

Intellect Publishing, LLC
6581 County Road 32, Suite 1195
Point Clear, AL 36564
www.IntellectPublishing.com
Inquiries to: info@IntellectPublishing.com

DEDICATION

For Andre J. Vleghels and Virginia D. Vleghels Fricke whose steadfast courage and sacrifice of self, mirrored the lives of hundreds of thousands of other Americans in like circumstances. They were ordinary citizens who answered freedom's call.

I have seen war. I have seen war on land and sea. I have seen blood running from the wounded... I have seen the dead in the mud. I have seen cities destroyed... I have seen children starving. I have seen the agony of mothers and wives.
I hate war.
Franklin D. Roosevelt

My Sister's Father

ACKNOWLEDGEMENTS

I have come to know many fine men from the 416TH Bomb Group who were always willing to listen to me, to answer my questions, and to share their stories. My search began with them. I have acquired a mound of correspondence and patient conversation from them—Marie Whitten, widow of Dolph Whitten, Ed Renth, my first contact, Billy Brewer, Ralph Conte, Wayne Downing, Bob Basnett, Floyd Henderson, John Geyer, Claude Brown, Robert Bower, and Willard Land. They have all been kind and gracious and welcoming. I will hold them dear, always.

I am grateful to Andy and Ginny for leaving a written legacy. Your words have illumined our family's past and revealed your humanity. I love you for it.

I owe a debt of gratitude to my sister, Sharon, who generously shared her father's missives with me and accompanied me on the pilgrimage of a lifetime. Together, we created new, unforgettable memories, healed old wounds, and cemented a love that binds. I am glad it was just the two of us.

Maurine Vleghels DeBusschere, Andy's sister, helped me to piece together the Vleghels family history. Through our regular visits over lunch, I have had the opportunity to know her and to love her.

The Suurland and Oosdijk families--their continual accommodation and infinite attention to detail made our pilgrimage all it could be and more. We know that we now have an extended family across the sea.

Mr. Zuurdeeg, the Keeper of the Records, never let me down. He always responded to my inquiries. The information dispensed by his office led us to our Dutch families and gave details of André's burial, previously unknown.

Nico J. van Vliet, a Dutchman from Utrecht, the Netherlands, enjoyed a remarkable career in communications, in the U.S. and abroad. When I caught up with him, he was living in Charleston, South Carolina. He didn't know me. He only knew of my mission. He happily agreed to translate Dutch records from Tholen documenting Andre's recovery and burial. He died on June 13, 2019 at the age of 92.

Mayor Nuis and Perry Bakx prepared a wonderful welcome for us and allowed us to be a part of their National Day of Remembrance on May 4, 2001.

Urged by his friend, Ralph Conte, the late Frank Perkins wrote an article about my endeavor that appeared in the *Star-Telegram*, Fort Worth, Texas. He told me that my story was unique and that I should "Continue the March".

My good friend, Susan Pearce, has been invaluable to me. A former English teacher, she read my submissions and made some constructive suggestions that helped the story expand and evolve. She believed in my pursuit and continually urged me to work toward publication.

My husband, Jeff, has always been there to assist me with his technical know-how. He supported all of my decisions to pursue my dream, without question, and "held down the fort" during my seventeen day absence.

CONTENTS

PART I

1. An Awakening	5
2. Romance Interrupted	11
3. Basic Training	37
4. Advanced Training	43
5. The Furlough	57
6. Wedding Plans	71
7. The Newlyweds	92
8. The Separation	108
9. Over There	130
10. Somewhere in England	142
11. The Invasion	159
12. A Soldier's Duty	164
13. The Purple Heart	203
14. Back to Reality	218
15. The New Mother	234
16. Unknown Territory	249
17. The Vigil	266
18. The Aftermath	284
19. Digging Deeper	289
20. Touchstones	294
Photographs Part I	309

PART II

1. The Search	319
2. The Reunion	335
3. For Prosperity	345
4. Digging Deeper	351
5. An Ocean Away	366
6. In Our Stead	384
7. Hamm, Luxembourg	416
Photographs Part II	425
Notation	433
Epilogue	435
Bibliography	437
Citations	439
About the Author	444

My Sister's Father

My Sister's Father

AUTHOR'S NOTE

My passion to unearth the truth, coupled with my insatiable desire to know a loved one my family was denied knowing, propelled me on a mission to document the story of Andy and Ginny. I soon realized that by sharing their story, others could learn through their letters, what Andy and Ginny, and by extension, millions of others, world-wide, were up against during the war of the twentieth century—all encompassing, all consuming, altering the course of history and the future of every man, woman, and child on the planet for generations.

Countless books, important books, have been written about the events of the war. We have Anne Frank's incredible diary to testify to the horrific, relentless hunt for Jews and Hitler's maniacal plot to render them extinct. My intent has been to give life to the human side of war's exacting calculus through the faithful missives of a single soldier and those who loved him; the side where families endure the empty place at the table--the son, who will not outlive his parents, the husband, who will never again embrace his wife, and the father who will be denied the joy of rocking his child to sleep. These are the daily experiences of the every-man that enrich our lives and remind us of what it means to be human.

Recognizing that war is sometimes a necessary evil, a last-ditch antidote to tyranny, my hope persists, that by being vicarious witnesses to one couple's sacrifice and intimate exchanges, we will all come to appreciate the collateral damage of war, and in so doing, set out to avoid conflict when possible and to compromise when feasible.

I wish the world God's peace.

MY SISTER'S FATHER

Reclaiming Andre

My Sister's Father

PART I

Fare thee well
My own true love
Farewell for a while
I'm going away
But I'll be back
Though I go 10,000 miles
10,000 miles
My own true love
10,000 miles or more
The rocks may melt
And the seas may burn
If I should not return
Oh don't you see
That lonesome dove
Sitting on an ivy tree
She's weeping for
Her own true love
As I shall weep for mine
Oh come ye back
My own true love
And stay a while with me
If I had a friend
All on this earth
You've been a friend to me

10,000 Miles
Fly Away Home, **1996, Columbia Pictures Inc.**

My Sister's Father

Catching a breath of moonlight, humming our favorite tune
This is a lovely way to spend an evening
I want to save all my nights and spend them with you

A Lovely Way to Spend an Evening
Harold Adamson

Chapter One
An Awakening

July 23, 1998. Feeling great trepidation, I took a deep breath and slowly nudged the door a crack, peering in. The glorious morning light cast a glow over her body and her pale pink nightgown. Though her complexion had yellowed, her countenance radiated joy. My mother's body was stretched out across her bed. Gently, I eased myself down next to her and used this precious time to softly stroke her cheek, tears streaming down my own. Her eyes were open. They would dance no more.

In the midst of my new-found sorrow and loss, I experienced a most astounding encounter. Mom transcended the spoken word. Her spirit lingered. She was communicating with me, mind to mind, soul to soul; it was mystical, but it was real. She assured me, as mothers do, that she would be alright; she was free of her shackles, free of the trials and the pain of life. Death laid bare all pretense. She had made mistakes, yes, but she had done her best. She had given us all that she could, and now it was her time to begin a new life. My post-mortem glimpse into her soul consecrated me with an intimacy my mother and I had never known in life. I never loved her more than at that moment. Great grief and comfort filled me.

The urgency of her funeral preparations jolted me from my reverie. And so, I began. The representatives from the funeral home would be arriving soon to take my mother's body away. Reaching into a dresser drawer, I drew out a box, tucked away in the back. Its decorative cover, embossed with yellow roses, told me it contained something significant. As I opened it, I burst into tears all over again. It was filled with irreplaceable mementos of Andy, mom's first husband and World War II hero. Picking through its contents, I noted various English coins, a machine gun bullet, pilot wings, a scapular medal, and a sterling silver rosary. The rosary had been a wedding gift from his bride. I handled the beads, blackened now after these fifty-four years, letting them run through my fingers.

By evening, the grueling tasks of funeral preparations behind me, I felt compelled to seek solace in my mother's room as she had done so many times. Her death left me with a pain in the pit of my stomach, piercing, that refused to abate. I was emotionally spent and engulfed in sadness. I was not ready to let go. I needed to feel close to her. Dusk was falling--the time of day when she would be lost in prayer. Balanced on the edge of her bed, I began to sift through her prayer cards and inspirational books stacked up on a tiny table nearby. I longed to read what she had been reading, pray what she had been praying.

Settling down on the bed, my eyes drifted to a larger bedside table. A framed photograph, circa 1920, of Andy as a toddler, held in his mother's arms, stood to one side. It was then that I noticed it. A letter lay open. Through watery eyes, its sheer sheets appeared to be veritably floating. Was I seeing things? I blinked. It appeared to be airmail stationary. Instinctively, I knew it was a letter from Andy. Mom must have been reading this letter just before she died! Eyes squinting, I fought to read the unfamiliar pen. Guilt flushed over me. These private love letters entombed in my mother's bedroom closet all these years were privy to no one. She kept them in a shoebox, brimming, faithfully written to her throughout Andy's days of military service. I suspect that she had turned to Andy's letters for comfort in recent years. Most likely, the death of her second husband had triggered intense feelings of grief, lying dormant like a cancer, since the loss of her first love.

My curiosity proved stronger than my guilt, so I began to read:

July 12, 1944
My Dearest,

Today I received three letters from you and my sojourn in the home for the sick and ailing was brightened very highly. [Andy was being treated at a local hospital for follicular tonsillitis.] I had more than one laugh from your letter, and I suppose my cellmate thinks me quite insane. And the snapshot of Tommy was very cute. He certainly has big eyes [Tommy is their nephew, born the previous February].

Those gal friends of yours are going to find your husband rather irate if they don't cease pulling for a girl. Just like a woman. Come October, I'll bet they really will be envious when you bounce that wonderful baby on your knee.

I've been listening to the British radio all day and as yet they haven't played any jive. I'll admit they have no commercials, but the programs really stink. I can't see what they have to be so aloof about. Any hick town in the States is far ahead of them.

Reading your letter about our reunion last October, it struck me as rather a coincidence that a year, almost to the day, Junior will be born. Looks like October is our month. It always has been my lucky month. Remember our date that Friday night at the Statler? It seems funny now, recalling that we were still quite reserved towards each other until we began dancing, but then once I had you in my arms, my knees seemed weak and I thought I was trembling. At that moment, I needed a couple of drinks to fortify me. I remember clearly that my head was in the clouds and my feet treaded on air (or was it your feet). Then when I softly kissed your cheek, it thrilled me beyond all comprehension and I knew I would never let you go again. Little did the bandleader realize what beautiful music we were making, music no composer could ever attempt to put on paper. I don't believe I ever danced better in my life.

Then the unforgettable night when you said "yes". I wasn't afraid because I could see the answer in your eyes, which must have seen the deep penetrating love that shone in mine. What ecstatic days.

My Sister's Father

Darling, when I come home, let's do it all over again. You know what I mean, the first and second night anyway and we'll be married the third. Am I being too silly? I can't help it though; loving you makes me do all sorts of crazy things.

Finally have some good jobs. It isn't the fault of the Limeys though, it's "Command Performance" from the States.

I still get pretty blue when I hear "Lovely Way to Spend an Evening". I feel all right now, but the sulfa makes me a little weak. Can't fly for five days after I get off the stuff.

Well baby, that's about all for now. I miss you very much and love you with all my heart and soul.

*Yours always,
Andre*

For me, Andy's letter was a door, finally opening. Until I read his words, I did not have the slightest inkling who Andre Vleghels was as a real person. For my entire life, he was a mere shadow, relegated to the background. Mom had made the decision, long ago, to slam the door shut on their life together. But now, with Andy's voice rising, everything changed. His romantic reminiscences transfigured an empty visage, a soldier once married to my mother. Haunting questions from the past awakened within me, pressing me to learn more about Andre Vleghels and the love and marriage that he once shared with my mother, Virginia Egan, a lifetime ago. When I returned to my home that evening, I had a deeper understanding of mom's devastating loss. I had arrived at a threshold. I decided to walk through the open door and discover what was on the other side.

This is the G.I. Jive

Man alive

It starts with the bugler blowin' reveille when you arrive

Jack, that's the G.I. Jive

Roodley-toot

Jump in your suit

Make a salute

Boot!

G.I. Jive
Johnny Mercer

Chapter Two
Romance Interrupted

Letters, it turns out, became the lifeblood for Andre and Virginia. The two began dating in 1937 when Andy was a senior at St. Philip Neri in Detroit. Virginia, or Ginny, as her friends called her, was a year behind him, yet they were both seventeen at Andy's June graduation, the second-high school graduation class at St. Phil's. Ginny had repeated a year in early elementary school due to illness. According to the graduation issue of the "St. Philip News", Andrew Vleghels' favorite study was "Junior Femininity". His "Last Will and Testament" read:

"I, Andrew Vleghels, do hereby will to Robert Mosseau the pleasure of escorting Virginia Egan to and from school for one term ONLY and to Bernadette Paquette my bowling ability and may she long be remembered as the best bowler at St. Phillip's."

At some point following Ginny's graduation, a year later, she and Andy inexplicably drifted apart and started dating other people.

I think it is fair to say that Ginny had a serious nature, which made for a serious student. Unlike Andy, who breezed through school with little study, Ginny spent four hours most school nights "hitting the books." Fellow classmate, Robert Mousseau, remembers her as a "whiz student—top of her class and all business." Her approach to study was methodical and disciplined. She was willing to do whatever it took to achieve her academic goals. By high school's end, her efforts were rewarded as class valedictorian and several medals of high achievement. So when her college ambitions and aspirations of becoming a teacher were dashed by financial constraints, it was a hard disappointment for her. She accepted the news from her Dad who she only described as kind. Instead, she settled for a one-year secretarial program at St. Mary Commercial School in downtown Detroit.

Her closest high school girlfriends joined her at St. Mary's--sisters, Ruth and Bettie Dykeman, along with Jane Mahoney. They had palled around together since the girls first welcomed Ginny into their circle, freshman year at St. Phil's. Due to a change in parish boundaries, Ginny transferred from St.

Ambrose where she had attended elementary school for eight years.

The foursome remained close friends throughout high school and beyond. Lazy summer days were spent on Harsens Island on the St. Clair River, thirty miles north of Detroit. Families retreated to cottages there during the summer months. Friends of the Dykeman's kept a place there that they were welcome to use. From time to time, Ginny was invited to join them. In 1940, the Dykeman girls and Ginny spread their wings and took an exciting trip to New York City. Another year, they ventured off to Mackinac Island and stayed at the Grand Hotel. On weekends, the girls and their boyfriends usually gathered at a friend's home, cut a rug at the local dance hall, or went to the local movie house. During this time, Bettie's cousin, Ralph Krass, became Ginny's steady beau.

Many of Andy's evenings were spent pounding the typewriter keys to the rhythms of the latest jazz. Following graduation at St. Phil's, he enrolled in a two-year program at The Detroit Business Institute. After graduating in 1939, he joined his dad, Maurice, and cousin, Frank, at Gray Marine Motor Company where Andy assumed the responsibilities of accountant and office manager.

In the first of many ironic twists, Gray Marine Motor Company was to become a cog in the wheel that turned the great Allied war machine on the home front. Detroit, coined the "Arsenal of Democracy", converted its manufacturing capabilities to supply tanks, planes, and Jeeps. Gray Marine made no small contribution to the war effort by producing a 250 horsepower diesel engine that propelled the landing crafts for vehicles and personnel also referred to as the Higgins LCVP.

Eisenhower would later proclaim that Andrew Higgins, its inventor, won the war for the Allied forces.(1) The Higgins Boats made it possible for the Allied soldiers to storm the beaches of Normandy on D-Day and beyond.

Typical of many post-depression families, the Egan's and the Vleghels' lived in modest, neat, blue collar neighborhoods where fathers, and, sometimes, mothers labored to scratch out a living. Sacrifice, conservation, and cooperation were the virtues of the day that enabled them to pay their bills and raise their families.

[As a young child in the '50s, I recall visits to Grandma Egan's, and our trips to the neighborhood grocer, Landau's Market. It was somewhere between an excursion and an ordeal. We would traipse through the alley-way, following our grandmother like ducklings as she pulled her shopping cart behind her. The butcher knew that Mrs. Egan would not settle for tough cuts of meat, so he did his level best to keep one of his faithful patrons, happy. Sharon and I were often enlisted to search out the dented cans, because they were a few cents less, a throwback to the days of botulism. At the checkout counter, perhaps as a reward for patience and good behavior, Grandma would oblige us by treating us to something sweet. Usually, it was Cracker Jacks or spicy Windmill cookies. Once home, she always abided the same ritual. First, she placed each item atop her oil-cloth-covered kitchen table. Determined not to be overcharged, she methodically checked off each purchase on her sales receipt. It seemed like an eternity before we could quiet our rumbling tummies with boloney and catsup sandwiches on Wonder bread. Coffee, with lots of cream, helped to wash down the bake good of the day.]

My Sister's Father

After years of no contact, it was letters that reconnected Andy and his former high school girlfriend, Ginny Egan. They had both been experiencing the working world for a couple of years now, dating other people. America had begun providing ancillary assistance to a battered Britain, swelling draft quotas in anticipation of eventual military engagement. The draft caught up with Andy in June of 1941. On August 22, he sent Ginny what was to become the first of many missives.

Dear Virginia:

I'll bet you're surprised to hear from me, aren't you? I feel rather ashamed that I have not corresponded with you before this, but after I explain the circumstances which caused this delay, I believe you will exonerate.

As you probably have guessed by now, I am now affiliated with Uncle Sam's Army, and I'm stationed at Fort Leonard Wood, Missouri, in the heart of the Ozark Mountains amidst all the hillbillies or if you prefer, hillwilliams. If you will bear with me, I'll try to give you all the pertinent information I have to offer.

On the momentous day of June 11, 1941, I was inducted into that great organization -- the Army. Naturally knowing my mother, you can realize how she felt when I left. After all, I had never been away from home longer than two weeks.

From Detroit I was shipped to Fort Custer for the duration of about six days. I really enjoyed my stay there, for the simple reason that it was only five miles from Battle Creek and I was able to raise a little general h---. But now here I am at Fort Leonard Wood, Missouri, and miles from nowhere. In fact, the nearest town is 32 miles away. The only consolation is my radio. You know how much I like swing; well every morning after breakfast I have it going until 7:00 A.M. at which time I go to work. By the way, that incidentally is the only real break I have received in this man's army. I'm working as stenographer in Regimental Headquarters, taking dictation from the Major and Colonel, which is quite interesting. I acquired this position the second day of my arrival here and I consider myself quite fortunate. In fact they appreciate my talents so much, that they will probably keep me here for a period of two and a half years.

I'll give you some idea of my day--not Mrs. Roosevelt's. We lay around in bed every morning until 5:30 a.m., which gives us plenty of time to shave, dress and wash, make our bunks by 5:45, then some #~%#~% blows a bugle and we fall out and stand at attention while the sergeant calls roll. After that we have a little calisthenics, such as, grabbing ourselves by hair and holding it out in front of us. On Mondays we had both feet in front of us. Calisthenics being over, we grope our way to the mess hall, where delicious repast on either rye or white crusts is to be had. After gorging ourselves we go back to the barracks and having nothing to do until 7:00, we sit around and scrub toilets, mop the floors and pick up all cigarette butts and matches within 150 feet of the barracks. At 7:00 I stroll over to Headquarters and begin my wearisome toils. This continues until 11:30, at which time we knock off for lunch. Of course I only get two hours for lunch. I resume my arduous labors at 1:30 p.m., and at 4:30 p.m., I go home for the day--gee, am I tired.

There you have the gist of my daily occurrences. About the only diversion I have in the evening is either to go to the show or listen to the radio. I went to the show about four times last week.

My parents and Maurine were down here last weekend; it was really wonderful to see them again, after such a long absence.

How are you getting along with your work? I hope your family is feeling fine, tell them I said "hello."

During the past month, I'll bet I've had my picture photographed about eight times. I'm really getting mugged. I'll probably be an old man by the time I get out of this army. It really gets monotonous at times. Detroit still the same? The weather down here is slightly warm, only about 110 degrees, so don't think it's hot in Detroit. I get the Sunday Detroit News every week, through a subscription sponsored by my cousin Julia. [Julia and Edna were sisters, who married Andy's cousins, Frank and Charlie, in a double ceremony.]

Well, since I'm typing this letter, or rather this short novel during working hours, I'll have to sign off now and return to my work. Please let me hear from you. My address is Hq's Btry, 182nd F. A., Fort Leonard Wood, Missouri. So until later, so-long.

Yours,
(Andy forgot to pen his signature)

MY SISTER'S FATHER

Ginny probably answered Andy's initial letter, but evidently, suspended correspondence. Months later Andy tried again.

HEADQUARTERS 182ND FIELD ARTILLERY

March 7, 1942
Dear Ginny:

You probably gasped with surprise when you received this letter. Evidently you thought that I was dead by this time but no such luck. How are you? I suppose that you are a big success in the commercial world. I can still remember the time when you abhorred the very idea of working in an office. Have you still the same attitude?

It really has been a long time since the last time that we corresponded hasn't it? I am still employing my talents, what there is of them, as a stenographer. I have made application for the Air Corps and expect to take my examinations any day. I received a grand letter of character recommendation from Fr. Vismara, which was needed before I could make an application for the Air Corps. The prevailing conditions here don't exactly agree with me and I am trying to get into a more active branch of the Service. Therefore I chose the Air Corps

Andy's parents were not happy about their son's decision to join the Army Air Corps. Due to his experience as a stenographer for the military court, he was offered a position at Eisenhower's Headquarters, but he turned it down. Maurice and Rachel wished their son had made the "safer" choice.

I still see Bob Griffith and George Noe frequently and George has also submitted his application for the Air Corps. Right now there is quite a demand for officers of all kinds and I would say that 75% of the regiment has made application for Officers Candidate School.

Bob and George lived in Andy's neighborhood on Coplin Street. The three of them were good chums, spending time ice-skating and playing baseball. When Andy's kid sister, Maurine, had to remain in isolation due to a bout of scarlet fever, it was the Noe family who invited Andy and Maurice to board with them. Rachel would prepare their daily lunches and pass them through the milk chute for pick-up. Bob Griffith and George Noe did not return from the war. George, a nose-gunner on The Black Cat, the last American bomber to be shot down in the European Theater, was lost over Germany.

I understand that you met Ginny Lynch the other day under rather peculiar conditions. She told me how embarrassed she was when the elevator operator in a rather loud voice introduced her to you more or less informally. What do you think of her?

Apparently, Ginny Lynch and Ginny Egan both worked in the same building that housed the Chancery Offices for the Archdiocese of Detroit. Miss Lynch and Andy were dating at the time that he was drafted. Maurine described her as an out-going, fun-loving kind of gal who reached out to a preteen Maurine, exchanging girl talk and experimenting with hairstyles and make-up. Maurine appreciated the special consideration.

Incidentally, who do you know in Service Battery, 1st Battalion, 182nd Field Artillery? How do I know? A little bird told me. So, you know Fr. Cavanaugh too? I have met him and think that he is really tops. Was I just a private the last time I wrote to you? Well, now I'm a Private First Class, which I have been since October and make the enormous sum of $51.00 per month. I was home at Christmas for seven days and it was really wonderful. There is a rumor around now that we may get furloughs in the beginning of next month or the latter part of this month. But I'm not building up my hopes for I may be in for a letdown.

My mother and dad are fine and Maurine is now completing the sixth grade. Of course her grades aren't as good as her brother's, will you listen to the egomaniac. Remember what I said once, "Fr. Vismara said that if a person knows that he is good, he should tell the world about it" and I am certainly living up to his teachings.

Well, Ginny, I'll leave you now and give my regards to your mother and dad. Till later, au revoir. Write soon.

Sincerely,
Andre

Nearly a year went by before Ginny answered Andy's letter. I surmise it was out of loyalty to Ralph, believing that it would be improper to correspond with two fellas, simultaneously, and Andy being a former suitor.

My Sister's Father

January 8, 1943
Dear Andy:

No doubt you will be very surprised to hear from me once again, but I couldn't resist writing you to tell you how much I enjoyed seeing your folks during the Christmas holidays. Naturally, I suppose you are wondering how this came about so I shall explain. Your mother never forgets to send me a Christmas card and with her card this year came a note asking me to pay them a visit during the holidays. When I received the note, I thought it was so sweet of your mother to remember me after all these years. So, one Sunday afternoon I dropped in on your mother and dad. I only intended to stay for a short time, but they insisted that I stay and before I realized it, supper was over, and I had spent the greater part of the evening with them. Maurine has surely grown to be quite a young lady. If I had met her on the street, I would not have recognized her. I don't believe your mother and dad have changed in the least. They are both looking just fine.

What Ginny does not mention here is that Mrs. Vleghels let her know that Andy would really like to hear from her and encouraged her to write.

Of course, they told me all about you and that you had enlisted in the Air Corps and were now stationed in California. I was not too surprised at this news, because the last time I heard from you, you were contemplating entering this branch of the service. How do you like it? I am confident that you will come through with flying colors. Do you find the courses difficult? I believe you are stationed in the vicinity of Hollywood. I can just imagine the fun that you must be having on your free time. I suppose you have seen many stars of the stage and screen.

As for myself, I am still working in the Chancery Building as secretary to Father Raymond Clancy Director of Social Action for the Archdiocese of Detroit. I enjoy the work immensely. Father has such a magnetic personality and is always so pleasant that it is a joy to work for him. In March I will be working for Father just two years. Time does fly, doesn't it? It seems ages and ages to me since our High School days at St. Philips. How about you? I don't recall what brought the subject up, but the other day mother happened to mention something about you and when you were learning to dance. I guess I will never forget that box step. I imagine that you have come a long way since that time.

As Ginny attests, working for a priest was a comfortable fit for her. A former president of the Children of Mary at St. Phil's and strict in the practice of her Catholic religion, Ginny had considered entering the convent right out of high school. However, her mother, being the pragmatic sort, did not support the idea. She wanted Ginny to work for one year following her graduation from business school to get a taste of the world. If she still felt "the calling", she was free to enter. Working in the Chancery office allowed Ginny to meld her religious leanings with her secretarial skills.

You will undoubtedly be surprised to hear that my brother Leo was married last summer - in fact - August 1. He married

Patricia Minnie from his class at St. Philips. I don't think you would know her as I believe you had graduated before she attended St. Phil's. They were married at St. Margaret Mary's Church at a Solemn Nuptial Mass performed by Father Vismara. It was a beautiful wedding. You, I am sure, remember Tubby Fuhs and Donald Beattie. Don was Leo's best man and Tubby was an usher. Incidentally, Tubby and Florine Walker have been married now for over a year. The wedding breakfast was held at the Savarine Hotel on Jefferson Avenue and also the Reception in the evening. Leo and Pat are now living in an income on Algonquin Avenue. They are getting along just wonderful and if it wasn't for the "draft" everything would be perfect.

Andy, I was very sorry to hear about the break-up between Virginia Lynch and yourself. Naturally, working in the Chancery Building, I was one of the first ones to hear about it. I only had occasion to meet Virginia once, so I really don't feel that I know her.

Ralph and Egon Fricke both received furloughs together, after maneuvers in Tennessee, during the latter part of November. I believe you know Egon, don't you? He is a grand fellow and lots of fun. From all report's maneuvers were quite tough in Tennessee. Ralph didn't mention it, but Egon told me that the boys met you in Tennessee. I was quite surprised. While Ralph was home on furlough this last time he and I broke up. At first I wasn't going to mention this to you, but then I changed my mind.

Well, Andy, I think it is about time that I stop all this rambling and conclude for now. Mother, dad and all of the family send their best wishes to you. Even though I have not corresponded with you in a long time, I want you to know that I have often thought about you and hoped that you were safe. I realize that it takes a great deal of courage to do the job that you are doing, and my best wishes and prayers are for you.

This single letter is the only one I found that Ginny wrote to Andy. It was typewritten and unsigned, most likely a copy of the original. I do not know for sure what became of all the daily missives that Ginny penned to Andy as the war progressed. But she was forever vigilant not to reveal too much about herself and fiercely guarded her privacy, so I can only conclude that she destroyed them.

I was more than delighted to read mom's description of Egon Fricke, the man who would, one day, become my father. In a strange twist of fate, Ralph, Andy, and Egon were all stationed at Fort Leonard Wood in Missouri when Ginny visited. "Never in my wildest dreams", mom would tell us, did she suspect that she would eventually marry two of these men, neither one being the object of her affections at the time.

The postmark of the following letter was Oxnard, California. For several letters, up until the end of March, Andy dated his missives, 1942. However, the year was 1943.

January 22, 1943
Dear Ginny:

You surmised correctly; I was surprised to hear from you but very pleasantly so. It really has been a long time since I had heard from you. My mother wrote in a recent letter that you had accepted her invitation, and of course the usual comments followed as to your inevitable disposition and so on.

I am surprised that you and Ralph came to a parting of the ways. I thought he was a very nice chap. We had a lot of fun together, but I must admit that I caught myself musing a few times, just how you two ever got along because I do know he likes a lot of people and shall we say considerable noise, whereas knowing you, I just couldn't see the two together, but I usually brought all this to end by concluding that you had changed. It was rather hard to take at first, breaking up with Ginny I mean, but the longer I thought about it, comparing bad traits and attributes and various incidents, I came to the conclusion that I was better off. So I find myself living a normal life, flying and very happy. I have wonderful parents, I have friends, what more do I need?

As you say, it is years since we last held hands in high school and you had the patience to teach a perfectly clumsy boy to dance. That box step was really the thing and I shall never forget it or you either. In fact, about a month ago I was teaching that very box step to one of the fellows who couldn't dance and needless to say he is also progressing well.

I would have answered this letter sooner but it just arrived today. Reason for the delay in delivery was the fact that it had been sent to my old address at Santa Ana. I am now about 100 miles north of there in Primary learning to fly. (1) I now have seven hours in the air and I really love it. There are only about 380 cadets here and we live in 4 room cottages. Our meals are also served by waitresses. Conditions are rather ideal, insofar as living quarters are concerned. As to free time, that madam is something that is practically unheard of. We are allowed to leave Saturday at 6:00 P.M. and return by 10:00 A.M. Sunday, so we don't have much time. Although while I was at Santa Ana I did frequent quite a few places in Hollywood and it's environs and I must say, that they are tops. Popular bands are here year-round.

Ralph had told me that Leo took the fatal step, also showed me a few pictures of the affair. You really looked fine.

Yes, I knew Fricke, in fact my last weekend in Nashville was spent in the company of Egon and Ralph; we had quite a time. Incidentally, is the 182nd still at Wood, I am anxious to know because they still have some of my personal belongings and I receive no answer to my letter?

I do hope you will continue to write to me because I do want to hear from you. Now that we have both resumed a normal life, free I mean, there is no reason why we shouldn't write. Agreed?

So I hope I get a reply from you in the near future. Thanks a million for your interest in me. I appreciate it very much. My best regards to your mother and dad. Au revoir.

Sincerely,
Andre

And so, the romance, interrupted, was rekindled. A couple of carefully scripted letters altered the course of the lives of Andy and Ginny. Though Ginny's responses are absent, much of the time, it is not difficult to read between the lines of Andy's missives.

February 3, 1943
Dear Ginny:

I was really elated to get a reply from you so soon, I hope that it will continue in this way in the future.

It is now about a half an hour before I enfold myself in the arms of Morpheus, which is at the very late hour of ten o'clock. Before it slips my mind and maybe it is a coincidence but the band I am listening to at the moment is none other than Sammy Kaye. Remember him on a certain June night back in 1937? Seems as though that was the beginning of the end for us, then anyway.

Thanks for giving me the idea of writing to Father Maino. I still have some personal effects back at Wood, where they have been since I left for maneuvers in September. There is a possibility that he can do something about them.

Father Maino was the chaplain for the 182nd Field Artillery. (They eventually became attached to Patton's Third Army on his march through Europe.) Ginny may have known Father from her work at the Chancery.

I understand perfectly well why you couldn't write to me at Wood and I certainly wouldn't have wanted to cause any friction between you and Ralph. Consequently, I never did think it strange that you didn't write to me, but we can forget all that and think about now.

A momentous little episode happened in my young career yesterday; I advanced from the lowly rank of dodo, by the important step of a solo. I really felt wonderful when my instructor got out of the ship and told me to take it up alone. I'll bet I had a very silly grin on my face. I was singing all the time I was up which was 20 minutes. Today I was up 40 minutes much to my elation. Really, there is nothing like flying.

It is odd that Father Maino always connects you and I together. He only knew of our high school days. In plain words; it beats me.

I have met Father Cavanaugh on different occasions and he is really swell. We get along fine together. And speaking of bowling, I still haven't lost the craze and hope I never will; do you still bowl?

Bowling, a sport popularized in the thirties and forties, became a great pastime and passion for the Vleghels family-- well, most of the family. The employees of Gray Marine, a family unto themselves, sponsored a family bowling league. Feeling inferior to the honed skills of her parents and brother, Maurine tried to content herself with score-keeping duties.

So now I have the pleasure of knowing a USO hostess.(2) Nice going. Hope the fellows realize what a break they are getting when they can dance with you and pour out all their troubles too. You still are tops on my list. Someday I hope we can get together and have a nice long talk. Maybe you will listen to some of my troubles, mostly the ones in the past. As a matter of fact I attended a USO dance last Wednesday and I certainly have been to diverse USOs throughout the country. I agree they are doing a wonderful job.

Well, Ginny, I have just a few minutes left, so I'll sign off with a fond adieu and with the anticipation that you will write again and soon. Au revoir.

As always,
Andy

P.S. *Strange that I still remembered your address after all this time.*

Andy begins his next letter with all the enthusiasm and encouragement of a football coach:

Feb. 11, 1943
Dear Ginny:

Now you are showing the spirit I like to see in your correspondence. No delay or anything. I am very glad that we are getting together and before long we should be up-to-date with events past and present. You admit a liking for Artie Shaw now; this is a fine time to enjoy his music after he has disbanded after all these months. How about my boy, Harry James? You must be dancing with some G.I.s who are jitterbugs, how do you cope with this predicament?

It was a surprise to me upon learning that Bob and Dorothy had been married, and that he is in the Marine Corps. Too bad he didn't become a father before he was endangered by the draft, he would have had a little deferment. If he is stationed in California, he is probably at San Diego. He was fortunate to get a furlough. I have forgotten what it is to have a furlough, but I wouldn't mind finding out anytime.

I appreciate your confidence and pride in me. Hope I don't let you down, because there are some days when I feel an utter lack of confidence in myself. I was rather, shall we say, melancholy yesterday and I gave my instructor a poor ride but today it was altogether different and my morale zoomed up a 100%.

Your description of New York and your liking for it describes my attitude about California. Wish I could squire you around to the different night spots in Hollywood and L.A. We could take in the Mocambo, (3) Ciro's, Beach-Comber, 7 Seas, Slapsie Maxie's, though I don't think you would enjoy the ribald floor show. Then there is T. Dorsey at the Palladium and Freddy Martin at the Ambassador. I could write reams of paper of the various spots. I think the spot that has the most beautiful show is Earl Carroll's. (4)

Got in 2 1/2 hours of flying in today and I didn't have any time to do any joy riding. You have to work constantly on spins, crossroad eights, pylon Os, stalls and what not, but I can't think of anything I would trade it with.

I may get to L.A. this weekend providing I don't have to fly Sunday. I haven't been there in three weeks and I feel I must be missing out on something.

Every time someone plugs in an electric razor in one of the surrounding cabins, it causes static in my radio and just when I am enjoying a program. Incidentally, does your dad still get such a kick out of radio comedians?

Well, it's time for me to say au revoir, so till later. Write soon.

As always,
Andy

Feb. 19, 1943
Dear Ginny:

Speaking of favorite songs, it is rather difficult to select a favorite tune, I think mine is "Black Magic" it's good by Freddie Slack or Miller. Kate Smith is now "giving out" with "I don't get around much anymore" rather ironical.

I have vivid memories of Kate Smith's appearances on The *Ed Sullivan Show* as a youngster in the fifties. The Sullivan Show aired on Sunday nights, which coincided with family visits to Grandma and Grandpa Egan's. You could usually find us kids sitting cross-legged on the floor, huddled before the television screen. Typically, Sullivan would save Kate for his closing act. A buxom woman, in those days, she would belt out a rendition of *God Bless America* as only Kate could sing it. Her name had become synonymous with Irving Berlin's composition.

When she finally appeared on stage, the adults would bellow, "Ginny, she's on!" We would all freeze in our places, barely daring to breathe, as Kate mesmerized us in a wave of patriotism. Of course, mom cried.

Since I have been away from home so long, various desires have piled up until I can't see where I am going to find time to fulfill all of them. There are so many things I want to do, so many people to see that it promises to be a large furlough if ever I get one. Most of all I want to see my family, gee I really miss them. Just think it has been ten months since I last saw my humble abode. Well, someday I'll resume a normal life again; right now

I just want to help get this little fracas over with. My one ambition is to get tight in Berlin, that is if anything is left standing.

I imagine most soldiers had some plan in mind to celebrate an Allied victory when it finally came. Andy was not atypical. General Patton marked the occasion of crossing the Rhine, by urinating in it.

Speaking of your radio, if I didn't have mine, I would miss a lot of the relaxation that I derive from music. It really relieves pilot fatigue, because after keeping your mind and nerves keyed up to a high pitch for several hours, I can stand 8 hours sleep and that my dear, is where I am heading for in a very few moments. Write soon. Adios.

Sincerely,
Andy

March 3, 1943
Dear Ginny:

Here I have only four more hours to fly and to fix matters up, we are being deluged with a constant downpour. I would have finished up today, but that's the way it stands.

We leave here the morning of the 10th for Lemoore Field pronounced like Lamoure, only no Dotty. (5) We graduate on the 9th and have our dance on the 8th. We are paying $125 for *the orchestra. I may run into L.A. this week-end, for it may be quite a while before I see the old town again.*

Lemoore Army Airfield was built as a training field for the Army Air Corps, boasting 6,500 feet of hard surface. It was, however, only operational in dry weather, because it was made of compacted dirt.

No, I don't receive my wings when I graduate here, from here I go to Basic where I will put in about 70 hours flying a ship that is about 50 or 60 miles per hour faster, learn night flying and formation. From there I go to Advanced where the planes are still faster around 250 MPH. Upon completing Advanced, I then receive my 2nd Lieutenant's bar and wings. Graduation should be sometime in July, which is only about 4 months off. The thrill of that moment, the final graduation I mean, would be if my mother could be there to pin my (sketch) wings on. It would be worthwhile to go through all this, just the idea of it all, thrills me beyond words. Hope I can live up to my parents' pride and fulfill all the promises I have made to myself.

Andy recognized the many sacrifices that his parents, Maurice and Rachel, had made. The three of them had emigrated from Ghent, Belgium, the Flemish end of the country, in 1923 when Andy was four. Together, they had weathered many storms and survived numerous setbacks, forging a strong bond of mutual love and respect. He was a dutiful and grateful son and they, his proud parents. And although America was the land of opportunity, it was not a panacea. So when the Great Depression hit in October of 1929 and the banks closed, Maurice and Rachel were forced, once again, to give up, not only their home, but a neighboring lot they were saving to purchase. It all disintegrated in a flash. Like so many other victims of circumstance, they rolled up their sleeves and started over, yet again. For them, that meant renting a home on Coplin Street.

It was kind of Sister Marie Eugene to remember me. She taught chemistry didn't she and I always thought that she didn't particularly care for me. Seems like many years ago that she was trying to get something into my thick head. Gee, it is six years at that, isn't it? Must be getting old.

I have open post tonight from six until ten. I can still recall the good old G.I. days when I didn't have to be in until reveille. I really had a great life then, but I still wouldn't trade it for this.

Benny Goodman replaced Tommy Dorsey at the Palladium in Hollywood last week, may run in and see him. At the present moment Artie Shaw is emanating forth from my radio in "Concerto for Clarinet" one of my old records I had at home.

Andy's love of music, in general, and the clarinet, in particular, came quite naturally to him from his dad, who loved to play clarinet with a band back in Belgium. Surely, as a young child, Andy would have heard the rich, mellow tones of the clarinet, emanating through his home whenever Maurice practiced or played for his own enjoyment.

Just listen to that rain come down, can you hear it! Sure hope it clears up by tomorrow so I can finish my flying.

So Ginny again I will bring an end to my manic chatter, do write soon, for your letters are grand and appreciated very much by your humble correspondent. Till then, au revoir.

As always,
Andy

Keep 'em flying, every headline screams
Keep 'em flying, army fighting teams
On thirty thousand different beams
Keep 'em flying, Uncle Sam
Keep 'em Flying
Bill Coleman

Chapter Three
Basic Training

Basic flying school, the next rung on the commission ladder, molded the novice flier into a military pilot, again, over a nine-week training period. Seventy hours of flight instruction were required. Cadets transitioned to heavier, faster planes and began to learn the rudiments of instrument, night, and formation flying. They were introduced to the art of cross-country flight, learning to fly from one point on the map to another.

March 28, 1943
Dear Ginny:

Please excuse the stationary, but it was all I had available; I dislike using it because I detest to write on lined paper. If I write on every line it becomes all jammed up and every two lines is too spaced.

Sorry that I haven't written before now but I am so busy that I can't find a moment to myself. Today being Sunday makes no difference in our schedule, it's just another day, I have to go to Mass in the evening, as a matter of fact in about 20 minutes.

The old confidence is returning once, especially after, I passed my 20 hour check yesterday, so I have about 40 hours to get in by graduation. I decided I would experiment and use every line, maybe you can still read it. At the present moment I am listening to a records program of Glenn Miller's (6) records; mellow.

Last Monday night, we had our first open post and some of us traveled into Fresno and had quite a time. Had a rendezvous at the Bamboo Room with a Cuba Libra and later we went to hear Jan Garber, who incidentally has quite a band now and consequently I can't call him Jan "Garbage". Next Monday night, or rather tomorrow night, I have a date with a Delta Epsilon from Fresno State U., and I plan to hear Tommy Dorsey. Seems as though all the big time bands make one-night stops at Fresno on my open post night, much to my elation.

Incidentally, Ginny, why don't you drop in and see Mom and Dad, I'm sure that they would be very glad to see you, also you might like to see a few pictures of Oxnard and of one flyer named A.J., which undoubtedly they will show you upon the slightest provocation.

The weather here is getting very warm and in the afternoons it is a little too warm.

And the calisthenics, oh my poor back. Upon the termination of this period, all the fellows limp back too tired to talk and groaning with every step. Honestly, I thought training for football was tough but this has it all beat. Just try bending down, up and back and down again touching your toes for about 10 minutes straight, or lying on your back, feet about 10 inches off the ground, legs rigid waving back and forth for an interminable period. Every drink I ever had shrieks in protest. Man, it's murder.

One of these evenings if I have any energy left, I intend to play a little tennis. We have a bowling alley about a block from the barracks. So far I have only entered it once, time being as scarce as it is.

Well, Ginny, I must sign off for now because I have to leave for Mass. Do write soon and say a prayer for my success. I need it.

Sincerely,
Andy

April 15, 1943
Dear Ginny:

Listen dear, I'll send you a picture of my gruesome little self but it will be a week or so because I send them out to get developed. ("As Time Goes By" is now being played, also my favorite) In reciprocation, may I ask for a picture of you? Please, I haven't had one in quite some time. Ginny, I have never told you this before, I have often been sorry that I didn't but one of the things that broke us up was a picture. That's the truth. Remember your graduation picture, well, I never did receive one and I was very deeply hurt at the time and came to the conclusion that you didn't care about me. Darn it, you never got jealous, you never contradicted me, everything I said was alright. Strange I should tell you all this now, years later, when I should have told long ago. Many things might have been avoided.

Say you really painted the town a little and wish I could have been with you. Especially when you mention some of my old haunts. ...

I do hope that you will write again and soon also the granting of my request. Au revoir.

Sincerely,
Andre

April 28, 1943
Dear Ginny:

You begin your letter giving an ear to Fred Waring and I am listening to a little jive as played by the one and only Harry James. Thanks a million for the grand picture. Makes me realize just what I am missing. Sorry I am not able to send you my picture at this time because as of yet I haven't received them from the film company where I sent them. I can assure you however, you aren't missing a thing. Here comes my boy T. Dorsey.

Look Ginny, I'm the one who is puzzled now. It was so long ago that frankly I don't remember what I did to hurt you. Please relieve my mind and tell me what it was. I guess we can blame it all on youth. You were the first girl that I ever went with longer than a week or two and I guess love and such never meant anything to me but looking back on the whole situation, how could I have been such a fool? Do you happen to remember the day I walked home from school with you and described as being patrician? I shall never forget that. Well, I hope the day is near when we can really talk and not try to put it down in writing.

Andy's home was only a couple of blocks up from St. Phil's, but Ginny's home was several streets further. Consequently, in order for Andy Vleghels to escort Ginny Egan to her door, he would have extended his walk by nearly two miles round-trip, thus affording her "the royal treatment".

Thank you again for the medal. I have it hanging around my neck with a Sacred Heart medal.

I believe that Ginny's gift to Andy was a scapular medal. It depicts the Sacred Heart of Jesus, and the Mother of God on the obverse side. The medal could replace the woolen scapular. Back in the thirteenth century, Our Lady promised Simon Stock, Superior General of the Carmelite Order, that those who strived to live a Christian life and wore the scapular would be saved from eternal damnation and on the first Saturday after their death, would be taken by her to heaven.

... I am in hopes of a leave when I receive my commission. I shall be very disappointed if I don't get same because I have formulated extensive plans in which you play an integral part...

*Sincerely,
Andre*

May 12, 1943
Dear Ginny:

One more day of ground school and we will be all through here.

I'll need a little assistance on your part in the way of prayers that I will succeed in Advanced. I just can't fail now.

We have a new attraction on our post -- the WAACs came in the other day. About 65 of them and the boys have been pretty eager to get acquainted. We aren't supposed to go out with them because they are enlisted personnel and we are supposed to be officer material. However, last night quite a few of us went over to their recreation room and learned all about the WAACs...(7)

Do write soon.

*As ever,
Andy*

I remember you-ooh
You're the one who made my dreams come true
A few kisses ago

I Remember You
Victor Schertzinger & Johnny Mercer

Chapter Four
Advanced Training

The sole purpose of Advanced Flying School was to instruct the cadet to fly either a single-engine or multi-engine plane, depending upon the ship he would eventually fly in combat. For those assigned to the twin-engine school, like Andy, the expectation was to hone their instrument, as well as night and formation flying skills. But, the first order of business was to master flying a plane with more than one engine. Cadets were required to accrue seventy hours of in-flight training over a nine week period.

May 27, 1943
Dear Ginny:

I'm still alive and kicking should you have wondered just what happened to me. But then I haven't heard from you in sometime.

I am basking in the sunshine here at Yuma, Arizona, or should I say roasting. The temperature was only 109° yesterday. The scenery is really beautiful here, nice sand everywhere you look, of course, this monotonous scene is alleviated by superb cactus and mesquite.

We arrived here in the morning of the 21st and the sight of the base wasn't very encouraging. We miss quite a few of the conveniences we had at Lemoore. The constant heat causes an unquenchable thirst. The only consoling thought is our graduation on July 28 and the hope of a furlough at that time. The class that just graduated all received about 14 or 15 day furlough!

My day is rather long; reveille at 5:30 and it is 9:00 p.m. when I finish eating dinner. So you can see just how much time I have.

I'm flying a twin engine AT-17 now and I'm not so crazy about it because it is not capable of doing acrobatics. Wings come off too easy.

We had a delightful trip down on the train plus a 13 hour layover in L.A. Toured RKO studios and watched a picture in the making. Later we went for a swim at the Beverly Hills Hotel pool and it was marvelous. The homes there have anything we have in Detroit beat. I spent the remainder of the evening at the Coconut Grove listening to Freddie Martin.

Last Sunday, Carole Landis, Gloria Jean and Marjorie Woodworth put on a show for us here and it was pretty good.

I would say, the temperature at the present moment is about 120°.

Here I am again back from the flight line and ready to go to supper in about 10 minutes. It's rather late to be eating, 8:30 p.m. I received your letter today that you had mailed to Lemoore. No doubt you have received the picture by this time.

I'm due to graduate on the 28th of July and next day I celebrate my birthday. I thank you very much for your prayers as I shall need them.

I hope you will find time to write very soon. Till then, I'll say adieu.

Sincerely,
Andy

June 6, 1943
Dear Ginny:

According to an affidavit I signed this past week, I shall assume my baptismal of Andre and shall henceforth drop the name of Andrew forever and a day. Only correct I guess, because my name never was Andrew until the kind Notre Dame Sisters tacked the "w" onto it.

Although the name, Andrew, followed him throughout his school days, to his classmates he was simply, Andy. Each of his family members had their own pet name for him. His dad called him Petit (little one) from birth, while Rachel addressed her son as André or Dré; for sister, Maurine, it was Nannie, a name she had assigned to her brother as a toddler, unable to pronounce Andre.

With Andy's commission on the horizon, slated for July 28th, the Army Air Corps saw to it that everything was in order and "by the book". In spite of Andy's naturalized status, that included officially becoming a citizen of the United States. Andy completed the required papers and pledged his allegiance to his adopted homeland.

Glad you liked the picture such as it is and being on the night table reminds me of another picture of me on that table in a very different garb. Have you still got it?

I hear that my former heart-throb is getting wed this month, well I feel no pangs of sorrow and hope he can understand her better than I did.

If and when I get my leave, I hope to fly home in order to save some time because I don't want to waste a minute. I believe I am going to encounter difficulty in my attempt to get transportation from here when I do get my leave.

Some dope from the Chamber of Commerce is elucidating on the charms of Yuma such as--"where the winter spends the summer, leafy palm trees, lovely sunshine, flourishing and growing until Yuma has become a leader"--what drivel and perjury.

It appears that I will be home just in time to see you. Would have been a catastrophe if I would miss seeing you.

Incidentally, why don't you drop in and see mother and dad. I know that they would be very happy to see you. After all you haven't been over there in sometime.

I have about 15 hours in the bamboo bomber (8) now and find I like it a little. Begin formation flying next week followed by gunnery. Haven't decided yet whether I would like to fly a P-38 or A-20 when I graduate. Would you have any qualms about going up with me?

Believe I'll go to a movie tonight and see "Mission to Moscow" the cinema is just about the only diversion I have.

Quite a celebrity aren't you, giving a speech before such a large body, if I know you, it will be good, lots of luck.

Well, Ginny, that's about all the gossip for now, do write soon. Till then adieu.

Sincerely,
Andy

June 25, 1943
Dear Ginny:

I offer my most sincere apologies for my delay in writing to you but I am being kept busy continually.

I finished up my day flying today and all I have left is gunnery and night flying. The former will be exciting diving at a target blazing away with a machine gun and pulling within 100 feet off the ground.

On July 18, the colonel is going to inspect us in our officer attire. Ten days later comes the grand finale.

I'm listening to a jive rendition of "Moonglo", really solid.

I'm glad that you kept your promise to see the folks. Mother and dad were glad to see you I know and knowing my mother that she considers you welcome at any time, don't wait for an invitation, just drop in when you feel like it.

Glad your banquet and speech was such a success. I knew it would be.

The banquet that Andy refers to was the Fifteenth Annual Banquet of St. Mary's Alumnae Association given in honor of the 1943 graduates. Ginny served as toastmistress for the evening, welcoming guests, as well as making introductions and bringing the evening to a close.

Indicative that there was a war on, Lt. R. C. Coburn of the U. S. Navy Reserve was the guest speaker. Predictably, he spoke of the important role that the Navy was playing in the war, and acknowledged the contribution being made by women now serving in the Navy. (St. Mary's educated women.) However, he felt that woman's most important role would come when the troops, dearly missing the comforts and solace of home, returned from the battlefields. It was then that the American woman would be needed more than ever to provide sanctuary and peace of mind.

In her closing remarks, Ginny expresses the "hope that we will be together a year from tonight in a world that is celebrating the realization of victory and the happiness of a just and lasting peace."

Strange enough I managed to average about 95 in my ground school work here. No one was more surprised than I. Remember how I used to tease you with one of the Vismara sayings "if you think you are good, tell people you are" well I guess I'm still pretty much an egotist because confidentially, I think I'm a pretty hot little pilot. Boy, am I humble. ...

You know I am really looking forward to seeing you and I do hope I get that leave although I'm not as sure of it as I was but I'll wait until the time comes to worry about it.

How well I remember the days spent as a carpenter and the evenings we went swimming, centuries ago wasn't it.

Often, come Summertime, Andy would assist his cousin, Charlie, with building projects. One of Charlie's specialties was camping-trailers.

Did I tell you that I have a reservation on a plane leaving Phoenix on the 28th? Should arrive in Detroit the morning of the 29th. That leave had better come through.

Well, I believe I'll call it a night. Hope you find time to write soon. Au revoir.

Andy

July 2, 1943
Dear Ginny:

I shudder to think of my near confinement in the doghouse. Methinks, I would not like it there. Saved again by the Pony Express.

Have had even less time to myself this week, due to night flying which lasts until four in the morning. We sleep until noon, get up for dinner, indulge in athletics and then we go to the skeet range. It's really a lot of fun. Quite a little thrill blowing the clay pigeons to bits. We have to shoot them at all angles, also two at a time. Got 14 out of 25 today including two doubles.

"Human" targets were never used for combat training during the Second World War. Consequently, there were incidents when soldiers, in the heat of battle, froze, unable to fire their weapon, placing their comrades in mortal danger. Lesson learned. Thereafter, the military used human forms for weapons training.

The outlook for a leave doesn't look too good, so I may be very disappointed in not being able to see you.

I remember that ride to Mt. Clemens very well and if I remember correctly, you were rather aloof that evening. We also stopped for ice cream, remember? I often wondered after that just why I had taken you out that evening and the only conclusion I could formulate, was that I was trying to resurrect an affair that had gone astray but somehow your attitude frightened me off and I never made another attempt, but I would like to take that drive again under the present circumstances.

One paragraph in your letter bewilders me, what have you been reading that makes you accuse me of being a glamour boy. Elucidate gate!

You don't mean to tell me that you aren't afraid of deep water anymore? I'd like to give you the opportunity to "duck me" maybe it would be vice versa.

Have you anymore recent shots of yourself? I really would like to see another pose of you besides the one holding flowers. The flowers are getting wilted from much handling.

In a few minutes I have to go and fly until four a.m. so I'll take my leave of you. Do write soon.

Sincerely,
Andre

July 20, 1943
Dear Ginny:

One week from tomorrow is the big day at last. It hardly seems possible that the time is so near at hand. Then too, the possibility that I may be home next week seems too good to be true. I won't believe it until the plane comes in for a landing at the Municipal Airport. [Now known as Willow Run Airport located about twenty miles from Detroit.]

I was out for a couple of hours today making the final arrangements for our flight party tonight. Details like ordering the liquor, chaser, ice, food, transportation and so on fell on my shoulders, why I don't know. This will be our last celebration as cadets and it will be a good one. Friday, we have a combination splash party, barbecue and dance. Also there are a couple of shows I want to see this week so my time seems pretty well taken up from now until next Wednesday.

I hope you get in the mood to go to the photographer soon because I would like a picture of you that I could display. Maybe you'll have it done if and when I do come home.

About the ride to Mt. Clemens, it has its possibilities and I don't see why we wouldn't be able to take it. Maybe it could be termed as the ride that made history.

Mt. Clemens is ten miles beyond Detroit city limits. Andy and Ginny would have taken the river route, meandering along the St. Clair River. Maybe it is why, when I was a child, my mother loved to take family drives along the river all the way to Algonac and ferry across to Harsens Island where we would have dinner and watch the freighters go by. There are some things adults fail to disguise from their children. It was evident, even to my young eyes, that these excursions made mom happy. A sense of calm came to her face and a smile to her lips, as she strolled out, alone, onto the dock. But when she returned, there were tears to wipe away. It left me feeling confused, having no idea what had just happened. I looked to Dad for an explanation. He just shook his head. Ginny's secrets were safe with him. We just continued on as if nothing had happened.

The heat is still terrible and my arm keeps sticking to the paper.

We have a couple of hours of lectures on the schedule before we have our little affair tonight. That's about all we do now is attend lectures.

Wednesday

Well, the flight party has come and gone and the boys look a little under the weather today. Got to bed about 2:30 A.M. and slept until 11:00 this morning which was very nice.

Next week at this time I shall be a shave tail (newly commissioned second lieutenant) *and no longer a cadet.*

Have had quite a bit of leisure this week for which I am grateful.

Here's hoping that I'll be seeing you next week. Till then, so long.

Sincerely,
Andre

Aug. 6, 1943
Dear Ginny:

This is the first time that I have had an opportunity to write to you and also to thank you for the lovely handkerchiefs. I'm almost afraid to use them. I appreciate the fact that you are so considerate.

As you may know, my hopes for a leave were disappointed. I felt rather badly about it and it was with a rather heavy heart that I sent my folks the fateful wire.

A slight consolation was a few days delay en route which I spent in Denver. That really is a great town and the sooner I see it, the better. Arrived there Saturday evening and left early Tuesday morning.

Steve and I spent some time in the various officers' clubs and they were superb, very exclusive. Also danced to Jack Teagarden. There are so many nice places to go and the people are grand.

Steve was Andy's roommate. By evidence of V-mail, I have come to believe that his name was really William M. Stephens. I surmise that "Steve" was a nickname. After multiple attempts, I discovered that Steve survived the war, but I was sorely disappointed to learn that he died before I was able to locate him. There would have been so much that he could have shared with me.

Graduation was really a thrill, receiving my wings and commission. I have never seen so many 2nd looeys in all my life. Of course, it was one of the hottest days we have ever experienced in Yuma. It was a great feeling to be free at last and I do wish you could have been there. I wouldn't have asked my most hated enemy to come into that country.

The climate here in La Junta is very favorable. Cool breezes and all. Now, this would be the ideal place for you to visit. Am I hinting?

I shall probably have a 10 day leave when I finish here in two months and it will probably be the last one before I go elsewhere. Please don't mention this fact to mother but she probably realizes it but I don't want to worry her if I can help it.

Andy's two-month stint in La Junta was part of "Transition Training"--further training to prepare him for the type of plane he would fly in combat. The completion of pilot training was arduous as well as dangerous. Only sixty percent of the men who entered pilot training saw it through to the end. More than 130,000 "washed out" for a variety of reasons. Some were casualties.

I called the family from Denver and it was wonderful talking to them.

I'm flying B-25s (9) now and it really is a ship. Never thought anything so large could fly.

Again many thanks for your remembrance, do write soon.

Love,
Andre

With this letter, love replaces sincerely in Andy's closing for the first time. I am left to wonder if Andy took the initiative in this next stage of his relationship with Ginny, or if she abandoned her reserve. My hunch would be the former, since mom never wanted to appear too eager. She was an unwilling fool for love.

The same old sweethearts
The same old place
A boy in Khaki—a girl in lace

He bends to kiss her
She lifts her face
The boy in khaki—the girl in lace

A Boy in Khaki—A Girl in Lace
Allie Wrubel & Charles Newman

Chapter Five
The Furlough

Aug. 16, 1943
Dearest Ginny:

I hope this letter finds you at the Grand Hotel. I can well imagine that you are having a good time and it would be trite to say--I wish I were there. I know it's beautiful on Mackinac because I have seen it a few times. You deserve all the fun you can get because I know you do work hard.

I certainly would like to see Father Maino again, it seems like a long time ago that he was razzing me concerning one Ginny and then there is the bowling league he and I started.

Have been doing a little flying in different states the last few days, yesterday we flew to a few fields in Texas including Amarillo, thence to Oklahoma and back to Colorado. I may get to fly home on one of my cross-country flights and perhaps remain overnight. ...

Well, I guess I'm a failure; I just couldn't convince you to come to Colorado. Especially after I gave such a vivid description of the beauties and wonders of Colorado, (I don't mean blondes or redheads a depiction that would have done wonders to the heart of the Chamber of Commerce). Guess I've really slipped. I do want to see you because there are a lot of things I want to prove to myself, things which have troubled me for some time.

Will you wait for me?

I wouldn't mind tasting some of that fudge right now. As I recall it was good and I consumed copious quantities of same.

Ginny, is your birthday on September 16th, I don't remember correctly, but then that's me, I don't even know my mother or dad's birthday. I'll retract that statement, I just discovered it by reading my birth certificate.

We have a dance in the club every Saturday but for people like myself, everyone brings his own girl or wife and I have neither, so I don't dance and that is torture.

Well, Ginny, have a good time and think of me once in a while and try and drop me a line.

Au Revoir,
Andre

Mackinac Island, a dot on a map on the Straits of Mackinac between the upper and lower peninsulas of Michigan, was a popular summer retreat and remains so today. The island, a mere four square miles, does not accommodate cars. Tourists must arrive by ferry or plane. Everything and everyone are transported by horse or bicycle, lending an old-world charm and tranquility.

One of its world-famous exports is chocolate fudge of various nuances. People flock to quaint Victorian store-fronts, like bees to honey, to watch the fudge-makers slide and churn mounds of chocolate across marble slabs until it is cooled and thickened and prepared for consumption, a decadent indulgence.

The Grand Hotel dominates the island and exudes exclusivity. Any debate about it is quickly quelled by the toll for a night's stay. Considering their working class status, it would have been a decided splurge for Ginny and her friends.

Built on scale to match its name in 1887, the hotel is Americana personified with its wooden clapboards, painted white. Boxes of red geraniums border the expansive pillar-lined porch, the world's longest stretching 660 feet. During the war, an American flag was mounted on every pillar. Today they have resurrected that tradition.

One summer, when I was a teenager, most likely in an attempt to recapture my mother's fond girlhood memories, our family made the 400 mile trek to Mackinac Island. We stayed at a modest Bed and Breakfast, but one morning we ventured over to the Grand to take in her breathtaking ambiance and possibly, lunch. But Dad balked when he learned the price of a hot dog. Instead, it had to suffice to walk the length of the porch and sneak a peek at the sumptuous buffet being prepared for a higher class of people. I turned away, flushed with embarrassment, when a waiter in a white jacket, caught me looking. Like Liza Doolittle caught in a daydream, I tried to imagine how wonderful it would be to be served a meal in such an exquisite setting.

Aug. 23, 1943
Dear Ginny:

I still say you should have come to Colorado for your last week of vacation, because after I leave here and get a leave it will probably be the last one I get before I go across.

What do you mean 24 is the shelf age, I'm 24 and I don't feel that way about it. Just beginning to live at that age, so banish that idea from your pretty head.

If I do get to come home on a cross-country flight, it will be near the termination of my course here, but the whole thing is just a possibility.

Now that mother has a phone, I can give her a buzz once in a while.

Well, I hope you have a very good time during the remaining days of your vacation. Do write soon.

Love,
Andre

Aug. 31, 1943
Dear Ginny:

So dad tried to pull a fast one. I agree, I don't think he could disguise his voice that well. Leave it up to him to think of something like that.

Hey dear, when do I get that picture of you? The one I have now is getting rather frayed. I never have had a large picture of you and I believe it very possible that I could reciprocate with one of me, if coaxed hard enough...

I'll be taking some long cross-country hops this weekend. Tentatively on the list are Chicago, New Orleans, Milwaukee, <u>Detroit</u>, Pittsburgh and others. I'm really looking forward to the culmination of youthful dreams and landing at Selfridge Field. (10)

I'd give anything to see home and you again. I realize now only too well that I have left too much water run under the bridge as far as you and I are concerned. What do you think? I think the time is at hand for the two parties involved to get together.

Well Ginny, the time arrives when I must say adieu. Please write soon and don't forget my request.

Love,
Andre

Sept. 7, 1943
Dear Ginny:

Naturally, I was very elated to receive your letter and as per usual got a kick out of the contents.

I haven't been doing anything very exciting of late, just a show or bowling in the evening. Have been flying instruments all week and it's rather tedious and today it was a relief to fly formation. One thing that rather peeved me tonight is the fact that I have to go to Link Trainer (11) from eleven to midnight. So I can see I'll be fortunate to get six hours sleep tonight.

Gee darling, I'm glad that you are getting your picture made, utmost to curb my impatience until I receive the picture. To reciprocate, I'll see if I can find a photograph in town. ...

I'm really proud of you Ginny, for doing so much. There are still a lot of women that prefer to remain at home and spend their *time worthlessly and I admire you because I know you work hard during the day.*

If God wills you and I will meet again in just a month. Doesn't it sound wonderful! Just saying the words "I'll be home in a month" thrill me beyond all comprehension.

I'm listening to Kay Kyser at the present moment and with the tune of the "Johnson Rag" in my ear, I'll sign off. Do write soon and often.

Love,
Andre

Sunday
Postmarked 9-27-43
Dearest Ginny:

I know, don't say it, I'm a cad, a low-lifer, I'll be in the doghouse for the duration on bread and water but believe me dearest, I have been busy. In fact I called my family this morning to explain the lack of correspondence from this end. Irregardless, I have been thinking of you very often and I hope that feeling is mutual.

Last weekend I was in Denver and as per usual "a good time was had by all and sundry." The usual routine, visiting the local spots and for a change I was imbibing a little champagne. I have planned a surprise for quite some time now and you can be sure that you will be present in it when I get home.

This time when we have that long awaited dialogue, I don't want to do all the talking and I do promise to be frank if you will let your hair down because I want to get a complete understanding about a lot of things.

If all goes well, that should be in a couple of weeks.

I have seven hours left to fly and then, and then children, papa goes home. Another bit of news, my instructor has recommended me for instructor, so if it goes through, I may be around a little longer. I don't know if I'll care for it because I really would love to go to combat.

Did I tell you that I ran into George Noe down at Geiger Field in Spokane? We really had a gab session. His wife is with him and is expecting a baby.

Wednesday, I flew to Sacramento, California and met a few of my former colleagues from advanced. The weather is very hot out there. Cold here.

Am anxiously awaiting the arrival of your picture. I can hardly wait to see it. So until a little later darling, I'll sign off for now. Do write.

Love,
Andre

About October 10, 1943 Andy's long anticipated furlough was finally granted. From his letters that follow, one can garner some of the happenings of those ten special days—days that, like the switch of a train track, diverted the course of the lives of Ginny Egan and Andy Vleghels. A postcard postmarked October 20, 1943 let his fiancé know of his safe arrival at his new base in Florence, South Carolina where he would receive additional flight training.

Wednesday
10-20-43
Dearest Ginny:

I finally have found time to write a letter. I have missed you very much and hope that you have thought of me. It seems so long ago that we were together. I have your picture before me to bring back poignant memories.

I am going to fly A-20s, a light bomber, called the Havoc. It is lighter and faster and a lot of low altitude work. I shall be here at least three months and then we will replace crews that have returned to the States or have been shot down.

I went into town yesterday afternoon and it is nothing to brag about. Practically nothing to do except go to a show. Rather a dirty little town.

Our officers club is pretty nice and they do have dances every Saturday night what they dance with is beyond me.

I guess I can tell you now as you probably have heard it already but I ran into Jane Quinlan in the station at D.C. and she was in the same predicament as Steve and I, so the three of us did the town. I guess she's getting married to some looey [lieutenant] in N.C. Said she was coming back on the 23rd. We managed to miss her later train, so I got her a reservation on a plane bound for Detroit. I swore her to secrecy, so you don't have to worry about anything.

I suppose you are catching up on that well needed sleep. I had my first good rest last night.

Gee darling, I miss you so very much and love you with all my heart and soul. I really feel wonderful having you to love me. Steve admires my taste very much. But I didn't need him to tell me that because you are adorable. I shall always love you. And the only way I shall believe that you love me, is for you to write me very often. So with this, I shall depart. Think of me darling.

All my love,
Andre

The following letter was typewritten.

Friday
October 22, 1943
Hi Honey:

My Sister's Father

Sitting here in the Operations room with nothing to do so it seemed like an opportune time to dash off a sugar report to the one and only. Gee honey, I miss you so much that it actually hurts and that isn't good. I think of you constantly and all that I do is show your picture off to the rest of the fellows and make them green with envy. Incidentally, speaking of pictures, have you received my pictures from Craine's yet? If so, what do they look like? Horrible, I'll bet.

Still love me darling? I love you more with each succeeding day and I don't think that the apex will ever be reached? The more that I think of it, the more I am convinced that you are wonderful. I know that I teased you quite a bit but you know that I wouldn't hurt you for anything in the whole world. The only thing that I want to do is to make you happy and keep you that way.

As yet I haven't been up in an airplane since I arrived here, in fact I haven't done anything since I have been here. Not a word was said when Steve and I arrived a day late and probably wouldn't have said anything if we had been a couple of days tardy. I imagine that once I start flying I won't get a moment's rest, so I may as well take advantage of this well-needed rest for I do need to recuperate after that little session at home. By now you should be back in the pink and ready for another furlough. I'll see if I can't arrange it.

I have been into town a couple of times and it seems that a sweater craze has hit the girls because all of them wear one of some sort. Tomorrow night, we are having a dance at the club and I suppose that they will chase the gals out of the hills put shoes on them and bring them to the dance, just a bunch of jokers.

Darling, I am going to cut this letter short and hope that you are writing just as often as I am. Give my fondest regards to your family.

All my love,
Andre

Monday
Oct. 25, 1943
Dearest:

I haven't any news of any impact so you may find this letter a little boring. As yet, I have to leave the virgin soil of South Carolina far below me. I haven't flown in so long that I shall probably be called a "paddlefoot" [ground personnel] before long. The only reason I can see why I'm not flying is the fact that the scarcity of planes here is appalling. I went to ground school this morning and I can't think of a more tedious way to spend time. Can't see why we have to keep repeating it. At this rate, I'll be here for some months to come.

I do hope your tea was a success and a surprise. When will your pictures hit the paper? I want a copy of each paper it appears in. I don't mean the whole paper, just the part in which you are exhibited. Shouldn't be too easy to find those three lines on the last page announcing your engagement.

As yet I have received no correspondence from anyone. Probably, the mail service isn't very good. I have been writing every other day now so this should be my third letter I have written plus one card.

The tea that Andy refers to was hosted by Ginny's parents, in her honor, to announce her engagement to Andy. Officially, they were engaged on October 13, 1943. The local papers ran a formal photograph of Ginny, (probably the very one that Andy had been hounding her about) which bore a striking resemblance to Vivian Leigh, famed actress of "Gone with the Wind". I found the following announcement that Ginny submitted to the papers, in one of her scrapbooks: "At a tea given Sunday, October 24, in honor of their daughter, Virginia Dorothy, Mr. & Mrs. Edward J. Egan of Alter Road announced her engagement to Lt. Andre J. Vleghels, S.S.A.A.C., son of Mr. & Mrs. Maurice Vleghels of Britain Avenue. Lt. Vleghels is at present stationed in Florence, South Carolina. Miss Ruth Dykeman, Miss Bettie Dykeman and Miss Jane Mahoney acted as hostesses at the tea." The papers used an edited version of Ginny's submission as a caption below her picture.

I do miss you very much, darling, and dread to think of how I will feel in a few more weeks. I know now that I have never loved anyone except you. Still can't believe you are mine because you are much too good for me.

My Sister's Father

After I complete this I am going into town and buy a pair of pinks. (12) The cleaners shrunk my other pair.

So my darling, do write soon and often, au revoir.

Always yours,
Andre

> *Don't dance all night with me*
> *Till the stars fade from above.*
> *They'll see it's alright with me*
> *People will say we're in love.*
>
> People Will Say We're in Love
> **Rodgers & Hammerstein**

Chapter Six
Wedding Plans

Wednesday
Oct. 27, 1943
My Dearest:

I was so elated to receive a letter from you and I read and reread it many times. You were very brave at the station darling and I am very proud of you. I had quite a difficult time as I was leaving you and my family and it was sweet of you to shed tears after I was gone. The memory of that last kiss will remain etched in my mind until I again hold you in my arms. It was a grand ten days and someday we will have a whole lifetime together and we shall be able to live a natural life. I love you so much darling and I do think of you constantly. Darling, there is only one girl like you when you were made, the mold was broken. Any man would be proud to have your love and I still can't believe I am the lucky one. Our love was meant to be and nothing will ever break it.

The napkin was very cute and I am sure your tea was a high success. Just another score I have to settle with those yellow sons of _____, for keeping us apart.

My cold is still pretty bad and the doctor gave me some medicine and told me to stay in my quarters, so I still haven't been in the air.

Every time I get near a jukebox I play "People will say we're in Love" because I think it is our song. I have your picture before me as a constant reminder of your loveliness.

I still have your mark on my face, who knows it may be a permanent scar but as long as you put it there it's all right but don't let it happen too often.

The weather here is rather cold and the sky is overcast and it has hindered flying, I'm afraid there will be a lot more of this.

How did mother take my departure? I suppose Dad had his hands full consoling two weeping women.

Well my darling, I shall take my leave now. Think of me as I think of you.

All my love,
Andy

Continuing to write faithfully nearly every day over the course of the next couple of months, Andy professed his love to his fiancé in a continual litany of admirations. He kept Ginny abreast of his seemingly endless training, as it progressed, and the happenings on base. Pertinent excerpts from these letters follow:

Nov.1, 1943
9:30 PM

Darling, I shall try and write to you every day from now on because I do want you to be happy. Sweetheart, I love you and adore you with all my heart and soul. I have never missed anyone the way I miss you. You are my whole life and inspiration. Knowing that you have faith in me makes my whole being feel wonderful and how grand it is to be alive, having someone like you loving me.

Darling, I wish you could see the expression on my face when I reach the squadron, make a bee-line for my mail box and find your daily missive there, I feel tingly all over so please don't stop.

Hope you got the wings alright. You will wear them, won't you?

Nov. 2, 1943
6:30 PM

Your picture really looked super and it really makes me feel proud to see you shining out of the pages. Now thousands of other people will know just how lucky I am. I like the caption "Bride-elect of Air Force Officer." Yeah, that did the trick.

I was just thinking darling, that in the eventuality I get a few days off for Christmas, and that is a remote possibility, I thought that perhaps we could meet in Washington. At least we would get to see each other. If you think the idea is any good, let me know.

Nov. 5, 1943
4:40 PM

I just arrived from Columbia S.C., where I spent most of the day. I had to rise at 4:30 this morning because we were going by truck to the pressure chamber there and it is about 90 miles from Florence. It is a chamber in which ascent to high altitudes is simulated giving the same effect as if we were in a plane. We went to 18,000 feet without an oxygen mask and then to 23,000 with a mask. Coming down to 10,000 my sinuses really gave me a bad time, never had any trouble with them before. ...

I would have written yesterday but I actually put in four hours of flying and then last night, Steve and I went to the Fair that was in town. We were just like a couple of kids going on all the rides, throwing baseballs and other gyp joints...

I would give anything to see you right now. God, how I miss you. I have lived and relived those happy and glorious ten days. Just to think that it is a sample of what is before us the rest of our lives.

And we will have our own home and at night when I come home at twilight, you will be there waiting for me with outstretched arms. Gee, it all seems too good to be true. But of one thing I am sure, I love you.

Nov. 8, 1943
4:15 PM

I'm so glad that you approve of my plan to meet in Washington. Of course, if I get anytime off and the duration is long enough, I shall endeavor to come home. I am going to apply for same tomorrow and hope I am successful...

I miss you so very much. If this town had any living facilities, I'd have you down here in no time...

Nov. 9, 1943
7:20 PM

Darling, the medal was lovely and it is now about my slim, little size 16 neck. I do like it very nice. Sweet of you to have it engraved...

This afternoon I went to Post theatre and saw Judy Garland and Rooney in "Girl Crazy" and it was really good, haven't laughed so much in ages...

I too never believed it possible that I could love anyone the way I love you. To me you are perfection. It still seems strange that the spark broke into such a big flame after so long apart. So I believe I love you darling.

Nov. 9, 1943

I was glad to get the news about Bill and I am very happy that he is alive. I know it must be terrible enough to be a prisoner of the Japs but he is alive...

One of the boys piled an A-20 up this morning. Reason; one of the engines or both cut out and he couldn't make the field. I'm pretty sure the plane is demolished and he suffered head injuries. As yet no one knows too much about it. At least he's alive and that's something.

Nov. 11, 1943

Although I want very much to write a long letter, I'm afraid that I am not in a physical frame of mind to do so you know, "the spirit is willing, but the flesh is weak." First of all I have an earache that is practically killing me, secondly, I got shot for typhus and cholera this morning and I don't feel too well.

At the present moment, I am in Navigation class and the instructor who had experiences in the South Pacific, is giving us a little bull session on combat conditions.

Nov. 14, 1943

I'll wager that this is the first letter that you have ever received written up at an altitude of 4,000 ft. I can't use my pen because I'm afraid the ink would gush out. We are now in a 30° bank and over a forest which looks like so many bushes from here. Also a dandy forest fire going on. Usually there are quite a few, sometimes impairing the visibility to such an extent as to prohibit flying.

Nov. 16, 1943

I am writing this under different circumstances because I write letters in unusual places, such as 4,000 feet up and from a hospital cot where I am now reclining.

To explain: this morning on my way to the flight line I was in the back seat of a car with two other fellows and we were sideswiped by a G.I. truck. Glass flew galore and I promptly proceeded to bang my nose against the front seat in a very forceful manner causing a couple of bones to go in the wrong direction and the red stuff to flow profusely. We wound up in a ditch minus a front wheel and a few other miscellaneous objects appending to a car. Strange too, I was the only one injured. At the hospital the bones were pushed back in place and my nose packed until about 2:00 PM. I have a headache but that's about all right now.

I immediately felt much better when Steve brought your letter. I did get a kick out of that letter from Gerry and Ellery. I didn't have the faintest idea where they were. We did have a lot of fun together. I wrote to them right away.

Sure hope that my nose doesn't acquire any more curves. Doctor said he could see the malformation of one bone caused when I was playing football at St. Anthony's.

Sure wish that you were here to nurse me.

Gerry and Ellery, two Army friends of Andy's, sent a letter to Ginny after they happened to come across *The Detroit News* article announcing his engagement. The letter was pasted into Ginny's scrapbook. Andy's buddies had a grand time razzing Ginny about her pending nuptials to their "partner in crime".

My Sister's Father

HEADQUARTERS
272ND FIELD ARTILLERY BATTALION
Camp Butner, North Carolina

November 4, 1943
Dear Mrs. Vleghels—to be:

You will, no doubt, wonder who we are and why we are writing to you in such an informal manner, but by a stroke of good luck, while pining our hearts out in the wilds of North Carolina, we ran across a two week old newspaper from our old home town—Detroit. While running through the pages we found inscribed therein, an announcement of your forth coming marriage to our old boozin'-buddy, Andy. You may call him Andre, but to us it will always be Andy.

Your picture and announcement were quite a surprise to us. You are really beautiful. We can't figure out why you want to marry him with stuff like us still free, however, the best of luck and a world of happiness to you both.

It has been just about a year ago to date, since we were last together—Andy, Jerry and myself, and that was in Nashville, Tennessee while we were on maneuvers and he was still a boot (new recruit) in the Air Corps. However, that night we took the boot off and filled it up with everything we could think of, and then some, in the Drum Room of the Andrew Jackson Hotel. Boy! Did we get plastered. So much, in fact, one of the boys was carried home on a shudder. Since that grand and glorious night our thirst has mounted, but has never been thoroughly *quenched. Somehow or other, we miss the lad that used to lead us into sin and temptation. When you receive this letter, we hope you don't mind the ribbing your future is getting, for we don't mean it much. It is just that we wanted to congratulate you, and let him and yourself, whom we have never had the pleasure of meeting, damn it, know we are still thinking of you.*

Upon closing, we hope that on your wedding day in case there is an extra drink laying around any place—have it on us.

*Lots of luck,
S/Sgt. Thomas G. Washburn
M/Sgt. Ellery J. Lynn*

P.S. Please send, 2 each, pieces of wedding cake—not G.I. [Government Issue].

Nov. 19, 1943

I too, am hoping with bated breath for the news that will give me a few days off for Christmas. I can't possibly imagine anything more wonderful than being with you again. It does seem like a year since I last held you in my arms and told you how much I loved you but perhaps with the Grace of God, we will be together again sooner than we expect...

We haven't seen any signs of coal around here for the last week or two and I can tell you that it gets plenty cold at night and in the morning until about ten. Can't figure the deal out. Must be the work of some paddlefoot.

Nov. 21, 1943

So you really are domesticated now, I'd like to see that sewing and all--know how to fix a steak medium rare yet?

Nov. 23, 1943

Did I say you were wonderful? You are superb and I adore you for your thoughtfulness. You can't imagine how very happy I was when I received your surprise package. Boy, it really is good and I thank you from the bottom of my heart and send you a thousand kisses. It's simple to see just why I love you--so considerate, loving, oh I could go on for hours but there is no need because you are ideal and my love for you goes beyond words or actions.

So I used to distract you in class, why didn't you tell me then, I knew my charms were not to be spurned but I didn't know that they carried such a fatal charge. It probably was all for the best that we were apart for we may never have loved each other as deeply as we do now.

Nov. 27, 1943

I was just thinking that if I have to spend Xmas down here by myself, I'll go mad. I get melancholy enough as it is but on that *day, the mere thought of you will be enough to drive me to the depths of despair. I was very thankful that God brought us together again and that you love me so much. I adore you.*

Nov. 28, 1943

I'm going to have to keep an eye on my dad, taking such an interest in you. You know, I have a sneaking idea that they both like their prospective daughter-in-law...

Speaking of turkey, why didn't you send me a few sandwiches--my favorite dish. Say that's an idea, I believe I'll have my mother send me a roast turkey for Christmas.

Nov. 30, 1943

I didn't have to fly this afternoon and was sitting on my bed trying to read but my mind kept turning to you so much that I just had to stop and write to you. I love you so much, I get such a thrill writing those words and it fills me with contentment when you write of having fun with my family. Just think how grand it will be when we will all be together.

Darling perhaps you have wondered why I have never mentioned it but I have thought of it constantly and that is our marriage. I still don't think it would be fair to you if we were married now, then having to leave you and perhaps not coming back and leaving you maybe with a child, oh I know I maybe all wrong and at times it's all I can do to restrain myself from asking you to come down and marry me. I do wish you could tell me what you want darling. Think about yourself, for my part I would have wanted to be married for the last six weeks because being away from you would be torture. Whatever you say goes because I want to do all in my power to make you happy. There wouldn't be any sense in getting married unless you came to live with me and that wouldn't be easy around an Army camp. God, I love you so very much and you are always with me in everything I do.

Darling, if I don't get any time off for Xmas would I be asking the impossible if I were to ask if you could come down and spend a few days or so with me? I know it's a large order but it would be the most marvelous gift I could ever receive.

Dec. 1, 1943

I'm enclosing the money order which should finish up the ring.

Say honey, there is just a hope that I will get either five days off for Xmas or New Year's. They took our names and my preference was Xmas and if so will come home. I do hope it will come true.

Dec. 3, 1943

Hold your breath but I believe I am going to get a leave for Christmas, don't get excited now, it's not positive but I believe I'll get it. I'm going to try and get a flight from the field here but if that fails, I am going to try and fly home from Columbia via Eastern Airlines. I am going to try and get away the evening of the 21st and I have to report back by midnight of the 27th. So do *you feel happy now? I'm looking forward to it with all my heart and the excitement mounts with each passing hour...*

So if I get home on the 22nd, we will have five days together. I do think you should take time off, how about it! And if you want to, we can do something else with special dispensation, must I say more?

Dec.. 6, 1943

I received your letter today in which you believe we should be married. Well, I would like nothing more but I just happened to think of a certain matter which I hadn't given too much thought. The thing is, after I pay for traveling expenses, I won't have more than enough money to pay for the wedding ring. I know Christmas with my leave and all would be the most marvelous time to be married. Believe me darling, I want to get married. I want it more than anything in the world because I miss you and need you. I think we should be married because I believe I'll be in this country for a few more months at least. So finances are our only obstacle and at the moment I don't see how we can overcome it. I would be deliriously happy if I could have you at my side. If we do find some way out, it might be better if I came down first and tried to find some place for us to live. When we are married I'll make $321 per month and I think we should be able to live on $80 per week. I do wish you would talk it over with my mother and see if she knows any solution. If I were to know definitely that I would only be in the States a matter of weeks I wouldn't consider it but the way I have been flying it will be considerably longer.

So darling, tell me what you think, of course, I too would like a church wedding

I love you very much, darling, and I miss you dreadfully. I need you. Write.

On the day that Andy wrote this letter, Ginny decided to send him a telegram. Andy received the cable the morning of the 7th. Ginny writes: PLEASE CALL ME DECEMBER 7TH AT 7 PM AT MURRAY 3887 REVERSE CHARGES MUST ARRANGE OUR WEDDING PLANS LOVE GINNY.

Dec. 8, 1943

It was wonderful hearing your loving voice again. I really was thrilled and that is only a particle of the way I felt when I received your telegram yesterday. For the first time it really hit me that I was about to be married. Guess I went around with a very dopey smile on my face.

I called mother immediately after I had finished our call and naturally she was surprised and happy. Said if I'm happy then she is too. Talked to the rest of the family and Maurine and Dad said it was great.

Dec. 9, 1943
My Darling:

Nothing much to report tonight but I just had to write to you because the image of you is constantly before my eyes and this helps so much because it brings you close to me if only for a little while but soon we will be together and it will be Heaven. Oh darling, I still can't believe my good fortune and won't until I hear your sweet lips form the words "I do" that will make me the happiest man in the world.

I do wish I could be there to help you with the countless details that I know you have to contend with but I can only give my moral support and be with you in spirit.

I took my Wasserman (13) test today and will have the results in about five or seven days. Will that be too much of a delay? Darn it, I'm not used to this Remington Noiseless and I'm making mistakes galore as you can plainly see.

Darling, if it isn't too expensive, I would like to fly back here because otherwise we would have to leave on the 26th and that wouldn't give me quite four days at home, so I'll just add that little item to your already long list and know that you will take care of it. Of course, if it is out of the question, we will have to travel by train. Say honey, I haven't received a letter from you in the last two days. Please don't forget me.

I hope that you have talked with mother by this time and that some details have been straightened out.

I'm Alert Officer tonight which means that I have to post the guard, inspect them, have bed-check, and a couple of other details. Steve happens to be the same thing in his Squadron tonight so we have been whipping around the post in our jeeps and having a great time. He is very happy about our pending wedding and I am very sorry that he can't be here but such are the fortunes of war. He still doesn't know if he is going to get a leave but hasn't much hope of getting one.

Oh yes, if we are able to travel by air, don't forget that the limit on baggage is forty pounds and you could send the rest by Railway Express.

So my darling, I come to the end of another letter. I love you very dearly and miss you terribly. Soon we two will be one and so very happy. So pleasant dreams darling, I love you.

Yours always,
Andre

Dec. 13, 1943
My Darling:

Another day and as yet no letter. You really must be busy but I would like to hear from you and know how everything is going.

Darling, I'm in a quandary, could you give me some idea of what you would like for Christmas? As usual I am in a muddle and don't know what to get.

Looks like I am going to have to ask you to do something else for me. Would you buy a pair of pajamas, a white blouse and a scarf for Maurine, she takes age 18 pajamas, blouse 34. For mother a white blouse I think size 36, a night gown size 17 (she is 5'6" 140 lb) and a few pairs of stockings 9 1/2 long. Get Dad a box of R.G. Dun's (cigars) if possible, a couple of neck-ties and I shall try and find something else for him. Also, I suppose you have thought of something to get Leo and please buy something for your mother and dad for me. I'll have mother get something for Frank and Charlie.

I know I'm putting a big burden on you darling, but this is one of the many I shall place on you, maybe you can find some for me.

Oh yes darling, the major said he would try and get me up to Battle Creek on the 21st if we can land there, if not we shall have to land at Columbus, Indiana. I felt very good at hearing this because then I'll have a little time to help you with anything that has to be done.

Did I ever tell you how much I love you? As a matter of fact I adore you. Now when I go to town or eat at the club, I can just visualize you there with me and it's so wonderful. We'll be the two happiest people in the world. I miss you so much darling and with the grace of God we will be together in a week.

I'll sign off now thinking of you and loving you with all my heart and soul. Au revoir.

Yours always,
Andre

Andy's request for gift buying detail for Leo, Frank, and Charlie were wedding-related responsibilities. Ginny's brother, Leo, was to serve as their best man, while Andy's two cousins, Frank and Charlie, would be their ushers along with Ginny's youngest brother, Jerry.

Frank and Charlie were sons of Rachel's eldest brother, Alphonse. During their early years as Belgian immigrants, when Andy was just a boy in short pants, his parents shared their home on Theodore Street with their nephews. Being of working age, I imagine that they contributed toward household expenses. Maurice and Frank both secured jobs at Gray Marine Motor Company, while Charlie earned his carpenter's license. As a teen, Andy spent more than one summer helping "Uncle Charlie" with a variety of building projects.

Dec. 16, 1943
My Darling:

I was very elated to receive your wonderful letter and know that everything is alright.

It was a surprise to hear that your mother felt the way she did. I hope she is willing to accept me as a son-in-law. But I can understand how she feels, something very dear to her now is to belong to someone else.

I hope you receive the results of my Wasserman within a day or two. I sent it today special delivery.

I can't say I appreciated Fr. Clancy's sentiments. Doesn't seem very appropriate to persuade you not to go through with it. I realize he is losing a superlative secretary but I am gaining a wonderful wife. Can't blame him in a way I guess...

I think you had better get the ring at Meyer's and put it on account and I'll take care of it when I get home.

I have no definite assurance of the cottage and have other irons in the fire. But you are coming back with me even if we have to live in a hotel for a few days. Don't worry about it. Also don't bring too much clothes and all that. Do pack a formal because you'll need it occasionally.

Don't worry about finances for transportation, just get us reservations on a plane or a train. I have to report for duty sometime on the 28th.

What do people mean, times like these, what's wrong with the times. If all was to cease because of the war then we may as well stop living.

I love you so much darling, and each succeeding day, the excitement within me mounts until I'm afraid I shall burst with joy.

So please darling, don't worry about the housing problem, I'll take care of that.

Write when you have time darling. Perhaps it will be too late to write. I do miss you very much and love you with all my heart and soul.

All my love,
Andre

P.S. *It snowed 6" last night. Very cold.*

This was the last letter that Andy wrote to Ginny as a single man.

The Bells of St. Mary's
Ah, hear they are calling
The young loves, the true loves
Who come from the sea.

And so my beloved,
When red leaves are falling,
The love bells shall ring out, ring out
For you and me.

The Bells of St. Mary's
Douglas Furber & A. Emmett Adams

Chapter Seven
The Newlyweds

Despite advice to the contrary by some, Ginny and Andy moved forward with their plans. Fifteen days remained to plan their wedding to take place on the morning of December 23, 1943. More mementos began to fill the ebony pages of Ginny's scrapbook already begun at the time of her engagement tea--the press announcement of her engagement, a napkin imprinted with a gold script that read, Ginny and Andy, October 24, 1943, and dainty gift cards bearing best wishes from friends and family were neatly mounted, row upon row, page upon page. She included swatches of the bridesmaids' dresses, correspondence from area businesses offering their services tailor-made for "furlough weddings", and congratulatory letters from well-wishers. One such letter came from Sr. Joannella, her instructor at St. Mary Commercial School. In an excerpt sister writes:

November 26, 1943
My dear Virginia,

It was sweet of you to inform me of an event that announces a turning point in your life. Constance Turgeon had already sent me the clipping, but I was pleased to learn it from <u>you</u>.

With your parents' and Father Clancy's approval, I am sure that you are not making a mistake; and that the fortunate man is worthy of you. They surely are advising you to defer your marriage until he has finished his job with Uncle Sam. It may seem hard to see it in that light now, but you will not regret it, I assure you. Indeed, I shall continue to pray for you and Andy, as I have prayed for you <u>only</u> in the past, my dear Virginia.

Andy was right when he said that Ginny had a lot to manage. In addition to attending to all the details of the wedding, there was the long list of Christmas presents and keepsakes for the bridal party to purchase, in addition to packing-up for life on an Army base. I can imagine that she placed these responsibilities squarely on her own shoulders. Ginny's mother, Liz, ran an efficient household, but party-planning and fashion were not her strong suit. Ginny, on the other hand, was stylish and had an eye for detail, coupled with a tenacity to get things done. The constraints of the timeline were challenging, but not impossible for her to meet.

As with any wedding there was the juggling to be done among family members in an attempt to keep everyone happy, and yet, invariably someone always ends up feeling hurt. Maurine, who was just thirteen years old, was crushed that she was not asked to be part of the wedding party. Both of Ginny's siblings were included and Maurine felt left out on the most important day of her brother's life. Ginny had asked her friend, Ruth, to be her maid-of-honor; Bettie and Jane would be her bridesmaids. And then there was Andy, pining away in South Carolina yearning for a letter from his fiancé.

Even under ordinary circumstances, prenuptial emotions run high trying to keep in step with the frenetic pace of preparations, steeped in tradition and ritual. But these were not ordinary times. Uncertainty permeated these times like smoke in a house on fire. Maybe all the more reason to seize the moment and grab life before it evaporated before their very eyes.

And so, on Thursday, December 23, 1943 at ten o'clock in the morning family and friends gathered in St. Phillip Neri Church at the corner of Charlevoix and Lenox to witness the marriage of Ginny and Andy. A bitter cold wind whipped at the heels of the bridal party, dressed in their finery, as they scurried into the church to take refuge. Keeping with the spirit of patriotism, the attendants wore floor-length dresses of French blue velvet and carried generous bouquets of red roses and feathery ferns with full red satin bows. Ginny looked rather demure in her 1940's white satin bridal gown complete with the traditional long, flowing train. She held white roses with a matching satin bow, streamers of ribbons cascading to her hemline. A string of pearls accented their necklines. The men of the wedding party were outfitted in black tuxedos with white gardenia boutonnieres fixed to their broad lapels. With his trademark wavy blonde hair, Andy stood tall and handsome in his Army dress-uniform. Father Raymond S. Clancy, essentially, Ginny's boss, officiated at the Sacrament of Marriage and celebrated the Mass, uniting the lives of Lt. Andre J. Vleghels and Virginia D. Egan as they vowed to honor and cherish each other "until death do us part" before God and man. They were both twenty-four.

Following the ceremony, a breakfast reception was held at the Savarine Hotel on Jefferson Avenue, a neighborhood establishment. Wedding photographs capture Ginny's tentative smile. I suspect that the entire event was bittersweet, peppered with apprehension. Promises, happiness, good wishes, hope--all in the fore, while nagging possibilities that no one wanted to consider tugged at their hearts and minds. As the war escalated, and the Allied Forces began preparations for D-Day, such a scene became oh so familiar across America, repeating itself over and over so that the "furlough wedding" was becoming the norm.

At the rate of $6.50 per night, Andy and Ginny spent a couple of nights at the Hotel Statler Detroit in room # 822, checking out on the 26th. Maurine recalls that Andy and Ginny spent at least one night at the Vleghel's home. Rachel and Maurice lent their room to the newlyweds, while they slept upstairs in Andy's former attic room in a twin bed. Though ecstatically happy to be wed, Andy and Ginny extended consideration and sensitivity to the Vleghels family by making time for them. The hard truth was no one knew if they would ever see Andy again.

I am guessing that Andy and Ginny boarded a plane for Florence, South Carolina. Andy had to report for duty on the 28th, and in a letter, Elizabeth Egan mentions sending Ginny's trunk to her, a suggestion Andy had made if they were to fly back.

Andy and Ginny's precious time together in Florence as newlyweds was the one and only exception to my mother's aversion to conjuring up memories of Andy. Their home together was a furnished one-room apartment, part of a complex of adjoining units known as The Smith Cottages. Constructed of brick and siding, the units were devoid of even the most rudimentary appliances, including a kitchen sink. Dirty dishes were washed in the bathroom sink and were hidden in the shower when they entertained. Save the daily walks into town for a sundae with her new-found friend, Evie, I am sure that the dusty little town of Florence, South Carolina held no appeal for Ginny Vleghels. Without question, her good humor and contentment were solely due to the love and esteem that she felt for her groom.

Mom told and retold the story countless times, never tiring of it. And amazingly, she could tell it without crying. Most days in Florence began before sunrise. Half asleep, Ginny would struggle to prepare a hot breakfast for Andy. As he dressed for the day, he would patiently gaze upon his beautiful bride, contentedly amused, as she attempted to conquer breakfast. She readily admitted that she could barely boil water. Her wanton culinary skills were further hampered by her cooking appliance--two hotplates. How she hated those hotplates! They quickly became the bane of her existence. Now Ginny knew full well that Andy could have handily prepared his own breakfast, but she was determined, and her husband derived great pleasure from her willingness to please him, to care for him, and so he let her demonstrate her love for him in this way. It must have seemed a dream to him, at times, to have won the heart and hand of his love, nearly lost, now by his side to welcome each new day, safe in his arms each night.

And then there were the Saturday nights at the Officers' Club where they socialized and they danced--a real chance to let their hair down after the stresses of the week. Although Andy was still in training, accidents happened; men died in training too. Ginny found it especially worrisome when Andy had to practice night flying. It terrified her.

Once again, letters give witness to these fleeting and cherished days.

A verbose Father Clancy writes volumes on January 22, 1944:

Dear Ginny:

Pursuant to your instructions I am typing this letter myself, rather than dictating it to your successor. Hence you will have to be tolerant of any and all typographical errors.

We were all delighted to hear from you and to sense the spirit of happiness and contentment which permeated each page that you wrote. While we had every confidence in Andy (and you'll remember that I was "in his corner, pulling for him," long before I had the pleasure of meeting him), nevertheless we feared that you might encounter a housing problem and being so far away, alone and among strangers for so many hours each day, might become a bit home-sick. So we are all very much pleased to know that you are so happily situated as to your home and your neighbors and, particularly, that Andy can be with you so much.

For his sake I am glad that it is possible for you to eat at the Officers' Club; otherwise I should greatly fear for his well-being physically, while you are going through your basic training as a cook.

Father goes on for about another four pages, single-spaced. Mainly, he expounds in exhaustive detail about the many recommendations and subsequent interviews required to find a suitable successor for Ginny. Toward the end of his dissertation, he adds:

All of your many friends in the building, as well as Mother and Dad, join me in sending best regards to you and Andy. While we all miss you, we are reconciled by the knowledge of your happiness...

Cordially yours,
R.S.C.

P.P.S.—If you want subsequent letters from me to run as long as this one does, you will have to withdraw your strict admonitions to the contrary and permit me to allow Sally to do the typing. (Incidentally her full name is Sally O'Dwyer. Definitely, she is not Polish. Fearing that you might not be interested in a fuller description, let it suffice to say that she is decidedly on the blonde side, weighs ninety-five pounds and is very talented, lovely and efficient.)

R.S.C.

I found letters from the Egan and Vleghels families mixed in with Andy's missives. Family letters offer a window into the feelings and daily happenings of the parents and siblings of Andy and Ginny as the novices begin their life together. Their sudden engagement and wedding must have been a bit of a jolt to everyone. The war had imposed an urgency, nonexistent in a peace-filled world. Priorities changed. Ginny's seventeen-year-old brother, Jerry, was the first to write.

January 3, 1944
Dear Sis & Andy:

I did not have any school today; they gave us off in honor of that new priest who said his first Mass Christmas. I went downtown yesterday and saw Ina Ray Hutton and her all male band. Zink and I were sitting in the second row right in the center, it was a good show. Skippy (family dog) *was so sick for three days that he could hardly stand up. I don't know if it was because you went away or if he caught cold sleeping in the garage during the celebration. He is feeling very good now we had ma feeding him warm milk before he went to bed. It's a good thing you were not home a few nights ago. We were all sleeping when all of a sudden Skip started barking, as usual I did not hear him. Dad got up and started down stairs as he reached the first step he heard the coal in the coal bin come crashing down. It sounded just like someone running up the coal pile to get out the window. Dad did not waste time coming up stairs. By this time they had me awake. Dad got dressed and* *went outside to see if all the windows were locked. He found that they were. So Dad and I went down the basement. Skippy was chained up and still barking and looking straight at the fruit cellar. We both started sweating and flipped to see who was going to open it. Dad lost he opened it and what do you think was there. You could have guessed nobody there. Skippy was barking because he wanted a drink and his pail with water in it was next to the cellar. About the coal I guess that just slid down accidentally. We did not sleep good that night. I worked 30 hours in three days at the Saturday Night Press and made $25.00. No doubt you are learning to cook fast around there. I hope Andy is coming along okay with his flying. Take care of yourself, ma thinks your starving down there.*

Jerry

Ginny's mother, Elizabeth, writes a few days later.

Jan. 8
Dear Virginia & Andy

Just a few lines to let you know that we are all well and hope you and Andy are the same I just received your letter of Jan 1 it took 7 day to reach me that is a long time by air mail and Dad send your trunk the next day. You should have it by now and I send you a box of Sanders candy when you get it let me know. You ask me what I did New Years eve well we played cards till 4 and I did not have turkey for New Years we had chicken I ask Leo and Pat but they did not come they went out with Don so you see it was lone some I think you must be on the bus at 6 I look for you every night but some day you and Andy will be back home and we will have lots of fun Jane and Betty & Ruth Mrs. Dykeman call me up but they have not been over. I went down town last week and change that dress and got a pretty dark blue and new shoes patent leather you would like them I wash my kitchen last week and it looks swell how do you like house work I will send you the things you want this week. Virginia if you do not use those brown stamp in your book No 3 send them home in the next letter because they are only good for butter or meat it takes 8 for a ½ pound of butter (food rationing) *well dear Virginia this is all for this time hoping to hear from you soon*

With all my love and kisses From
Mother

Over the next couple of months, the Vleghels family write-- Andy's mother, Rachel, being the most diligent of the three.

January-16-1944.
Dear Virginia and Dre.

It sure was too bad that Dre could not make the flight to Detroit, you would not be lonesome Virginia, you have to get used an, a little at the time. That would have been swell. [The possibility must have existed for Andy to hop a plane from the base for a quick visit home, but it never materialized.] *We are very happy to receive such nice letters from you and to know that you are both happy. ... I bet you are getting to be a good cook Virginia, did you take some of your aprons along. Say Dre, what about you writing what your wife is cooking, getting lazy eh boy* and some more spoiled. Well you was in the paper again, not much, but in anyway. We haven't any news, don't go out much, so pa send all is love and Maurine too—he will write, I will make him do it, he is afraid his grammar is not very good.

>Bye. Till soon.
>Love
>Mom

January-21-1944.
Dear Virginia and Dre.

Just received both your letters and don't have to tell you, they made me very happy to know that my big boy is being taken so good care of, Virginia I love you for it and I am so glad also Pop that you are both so happy, we pray our dear God that he may end this war very soon, so all boys can go home again and be happy together... I guess we talked too much about dear pa's bowling he is rotten for the last two weeks. I will leave some space for Maurine and Pop. So I will say lets hope and pray that we all be together soon. A big kiss for both of you my darlings. Your Mom.

Dear Virginia and Andre,

School is getting along pretty good, and probably before I know it will be time to graduate. I am still hoping that you will still be there in June for I would love to visit you and see you very much. Lately we are getting quite a bit of homework. I hope you both will be home for good by the time I go to Dominican [parochial all-girl high school] *for I want somebody to help me with my homework. Our class pins are supposed to be here next week already. Well I've got a lot of homework now so I had better get at it or Sister will finish me off.*

That's about all for now. I love you both.

Your loving sister,
Maurine
Xxxx

Dear Angels.

Here is all my love and kisses, will write next week, as now Maurine as to take this letter to the mail.
God bless you
Your Lovely
Pop

Jan. 30-1944
Hello Ginny and Andre'

Here is your pop, better late than never, of course I am not very good in writing letters but I will take a chance.

We just received two letters from you and as always they make us very happy, How I like to see you both in your cottage, the way I read in your letter it must be beautiful, oh dear I will be right over for a cup of coffee, what no beer, it's a <u>scream</u>. Dear oh Dear, no good for pop. No speak English. Say Ginny how *come they always have coffee by you, what about them, don't be too good with these fliers let them furnish the grub for a change, no Justice; Can't write much news, Mom gets away with that, so I will just say these, take good care of each other and lots of luck.*

By the way, tootsie roll don't you dare two-time me, with all those fliers around you or I put you in the "cat house".

Yes my Boy we have seen the dog and the flea, really super duper as Ginny would say it, and the way pop says a short beer in a tall glass.

Yes, my Bowling is average for couple of weeks, but I am in shape for a 200 game I hope.

...My Boy, I am sure glad to hear that you are on your feet again and colds gone. Dre', do you think they will let you come home before you Leave?

News of the day, Red Wings [Detroit's pro-hockey team] *won 6 straight and 3 tie, take second place very good team.*

Well that's all for today dears, I send all my love and kisses to you all.

Your Pop

February-23-1944.
Dear Virginia and Dre.

My Sister's Father

Yesterday was parents day at school, so of course I had to go, they had diagram looked hard to me, and Maurine sure will appreciate your help when your home Dre you don't have to worry a minute about your wife we will keep an eye on her and I know she will on us and replace in a big way our darling boy, who we will pray so hard will come back soon, so darling promise and don't worry, but take always good care of yourself no matter where you are. When I was waiting in the hallway for Maurine I saw a big map of America on the wall, with small pictures and little ribbons, I said to myself, Maurine spoke of that could my darling flier be on it and jes there he was smiling lt. Andre Vleghels, Maurine's brother with a star and a ribbon attach that leads to the part where you are stationed nice don't you think, and sure not forgotten, big brute, myn baasken

As I said before Pop does not write a lot, just like son, but talks of you both all the time, believe it or not loves his daughter Virg. as much I believe as his boy...

Oh yes a very happy, how can I say it, 2 months anniversary jes two months today and don't you worry many happy ones are coming for you both. Hows the cooking, now you will have a chance to be a good cook Virginia by the time your husband comes home. So we send all our love and big kisses.

Your
Mom

*February-28-1944.
Dear Virginia and Dre.*

Just received your letter, sure came fast. We are glad that you will be here a few days more, you never write how and when Virginia is coming back, taught maybe they let you come for a couple of days, but that would be escpecting too much, and anyway its maybe the best way.

...and again don't worry everything will come out fine, but be very careful and don't go for medals. ? for them, take care of your own skin.

Oh yes I am going to work next week maybe, in the cafeteria of the vitamin production Co. on Gratiot and Grinell its past the airport, even if its only till I make enough to pay for Maurine her four years at school it will be escpensif and the war won't last long and money will be hard to get then, maybe you don't like it Dre, but we did figure a little on the time when you would make a lot of money as you always said, but instead got married, so I will have to see that Maurine has the same education as you had, because later on will be too old. So many do it so it won't kill me if only for a few months.

We are on pins to know where you are going but I guess you don't know yourself.

So Dre chin up you have a job to do, God will bless you and bring you home safe, don't <u>ever</u> think otherwise We will write all the time and V mail.

Lots of love from Pa also your sister we will be praying for you all the time. Virginia show everybody that you can take it and a few years from now, <u>both</u> of you will think about this as a bad dream.

I will send you, with this all my love and blessing and a very big kiss. Till not so long

*Your
Mom*

It's spring again
And birds on the wing again
Start to sing again
The old melody.
I love you,
That's the song of songs
And it belongs
To you and me.

I Love You
from **Mexican Hayride** by **Cole Porter**

Chapter Eight
The Separation

By the end of February, 1944, circumstances changed dramatically for Andy and Ginny. Andy had received word that he would be sent to Hunter's Field in Savannah, Georgia, a staging area for the Army. There, he would await his orders that would eventually determine his assigned Theater of Operations--European or Pacific.

The long anticipated and dreaded time drew near when the war would force the newlyweds to go their separate ways. They had just begun laughing and loving together and now, somehow, they had to learn to exist apart, at least on the physical level. And

Ginny had recently learned that they were expecting their first child, due in October. The war was intruding on their lives more and more. Like a storm off in the distance, they could see it brewing, they watched it as it edged its way closer, they even dared to step in its path, and now it was upon them; the vortex sending everything helter-skelter.

Since the Army kept the transfer and movement of military personnel a mystery to its ranks, Andy and Ginny had to guess at what to do next. Should Ginny accompany Andy to Georgia or return to her family in Detroit? Contemplating that the lay over in Georgia would be brief, and considering Ginny's early pregnancy sickness, they thought it best for Ginny to return to Detroit and her parents.

Andy expresses his feelings about their latest adjustment to his wife on a Wednesday in March:

March 8, 1944

My Darling:

I suppose as I write this you are being welcomed with open arms by all. I do hope that you made all your connections alright. You didn't get sick did you! God knows how much I've missed you already. Leaving you was one of the most difficult things I have ever done. I do hope that I won't miss you anymore than I do now because this hurts. Darling, please don't worry about me; you know I can take care of myself. Who knows maybe in six months we will be together again. Darling, I do love you so much, it really is strange, going someplace alone. Especially at night when I go to bed and I realize that your arms would not be around me. Honestly honey, you occupy my mind so much that I can't even write a decent letter.

This base is pretty nice, beats Florence a thousand ways. We haven't done a thing since our arrival Monday night and sleep as late as we like. The food has been good.

Sommers and I went into town yesterday but after looking around and the consumption of a couple of drinks, returned to the base. I just don't get any kick out of doing anything without you! If we did get a leave—and it seems dubious—I'd fly home because I can get a priority rating on airlines. The only reason I would dread coming home would be the renewal of farewells and I can't take much more of that, after all I am human and last Monday just about finished me. Guess I love you a little bit huh! So don't worry about me and take care of Junior.

I'm going to write mother now and break the news about the little one to her if you haven't already done so.

Write everyday darling and I shall do the same. I miss you terribly.

Yours always,
Andre

Rachel Vleghels writes to her son about Virginia and their baby news, along with some motherly advice for good measure.

March 9-1944.
Dearest Dre.

Virginia just called to tell me that you had called her, she was very glad about it, as she told you they came over last night and of course we were happy to see her, she look kind of thin but don't worry I will see that she takes good care of herself. So just forget about us all and take good care of yourself, be sure to gain back what you lost, I hear you have swell food where you are now, thats' good, When I come home yesterday Maurine, Ma you are going to be a grandma, I said so you open my letters, but she wanted to know how you were and could not resist. We are very glad about it and that will keep Virginias mind occupied. Pa said it has to be a boy. Well if it is a girl, so what, would our Dre say, but it will be a second Vleghels. ...

Be good and pray. We send all our love from your pa, sister and most of all from your Mom.

A big kiss.
The pictures are real nice just like you are, only on the lean side.

Although my mother's love letters to Andy were lost, miraculously, some other letters penned by her did survive fifty-five years and several moves. Whether by luck or divine intervention, they were resurrected from the attic of a friend. Following mom's death, I recalled that she had a friend with a military attachment to her and Andy, but the precise nature of their relationship was foggy. I knew that if I searched my mother's address book, I would be able to identify the name of this longtime friend when I saw it written on the page. Sure enough, the name, Evelyn Schaaf, (now residing in Florida) seemed familiar. I called Evelyn, explaining that my mother had recently died and that I wanted to learn more about her life during the war and Andy Vleghels. Evie was happy to enlighten me about their past. She and her husband, Phil, a fellow lieutenant, also lived at the "Smith Cottages". The four of them had great times together, which included a weekly sojourn on Saturday night to the Officers' Club. I had seen their faded images in the pages of Ginny's photo album, unable to put name to face. Evie explained that after my mother moved back to Detroit in March of 1944, they began to correspond. She felt certain that she had saved these letters and promised to look for them and send them on to me. I was ecstatic at my good fortune and dumbfounded that Evie had held onto these letters for more than fifty years. Simply to have these decades-old letters from my mother's guarded past in my possession was treasure enough, but they could also shed some light upon what it was like for her, a war bride whose husband was missing in action. A month went by with no sign of the letters. My anxiety obliged me to call Evie once again. The prospect of procuring letters in my mother's hand, written during such a tumultuous time in her life, expressed in her own words, was too priceless a gift to escape my grasp. Evie apologized for the delay, but living in Florida, she had been preoccupied with a lot out-of-town company. She reassured me that she would look for them the first chance she got, and send them on their way.

Not long after our conversation, a friend and I set out on a long walk on a brisk afternoon in early March of 1999. I was brimming with excitement and anticipation, waiting for the letters to arrive, astounded that they still existed. When I reached my home an hour later, my eyes honed in on my mailbox. A large manila envelope bulged from its slot. I yanked the parcel free. The return address read, "Evelyn Schaaf." I waved to my friend, pantomiming that my special package was here. I hurried inside, delirious to devour the letters. This was unbelievable! At last, I had a chance to uncover more truths of the hidden lives of Andy and Ginny Vleghels. I threw aside my winter clothes. A wave of dizzying emotions flooded me. I collapsed into my mother's favorite chair to read. Like a starving child, I wanted to gorge myself with the words that had been denied us for so long.

There were twenty-three letters in all that spanned March, 1944 through November, 1945. For me, it was a virtual gold mine, an intimate chronicle of those missing months. Back then, it took a mere three cents to mail a letter. The stamps bore a white eagle on a violet field encircled by thirteen stars with the words, "WIN THE WAR" emblazoned across its breast, its wings forming a V. A distinct, musty odor emanated from the stationary--the aroma of an attic. Though time had grayed the paper, my mother's flowing penmanship, written with a fountain pen, appeared fresh upon the page. Evie's cherished horde, as if by design, were now in my hands almost fifty-five years to the day that Ginny had written the first of her letters to her friends, Evie and Phil.

Along with her amazing gift, Evie included a note to me:

3-8-99
Dear Debby

I hope you enjoy these letters as much as I did as I reread them. It took me back to the happy times that we had in Florence and the Officers' Club with our "rum and cokes".

I remember Andy as a great fun-loving guy—he always had a smile and was very good natured. We were fortunate to make such good friends while we were there and we really were looking forward to a reunion after the war. It was a stressful time and it really was a devastating blow when we learned what happened to Andy.

If I find anymore mementoes, I'll let you know. I'm so happy that I saved these letters and I hope they help enlighten the past.

,
Evie

In the first of the letters, Ginny gives her account of her departure from South Carolina.

March 15, 1944
Dear Evelyn & Phil:

Please forgive this belated letter, but somehow it just didn't materialize. First of all, I want to attempt to thank you for all that you both did for me, and I certainly appreciate your thoughtfulness more than words can express. Without you I wonder just how I would have survived that last day.

My trip home was fine, although as you know, I had a brief delay in Washington. I finally arrived home about 10:00 A.M. on Wednesday. It really was cold in Detroit, with snow and everything, and it was quite a change from South Carolina weather.

No doubt you have heard from my husband by this time, for in one of his letters to me, he mentioned that he had written to you. He called me last Sunday and it was really wonderful talking to him again. He certainly has been in Georgia much longer than we anticipated, and if I had known that and also that he would have so much free time, I would have accompanied him there. But then that is the Army, you never know what to expect.

I went to the doctor's yesterday and I now have some "gruesome" medicine to take. I was in bed for two days after I arrived home, but am feeling much better now. I guess the trip home, together with parting from Andy, was a little more than I could cope with at the moment. But before long I am sure I will be in the "groove" again. I will let you know, Phil, when I need that "hot water".

Last Saturday night I thought of you both and wondered what you were doing, and whether you were at the Club. Both Andy and I shall miss those grand times we shared with you, and naturally, I miss those famous "rum" drinks.

How is everything in South Carolina? Is the weather still warm? Evelyn, how is the cooking problem coming along? I miss those shopping excursions we used to have especially our daily visit to the "Chocolate Shop". By the way, how did those pictures turn out? I hope good.

Thanks so much, Evelyn, for sending my blanket. It arrived safe and sound.

And so, kids, I think this is about all the news for now. When you have an opportunity do drop me a line for I would enjoy hearing from you.

Love,
Ginny Vleghels

Still in Georgia, Andy continues to write faithfully.

March 9, 1944
My Darling:

I never knew that I would be so happy to receive a card but the one you sent from Washington positively thrilled me. Gee honey, I love you so much. I only hope I get a letter from you soon.

We finished everything today and am just sweating out leaving here. Wherever we are going, it will be by boat, that much I know. Today I received a new wrist-watch (Elgin), .45 automatic, a nice long knife and sundry other items.

Sommers and I went to the Post theater and saw "The Uninvited" Ray Milland and it really was a thriller, in fact Sommers threatens to pull the covers over his head tonight.

My Sister's Father

Just think last week at this time I was at Charlie's house and you were in Florence, now look at us.

If you think I had an appetite before, you should see me stow it away now. It seems I can't satiate my ever-empty stomach, besides a few meals today, I managed to consume a couple of gigantic milk shakes with plenty of real <u>ice cream.</u>

I'm getting an early start at this father business because they informed us before we left that we should be like fathers to our gunners. Can't you just see me in the paternal role?

Well, my darling, it has been a long day and I must take my beauty sleep, not that I need it.

Write soon honey, I love you and miss you very much.

All my love,
Andre

(they serve French fries constantly)

When Andy mentions that "he was at Charlie's and you were in Florence," he was referring to an opportunity he had to hop an Air Force plane, along with his buddy, Phil, and fly to Selfridge Field back in Detroit. It was his last chance to see his family before shipping out. He was allotted one night. The next morning, close to dawn, his Pop, Mom, and kid sister, Maurine, drove him to Selfridge where he waved good-bye from the jeep that would take him to his plane and back to South Carolina and his bride.

From Hunter's Field, still awaiting his orders, Andy writes:

March 14, 1944
2:20 p.m.
My Darling:

This is a letter from a very happy boy, reason! I just received my first letter from you, my one and only wife. Gee, it really did wonders for me and hope I will get a letter everyday now. Honey, did I ever tell you how wonderful you are—I love you so much that it hurts. If I had known that I was going to remain here this long I would have let you come with me but I'm glad now that I didn't because you have been too ill and I am happy that you have your family to take care of you. So please don't worry about me darling, just take good care of yourself. I also received a letter from mother, and I know she and dad will take good care of you for me too.

I lay awake every night for hours it seems thinking of you and how happy we were in our little cottage. Just think if we would have decided to wait until some future date to have been married, all the happiness we would have missed. Now when Junior is born, you will have someone to remind you of me. I do feel your presence wherever I go because I know that you are with me in spirit. Someday, we will be together and nothing will separate us, we'll just be happy and blissful and raise more Juniors. Guess I love you huh!

I wish you would send me a small picture to carry around with me. All I have is the newspaper clipping. Honey I would gladly trade all the food here for one of your meals prepared by you, that's what counts and you were pretty good.

Your letter reached me in two days; can't understand the good service. I inquired today if there was any news about our departure but the answer was still "no, nothing."

I really miss not having a radio here as you can well understand. Especially, when Savannah broadcasts so much jive.

Just got some new information, which you could keep to yourself but we have to be in New York on the 19th. So that settles it. I'll try to call you from there. So don't go too far away Sunday or Monday. I'll conclude this now with all my love and missing you terribly.

*Yours always,
Andre*

Andy writes his last letter from Georgia on the 15th followed by this letter:

Mar. 20, 1944
My Darling:

Well, it looks as though I made it to New York. Of course, the weather was quite a change from Georgia, cold and about four inches of snow today. The reason I didn't put my return address on the envelope is because I am going to mail this in town and so avoid censorship, which is in effect here. [Gives present address, his A.P.O. number].

Got my first subway ride yesterday and have seen quite a bit of New York, Bronx, Brooklyn etc. We (Sommers) went to the Actor, Latin Quarter, Duffy's Tavern, Metropole, Zanzibar, La Conga, Diamond Horseshoe, and Tony Pastori. Really did the town. I can secure tickets at ½ price for Mexican Hayride through the Officer's Club at the Commodore. Aren't you envious? I do wish that you were here to help me enjoy all this; that's all I need now. I have never seen so many people in all my life, bars are crowded, lines for shows is fantastic. The dim out is not in effect, but they do have a brown out, all the lights still aren't lighted.

Until the time comes when we are alerted, we can go to town. Oh yes, I ran into York, Greene and all the boys here. They aren't leaving with us. In fact they will have gone when you receive this.

When you write don't ask any questions about my leaving, or where I am located because I won't be able to answer them.

Also saw the ship Gripsholm that carried American repatriated prisoners and the Nomandic. I am going to try to call you tomorrow hope I have luck. Hope you don't mind the reverse charges but I am lending my gunners money because they are in want of funds.

I do hope darling that you are feeling well again and eating heartily. Eat all you like because you won't have to worry about your figure for a while!

I miss you constantly darling and love you with my whole heart and soul. It will be even worse when the distance between us is lengthened.

So hoping I talk to you tomorrow, I shall sign off. So long baby.

Yours always,
Andre

March 24, 1944
1:50 p.m.

My Darling:

Nope, I'm not dead but I have been pretty busy around this place but I'm not going to offer any excuses and I should be writing every day. This doesn't mean that I don't miss you because I do worse than ever. It really burns me up to think we could have spent all this time together and if I had known that this would have happened, you would be with me today. Just think, all the time I had off I had at Savannah and a week in New York, why we could have had a marvelous time. But you know as well as I do that the Army tells you nothing in advance but it does peeve me because I miss you so terribly.

I have acquired a nice cold, nose running and a sore throat.

I haven't been to town yet to see about the wire but I hope it's there because I am getting rather low. My gunners have borrowed a hundred dollars already and still going strong. Saw the Ziegfield Follies the other night and it was great. Milton Berle is just about the funniest character I have ever seen, of course, the gals were pretty nice. Saw "Early to Bed" last night, it wasn't bad but I have seen better.

They really clip one in this town; money means nothing to them as long as they get yours. I have been getting my theater tickets through the Officer's Club at the Commodore. Had $4.40 seats for half price.

Heard a rumor today that we may go places in the near future.

Oh nuts, the only thing that keeps running through my mind is the thought of you and wishing you were here. I love you so very much. I'm still disgusted for not having you here but one never knows what kind of a deal they will pull.

Incidentally, I have tried to call you twice now and each time there was a 3 to 4 hour delay, I'll try again today.

So baby, I'll leave you for now, think of me. I love you dearly.

Missing you,
Andre

P.S. Tickets for Mexican Hayride $5.50 too expensive so no go.

Andy must have been successful in contacting Ginny that day, because she boarded a train for New York to spend whatever amount of time she and Andy had left, together. Near the end of her life, mom revealed to me that Andy had called her from New York City and wanted to know if she would be willing to get on a train and meet him at Grand Central Station. He cautioned her, however, that the possibility existed that he could be alerted in the interim and would not be there to meet her. If that happened, she would have to get back on the train and return to Detroit. Would she be willing to take that chance? Was she feeling well enough to withstand the trip?

With all the drama of a Hollywood movie, Andy waited at a mobbed Grand Central Station for Ginny's arrival. She must have been near frantic as she searched the faces of the crowd, not knowing if she would be met by her love or bitter disappointment.

Securing a place for them to stay was a tall order. The city was teeming with humanity and most hotels were filled to capacity. New York City, of course, was a port of embarkation (POE) during the war, so the streets were thick with military personnel. But with much perseverance and a little luck, Andy found a room at the Hotel Taft, Room #263 at a rate of $5.50 per night, less 10% (military discount). Located on Times Square at Radio

City (7th Avenue at 50th Street), the hotel stationary advertised that they offered 2000 rooms with bath, radio and circulating ice water.

Happily, they spent four days in NYC painting the town and squeezing as much loving as they could into the precious little time that remained. Andy decided to splurge and forgo the price of tickets to Cole Porter's musical extravaganza, *Mexican Hayride*. Their sweet time together must have been a cocktail of pure joy and excitement mixed with the somber prospect of yet another inevitable separation--a looming, menacing, threat too painful to ponder. Neither of them knew when it would all come to a crashing halt.

I suspect that Andy was obliged to spend his nights in the barracks at Camp Shanks, one of three staging areas on the eastern seaboard. Few passes were allotted, and once a soldier was notified that he was on "alert", he could expect to ship out within twelve hours. In the early hours of the morning of March 30th, Andy scratched out this parting note and left it at Ginny's bedside:

My Darling:

I couldn't bear to tell you but this is so long for a while. I was alerted this morning but I had to see you. It has been perfect heaven with you here darling and it will serve with memories for months to come while we are apart. Remember I love you more than anything in this world. Please be brave darling, I am only one of many in the same predicament. Don't worry about me, with the grace of God we will be together again soon. I believe you can get train information downstairs. I love you.

Andre

P.S. Empire leaves at 0900 A.M.

P.S.II I took $20 out of your wallet. I love you.

My mother had never dared to tell this part of the story—that Andy had left this farewell note instead of waking her. My mind cannot fathom the utter shock and sense of abandonment that Ginny undoubtedly felt upon waking to Andy's parting words. He was right there in the room and chose to leave a note? Andy's clandestine visit would have been in direct violation to military regulations. If caught, he would have been considered AWOL. But desperate times called for desperate measures.

Ginny found herself stranded in the largest city in America, with no one to console her. She had no real alternative except to muster every drop of fortitude remaining, gather herself up, and board the train for Detroit. She would have called her family to let them know when to expect her. Perhaps contact with them, even at a distance, helped to assuage her distress.

Departing Grand Central Station that morning would be a palpable contrast to Ginny's arrival. The exuberance and elation of the past few days melted into body-numbing sadness and abandonment. The grand station itself reflected Ginny's predicament--a place where train lines originated and terminated. For Ginny, married life as she knew it had come to an end. She was entering a new phase of her life now without Andy by her side, at least for a while.

As Ginny's train rumbled toward Detroit, Andy's ship churned across the Atlantic--destination, England. Simultaneously, bit by bit, mile by mile, the space between them grew. There would be soldiers on the train, some returning to a wonderful welcome home, their tour of duty satisfied, others with furloughs to visit their loved ones before shipping out, and still others at the very back of the train, in cargo, who had made the ultimate sacrifice. Ginny must have been exhausted by a litany of memories and dire possibilities ruminating in her head as the train tracks clicked off. Only God knew what the coming months would bring. The only thing that she could be sure of was her undying love for Andy and their child growing within her.

Following his shattering farewell message, Andy was quick to send a letter explaining his actions:

Mar. 30, 1944
8:30 p.m.
My Darling:

It seems like 24 years since I last held you in my arms but in reality it is 24 hours. I do hope you weren't angry with me darling for saying au revoir in the manner I did but I just couldn't bear to see you in tears again. Then too, I thought this way it wouldn't be so hard for you to take in my absence. Darling, leaving you this morning was the most difficult thing I have ever proposed. You were so lovable and sweet and unsuspecting but as I wrote you it was impossible for me to see you any longer. I do hope you made your train connection without any trouble. I shall remember these last few days as the most joyous in my life but it is only a sample of what is in store for us in the future which I hope is very near because I miss you already with a fierce pain that consumes my entire spirit. Words seem inadequate to describe my love for you but they will have to suffice for the present. Love like ours will never die and come fall you will have someone to remind you of me until I come home again.

So darling, do have fun while you can. It is irrelevant to remind you to write because I know you will every day. We did have fun these past few days didn't we? Being near you was enough to fill my cup of happiness to overflowing. Needless to say that when I do go across you won't hear from me for a while but don't worry. So my sweet, with your image implanted permanently in my mind and heart, I shall leave you. I love you darling and miss you. Au revoir.

Love,
Andre

As Andy nears the shores of the British Isles, his mother writes:

April 3, 1944.
Dearest Dre.

We wonder where this letter will reach you and hope you may receive it in good health. How are you getting along darling, you can imagine how anxious we are to hear from you, may God bless you. When Virginia came back from you, her dad, Jerry, and Maurine went to the station, I stayed by her mother and they came in at eleven o' clock, we all had a good cry, but made the best of it, said you was only one in a million, Dre don't worry about Virginia she will be all right as I told you before we will keep an eye on her, all she needed is a good rest and food. Pa told her to come and live with us for a while when I am home again, you could mention it to her if you want to, that if she likes the idea, it would do her good to be away from too much talk. Again dearest boy don't you worry about us here, but take good care of yourself and we will be happy then. Any more colds, that's odd you having them so often, don't doctors know the cause of it. Hope you have better weather than we have in Detroit, still winter even if it's spring, next Sunday is Easter, most of the people will be thinking about their boys and praying that this will be the last one that we are separated, if we all pray real hard God will give peace very soon. Darling we are thinking of you all the time, when I wake up during the night and say a prayer and ask God that he might keep you safe, and he will my dearest boy, chin up, bad things can't last for long, and then real happiness will be yours. Pa sends all his love also your sister, we will write very much... Time for bed, bye darling a very big kiss from Your

Mom

Maurine remembers the night Ginny returned from New York City and Andy. It was Ginny's appearance that struck her because it was such a departure from her usual way. She was dressed in her classic, tailored suit of dusty rose, Andy's "wings" fastened to her lapel over her heart. But her clothes were uncharacteristically disheveled and her stylish hat, askew. Her toes poked out of the holes in her silk stockings through her open-toed pumps, runs forming stripes up and down her legs. She had come undone.

> *I'll find you in the morning sun,*
> *And when the night is new,*
> *I'll be looking at the moon,*
> *But I'll be seeing you.*
>
> *I'll be Seeing You*
> **Sammy Fain & Irving Kahal**

Chapter Nine
Over There

V-MAIL--that was Andy's mode of communication once he reached Great Britain. A correspondent had a single sheet of full-sized paper on which to write or type their message. Later, it was reduced in size to a card measuring 4 X 5 inches. Although they were subjected to censorship as well, Andy preferred letters because they afforded more privacy. However, until he reached his permanent station in England, he was forced to tolerate its shortfall.

His first impressions of the "mother country" are reflected in his missive of April 8, 1944.

My Darling: Well darling, again I can resume my correspondence with you and convey my longing for you. I grant you that I cannot wax too romantic with limited writing space but I shall give my all. I am now in jolly, old England, my deah and what I have seen of it has been very nice. The countryside is very peaceful and war seems very remote but these subtleties are merely an illusion. The voyage was very serene and very boring, no, I didn't get sick. I'm still worried about you, I hope you aren't angry with me and I do hope you got the proper train connection. I have missed you terribly since we parted. Your mail finally caught up to me on the boat, five letters. I ran into Svenson over here, the others are gone. Listening to some mellow jive over Swede's radio. Darling, I love you beyond all human comprehension. I shall write to you again tomorrow.

All my love,
Andre

April 9, 1944 [Easter]

My Darling: Here it is a typical English day—rain. Went to Mass this morning and I couldn't help thinking of the time we went to St. Pat's. Sommers and I are going to the cinema this afternoon and this evening we intend to see the inside of the local pub. About all they have to offer is beer, warm at that. They just don't believe in refrigeration over here. We sure have a hard time sleeping at night because one of the boys really snores, sounds like a high powered buzz saw. This morning the countryside looked so tranquil that I could hardly resist the temptation to take a short walk but I still have plenty of resistance. I'm sure you would love it here. Gee, baby, I miss you terribly and my love for you cannot be measured. And I always thought that married people soon forgot how much they loved each other and here I am just as ardent as I was in the wooing stage before you caught me. Sizzle! So baby, write often. I love you.

Andre

Andy's reference to St. Pat's is none other than St. Patrick's Cathedral in New York City where he and Ginny attended mass when last they met. One year, in honor of St. Patrick's Day, I sent Mom a greeting card featuring an aerial shot of the cathedral, its Gothic spires resplendent in the sunlight. Before long, she framed the picture and hung in an expansive collage of artifacts that she constantly juggled and altered above her living room sofa. She pointed it out to me one day when I was visiting her and explained its significance. I felt pleased that, for once, Mom was forthright about an intimate memory of Andy.

April 14, 1944

My Darling: Joe Louis is just talking over the air as I sit here in my Nissan hut listening to the rhythmic beat of the rain and all that Erin go braugh, for your boy is now in Ireland. I'm finally with all the boys again, Greene, York etc. Sure am getting to see all of Great Britain. Guess I won't be fighting just yet, that is one of the mysteries that surround us. I really will be happy to receive a letter from you once again mainly because I miss you so much and memories of you become more poignant when Svenson and I reminisce over the good old times in Florence. They were happy days weren't they? Just like being a civilian.

Remember cooking the wieners with the skin, Swede reminded me of that and then when we hit Ireland he wanted to know whether the people were white or Irish. Gee honey, I love you very much and hope I hear from you soon. Putting on any weight?

> Love,
> Andre

True to his word, Andy wrote to Ginny daily. He attempted to abate his lonesomeness by watching a film or playing cards, or occasionally walking into town to visit the local pub. The rest of his leisure time was spent resting, listening to jive, and writing letters to family and friends and his beloved, Ginny. I've chosen a few lines from some of his early V-mails from Ireland.

4-15-44 Seems that everything I hear or say I try to associate with you hoping that the pain of missing you will be lessened but to no avail.

4-16-44 Baby, what I really need is some reading material, magazines, books, anything. No murder mysteries, however. Did I tell you that candy is rationed over here? Yep, some nice Hershey's or Nestlé's bars (chocolate candy bars) *would be ideal.*

4-17-44 Just about the only mode of travel is on a bike around here but the prices are too exorbitant so I haven't acquired one. I am sleeping under five blankets and I can use every one of them, gets right chilly at night. ...Don't worry about me, because characters like me always come out of it. I still haven't received any mail and I wish the ice would be broken.

4-18-44 Gee honey, I wish you were right here beside me. May as well ask for the moon.

4-19-44 I miss you very much darling and you are smiling down at me from your picture. I have been writing at least once a day trying to show in a small way how much I love you.

4-20-44 My Darling: The impossible occurred today; I received two letters from you making this boy unbelievably happy. One was dated the seventh and the other the ninth. My morale was boosted 100% because I had been feeling a little low—you being the reason. Did you see in the paper where A-20s made their first raid? Makes me feel good. Just finished beating York and Svenson at "Sweat the Queen". I don't know when you began writing but I believe there should be some letters floating around written before the sixth. Darling, we probably will spend next Easter together or I shall be greatly surprised—you mean all three of us will go. So you are working on post war plans already, seems very remote, thinking of a sane world again and in civilian clothes. It must be your imagination that your clothes are getting tight, little premature isn't it? I hope you can read this writing because V-mail will render it more difficult to do so, I know. I'll sign off now, remember I love you with all my heart and soul.

*Yours always,
Andre*

4-21-44 Here it is 10:30 and not yet quite dark, seems strange. . . . Say honey, would it be possible for you to buy a subscription to the Sunday Detroit News for me? I would like to see the paper from home once in a while, would you do that...? I'd give anything to know when we will be together again. I can't make pretty speeches but you are all I am living for, without you, my world would be bare and that is why I am fighting and that is a worthy and only cause.

4-22-44 I bought two dozen eggs for Sommers, Svenson and myself for our evening snacks and I just finished three, mighty tasty.

Tomorrow is Sunday and again memories of other Sundays with you. Guess our life in Florence was a fleeting bit of Heaven. . . . As per usual I am being educated again, I wonder if I'll ever finish with book la'nin.

4-23-44 Well, I don't feel too happy today because again I did not receive any mail from you, consequently, I decided to try airmail in the hope there might be more speedy. I hope so.

This morning, I went to Mass and received Holy Communion and offered them up for you and Junior. Honey, if this reaches you quicker than airmail, will you send me some airmail stationary, because I cannot secure any over here.

Oh yes baby, have you been receiving my allotments alright? If not, write to the Finance Department, W.D, Wash. D.C. and find out what the trouble is. There was a big article about the A-20 and it was highly lauded, using them quite a bit now.

4-25-44 Just heard a hot record "Sing, Sing, Sing" by Goodman, (14) really sizzling. Life is getting rather boring around here and I am ready to do a little fighting. This is strictly a gentleman's war over here; have to wear our blouses for supper and other uniform restrictions. Gee honey, I can't think of anything I would love better than to have your arms around me right now. Ah, fond dreams and I shall probably relive them for some time to come.

4-27-44 My Dearest: At long last I received a letter and an Easter card from you. Can't imagine where they were delayed. But I was so happy to hear from you, that it made no matter when it was written. Your letter was wonderful and I was lost in a reverie of you for some time after I read it. Gee, it was really great.

The episode in New York had me troubled for some time, but your letter of today eased my conscience. I had hoped it would make it easier for you if I weren't around but apparently I may have done the wrong thing. You can't possibly imagine how badly I felt when I kissed you for the last time and I broke it off as soon as I could because I would have probably spilled the beans in a few minutes. I don't believe it possible that there is anybody else in this world who are more in love than we are. You darling, are the motivating force in my life. (Cont.)

Hi Honey: This is continued from the other page. Hope they are arriving together. You should get a look at your husband, his face really looks a mess, I'll explain: Svenson and I were riding bikes and his back wheel hit my front wheel and the next thing I knew, I was sailing over the handlebars and landed on the road face first. Consequently, I have a couple of inches of skin off my forehead plus eyebrows, my upper lip, my chin and of course, my nose took a beating. My eye is discoloring as is my hand, some fun. Guess I'll need a nurse, hint, hint. Except for a banged up shoulder and wrists, I feel none the worse for the experience. I'll try not to emulate this incident. It looks as though I just can't get all I want to say on this sheet, so I'll have to start a third. Mind?

Hi Baby: This is part III and the finale, for I believe I'll tear myself away from you and write mother. See what one letter does to me. Another bunch (men) arrived from Florence and guess who one of the fellows was I met on the boat—Egon Fricke and Ralph Krass! No kidding they finally got across. Wonder if Fr. Maino is with them. If you can secure his APO number, send it to me.

The Army was quick to recognize that letters from home directly impacted the morale of the American GI. Consequently, they set up a system to facilitate the flow of mail to and from the military. APO stood for Army Post Office, FPO for Fleet Post Office. Between the World Wars, the Army and the Navy signed the Postal Agreement authorizing military personnel to serve in place of civilian postal employees overseas. They used official postal supplies and equipment and adhered to postal regulations.

Mail was channeled either through New York or San Francisco, and people living in the U.S. were only charged rates to these cities no matter where in the world their letter was being sent. There was no charge for a GI to send a letter. Postage was free. Each APO was assigned a number that supported particular units. When a soldier received a new assignment, he had to fill out a change of address card for the Replacement Facilities so they could reroute his mail. At times, however, the mailrooms experienced huge backlogs, delaying a GIs mail for weeks.

Now back to you, darling, always remember that wherever I may be and how long, I shall always be true to you. The only woman as far as I am concerned is you. None is worth your little finger. As yet, I haven't left the post area and I don't care to. I love you too much, darling, and believe me, I shall always be careful.

I really would like to get up in the air again, I really mean it. Well darling, this is all the news I have tonight. I miss you very much.

Yours always,
Andre

4-28-44 As you say, it is strange how we were united again after a period of two years. God must have willed it that way all the time. The separation did me good because it was then that it dawned on me that I had always been in love with you and I had been searching for a girl with your attributes and ideals but never did find one who even came close. And then that fateful evening I saw you again, I knew my quest was at an end because there is only one like you, for the mold was broken when you were created, in other words, mine is the perfect wife par excellan'ce. Love like ours will never die and rest assured darling, we have many years of happiness to come and I shall strive each moment to make a happy life for you, this is what I live and fight for and I'll win too because I play for keeps. That's why I'm a hard loser for I never play to lose, compre'?

5-1-44 Happy day in the morning, I actually had four letters from you today… Incidentally, what do you intend to name the baby—sad sack…? If you could only see me now, I'm now wearing a gas-mask, latest style by Dashi, practice alert is the reason.

Written on the underside of Andy's formal Army hat brim is his name, serial number and "Sad Sack", a cartoon often featured in GI publications. Did he identify with the comical character, portrayed as a GI who usually got the short end of the stick, or was it simply that he longed for Ginny? Maybe it was a little of both.

5-2-44 I have finished school now, and our time will be taken up with athletics which I believe will do me good because I played ball yesterday and today I feel crippled… When I come home we'll have a second honeymoon. The first night I shall probably have so much to tell you that it will take all night besides frequent interruptions to kiss you and tell you how much I love you.

5-3-44 Darling, did you compose that prayer? Irregardless, it's beautiful and I shall cherish it. It really is symbolic of you. Just saw a picture in "Stars and Stripes" (our daily paper) showing Café Zanzibar and Mexican Hayride and naturally my thoughts again turned to the glorious time we had together.

May 4, 1944
10:10 p.m.
My Darling:

I am enclosing a couple of clippings from our Army scandal sheet, "Stars and Stripes" portraying the work of the A-20s. As yet, the Jerries (German soldiers) *haven't shot one down and that's a fact. The only thing is they won't let them skip-bomb. As you can see from the articles, it's medium altitude work... As soon as I finish this missive to you, I shall endeavor to satiate my ever-questing appetite, by frying a couple of eggs. My mess kit is about to burn through because I have used it for this purpose so often.*

I know it seems rather premature but already I can visualize my homecoming and all the joy and happiness connected with it. My trend of thought in this direction had better stop or I shall be committed to a home for the feeble minded. I miss you so dreadfully but I am thankful that we decided to get married before I left instead of waiting. Think of all the glorious moments that would have been wasted...With the aid of your prayers, I hope God will see fit to bring us together again as an example of a perfect love. Darling, with you at my side, I can do anything because you fill me with all the confidence I need...

Good-night, darling.

*Yours always,
Andre*

5-7-44 *My Darling: Spent a tedious week-end in Belfast and I must say I was disappointed. People seemed more abundant than in New York. The food was poor and very little of it. They can give Ireland back to St. Patrick and the snakes. At the present moment I am listening to S. Kay and I am engulfed by nostalgic waves of memories.*

I received four letters from you today, and by the time you read this, I shall be back in England to start work. Had very nice rooms in Belfast, had bed warmers to warm up the beds, very quaint. Needless to say, I missed my wife terribly and could find no colleen to even faintly compare in loveliness, as a matter of fact, they are quite the homeliest things I have ever seen or have you spoiled all that for me? I love you darling now and always. Miss you.

*All my love,
Andre*

Missed the Saturday dance
Heard they crowded the floor
Couldn't bear it without you
Don't get around much any more

Don't Get Around Much Any More
Bob Green

Chapter Ten
Somewhere in England

5-8-44 My Darling: Well, here I am ready to begin my long awaited job. After three years in the Army, I am at last ready for combat. Everyone here is very congenial and we were greeted with open arms. I'm back with York now and also Sommers, Miller and Svenson are still with me. So whenever you read in the papers our particular airplanes, you can almost be sure I was in it. Anyway, I must say, I'm glad to be here and I'm sure I'll like it better than the last place. You are always smiling down at me from the shelf and that is always enough to give me fresh courage. You will notice my address is changed and I wish you would tell mother about it. (Incidentally, have you found any candy yet? I really crave some.) I'll be signing off for now, saying I love you very much and miss you constantly.

All my love,
Andre

Constructed of corrugated metal, Andy's "home" away from home was a Quonset- Hut, large enough to house eight men with a door at either end flanked by two small windows. A modest pot-bellied, charcoal-burning stove belching meager heat, stood at the center of this caterpillar-like structure, its exhaust pipe snaking its way up to the roof. Ten pounds of charcoal allotted per week per hut helped to stave off the cold, damp English weather, but only slightly.

A separate building marked with the sign, ABLUTION, afforded a place where a G.I. could wash up, cold water only. However, bathtubs with hot water were available, but only at designated times, rotating turns among four squadrons. Charcoal was in short supply and needed to fuel the water heaters, so conservation efforts required that each man should use no more than two inches of water, the same as the Queen of England. (I suppose they just had to take her word for it.)

May 10, 1944
My Darling:

Am gradually getting accustomed to my new surroundings which is made easier by the comradeship of my fellow officers. Was officially welcomed by a couple of colonels tonight, part of the old pep talk you know.

Haven't been off the ground yet but a few of the boys have done a little flying.

A lot of these men are West Pointers and second lieutenants are definitely in the minority. I probably will begin "sweating out" first looey after a few missions. Gets right chilly here at night and I am sleeping with my jacket on plus four blankets and a few coats.

This is the first place I have hit that serves real coffee—you know, the kind that sticks to your ribs. Besides our regular meals, we receive three eggs and fruit per week. Our huts are pretty nice since there are only seven of us in it. I have a rug, a table and a canvas-lined chair. Your picture gives it the homey touch. What I wouldn't give for our life in Florence! Just think how happy we were in a one-room cottage with poor cooking facilities, why we'll probably think we are in Heaven when we are together again and have a decent place to live. Darling all I can think of is you and how much you mean to me. Isn't it wonderful to be so in love? You would think that we were still in the courting stage but then I shall never stop wooing you. You are my permanent girl.

Now, I shall take my leave of you, missing you very much.

All my love,
Andre

With the planned invasion of Normandy close at hand, southern England was a virtual military encampment. When Andy finally reached his new base in England on May 8, 1944, he joined the ranks of the 416th Bomb Group where he was assigned to the 669th, one of four squadrons with approximately three hundred men per squadron.

Originally headquartered at Will Rogers Field in Oklahoma, the group had departed stateside aboard the SS Colombe on January 18, 1944. Following ten days at sea and a train trip originating in Scotland, it was February 1st when the 416th reached their secret destination and set up camp at Wethersfield, Essex County, about thirty miles northeast of London. By the time Andy appeared on the scene as a replacement, the group already had thirty-eight missions to its credit. There were no casualties for the 416th to this point, so replacement pilots were taking the place of those whose tour of duty had expired. Replacement pilots' role in the war was not to be underestimated. They helped to make the difference between victory and defeat. It was one of the reasons Andy signed on for the job. The Army Air Corps actively recruited pilots, recognizing that they were in urgent need of them. By March of 1944, the Army Air Corps accounted for 31% of the total strength of the U. S. Army. It proved to be inspired foresight for the Allied forces and the Achilles heel of the Axis powers.

The 416th were one of three A-20 groups who were sent to England to strengthen the IX Air Force Tactical Air Command in the European Theater. It was General Montgomery's (Monty) staunch belief that enemy air forces must be neutralized prior to the advancement of ground forces. Therefore, the 416th's assignment was to assist in gaining air superiority. In addition, they were to begin the systematic destruction of railroads, marshalling yards, and truck convoy routes leading to replacement depots behind enemy lines. Joined by other U.S.

and British Air Forces, specific targets would be designated in the battle arena once troop landings had been affected

A three-man crew--pilot, turret (mechanical) gunner, and tunnel gunner, manned the Douglas A-20 Havoc attack bomber, the aircraft flown by the men of the 416th while they were stationed in England. (In October of '44, the group transitioned to the A-26.) A lightweight bomber, the Havoc (Boston to the Brits) cruised at an altitude of 12,000 feet on the majority of missions. Although its service ceiling stood at 25,800 feet, the aircraft was not equipped with heat or oxygen. The A-20 was an exciting craft for a pilot to fly because it was responsive and possessed great maneuverability characteristics. With a maximum speed of three hundred and forty-two miles per hour and a landing speed of one hundred miles per hour, the Havoc was the fastest bomber of its class to date. Armament capability included six .50 caliber machine guns in the nose of the ship (operated by the pilot) and twin .50 guns in the Martin power rear turret, which boasted a three hundred sixty-degree rotation capability. The tunnel gunner, assuming a ventral position, operated a .30 caliber machine gun by aiming it out of a rear opening. The ship's bomb bay carried two, one thousand-pound bombs internally, but an additional two, one thousand pound bombs could be mounted externally on under-wing racks.

The cockpit of the plane was roomy and comfortable and its sleek design afforded the pilot good visibility. Isolated from his two gunners, the pilot communicated with them via a four-channel radio, one channel acting as an intercom. If it became necessary for the crew to bail out, the pilot could also sound an alarm. Escape from a doomed plane required that he manually push open his canopy, while the two gunners descended through a single hatch in the belly of the plane.

According to Jim Mesko's publication on the A-20, "The Havoc played a very important role in the eventual defeat of the Axis, particularly in the early days of the war. It was undoubtedly one of the finest warplanes used by either side in the course of the war."

May 12, 1944
My Darling:

I was so much in love with you today that I just couldn't wait until I could get my hands on a pen and tell you how much I adore you. I haven't any news but I did want to let you know how much I miss you and need you.

I just finished playing ball with the gunners and managed to raise a blister on my hand. So you can see how soft I am.

The weather here is right nice and it is much warmer than in Ireland. My cold is breaking up nicely and believe with a little more warmth it will vanish.

Say baby, have you picked up any weight yet? I don't suppose Junior is bothering your figure yet is he? Just wait until he starts kicking!

Say honey, you should see your old man now! I'm sporting a brand new mustache. Now that I'm away from you, I can raise one also I can smoke my big, black cigars of which I have an ample supply. I can just hear you raving now: " a mustache, cigars, I'll divorce him."

Yesterday, we got new, soft mattresses, makes sack time a pleasure.

Sure have a lot of big wheels around here. What are big wheels? Brass hats like colonels, generals, etc. So you have again learned something new.

New or old darling, the words, "I love you" may be repeated in my letters and I realize that they can't possibly convey how much you mean to me. Never thought it possible to care for a person so much. Gosh honey, I'd give anything to hold you close again and until I do, I'll keep on writing, I love you.

Yours always,
Andre

Andy continued to profess his love to Ginny through his missives, and she to him. Letters quickly became their lifeline, bringing purpose to their lives and relief to their lonely nights. Words of love and encouragement became vital, boosting their resolve to "carry on" despite the longing, despite the nagging uncertainty. As their days and nights eked by, Andy and Ginny kept a steely focus on the life that awaited them once the war was over.

Since a good portion of Andy's letters profess his deep love for Ginny and parrot similar sentiments, I have selected excerpts from his letters that either reveal an attribute of his character, or

Ginny's, or that relate events in his daily life for a pilot stationed "somewhere in England".

5-13-44 Saw a wonderful picture tonight "Song of Bernadette". I hope you get a chance to see it soon because it is very realistic and inspires one with awe and how great our religion is. I pity the Protestants who have no beautiful incidents like ours. I suppose a lot of them scoff at the picture and what it stands for.

Today, I was loosed from the bonds of Mother earth and again took to the call of the blue and it was a happy reunion for I spent some time in its' blue, azure playground. God, must be the romantic in me breaking forth. ...

We have one fellow in our barracks who differs on anything you care to talk about, he gets under everyone's skin. Thinks he's a wheel.

I realize honey that my letters are usually disjointed and perhaps desultory but you know how I am.

Hey baby, are you taking care of me back home? I need candy, literature and most of all—you. Oh nuts, I'll drive myself nuts thinking of you and the worst part is still to come.

5-15-44 The weather here has turned very cold and our stove, little as it is, is appreciated.

Gee honey, my morale is way up there tonight. Your letters do wonders for me and hope that they keep on arriving steadily.

5-18-44 I wish I could be with you when the happy day arrives for Junior to make his appearance.

I just want to see your face when again we meet. If it is night I'm sure your smile will make it as bright as the sunniest day...

I shall always be true to you irregardless of how many miles separate us.

Pray God that we may soon be together again happy for the duration of our lives.

5-19-44 [V-mail] *Say honey, why don't you move over to mother's for a while after she quits work. I'm sure it would be a pleasant change for a while.* [I believe that Andy made this suggestion due to the comment that his mother had made earlier in one of her letters. She stated that there was "too much talk" in the Egan household, implying that it would be upsetting to Ginny. It seems Rachel felt that a change of atmosphere would do her good.]

5-19-44 Honey, you are wonderful thinking that a little thing I may do now and then for you makes me so wonderful. Heck, I can go on for the rest of my life and never be really worthy of you. God was very kind to me when you became my wife. A lot of the fellows I know are always worrying whether their girl or wife is true to them but I never have to worry or even think about anything like that. But you are the only one I have ever known I could say that about.

You have an advantage over me, darling because you can describe your affections much better and more vivid than I can but you know however droll I may seem, my love for you will always endure and my only goal in life is to make you happy.

I'm glad that you enjoyed yourself so immensely at the party. I can just see Dad in the groove with a few beers under his belt. ... I have no desire for ribbons and rank, my only wish is to go home to you.

5-20-44 Dam when I think of all the things this war is prohibiting me from doing, a normal life, the opportunity to be with my wife when I want to, it fills me with a helpless fury and makes me avow to give these Jerries all I have.

5-22-44 Well darling, tomorrow is the big day. I've been looking forward to it for almost two years now and finally the moment has arrived. I realize tomorrow you won't be aware of this but I am sure God will prompt you to say an extra prayer. Coincidentally, we have also been married five months tomorrow so that should bring me luck. No, I'm not frightened but I shall probably have a sinking sensation in my stomach just like before a big game and which will vanish upon commencement of play.

It is grand of you darling and very wonderful to offer so many Masses in my behalf. Then too, catering to my every want makes it very easy to see why I was so lucky to get a girl like you.

Last night I went to town for the first time and indulged in a movie. But I wish I had stayed home. This is the third time I have gone anyplace since I left the States and I have as yet to enjoy myself. I guess I never shall until I can go out with you once again and talk about things intimately important to us only.

5-24-44 My moment didn't come yesterday, but I had my share today. <u>I was near my birthplace twice today</u> and everything went along fine.

According to the Operations account, the two missions that became Andy's first missions were mission #53 and #54. As it turned out, neither mission yielded very good results since the bombs detonated shy of their targets. Heavy flak was anticipated on mission #54 over Abbeyville-Drucat Airfield, but was not encountered. In fact, the flak was nonexistent. Extra precautions had been taken by having window planes precede the boxes along with P-47s that accompanied the formations. Window planes dropped streamers of foil in an effort to scramble enemy radar.

5-25-44 Well the enclosed clipping will give you an idea where I went yesterday and was my initial entry into combat. Made another sortie the same day... No, I wasn't scared, yet. Hope they are all like yesterday's...

Was just listening to a jive program put out by the Jerries and broadcast by some gal with a sugary voice. Honestly, she fairly nauseates one to listen to her. She attempts to make the boys homesick by playing a number a few years old and endeavoring to restore memories of those days in their minds, however, I believe her plan seems to be back-firing for all the boys have dire plans for her future.

5-28-44 *It's just like a ten minute furlough every time I read one of your letters.*

I have now been on five missions and was on a rough one last night when I so abruptly ceased my letter to you. I came very close to winning the Purple Heart, which is no design of mine. Have a few flak souvenirs now. However, I did win the Air Medal, which is no great accomplishment.

This morning I flew practically over my home-town and had a good look at it. We did give Bruges a bad time. ...

Heck, I don't have any idea on a name for Junior. That's rather a penalty to hang a name de-plume like Andre on that poor kid. You submit your ideas and I'll give my opinion on them...

Since I was on a mission this morning I was unable to attend church much to my regret...

P. S. I'm supposed to come home for 30 days after 50 missions. I hope.

Amiens marshaling yard was the target of Andy's fifth mission and the group's fifty-eighth. As Andy attests, it was rough. An official accounting reports that three crews were shot down, with a total of two pilots and six gunners bailing out of their flak-ridden planes. In spite of being hit by antiaircraft fire (FLAK) as he approached his bomb run, pilot, Lt. Thomas J. Simms, dropped his bombs, called to his gunners to bail, and returned to England in his hampered plane, himself bleeding and growing faint. After crash landing, he passed out and was sent to a hospital.

That Andy would disclose the near miss of this harrowing mission to Ginny, knowing how much she worried about his safety, more than surprised me. In an earlier letter he explained to her that he believed a soldier was only awarded the Purple Heart if he was killed in action. The implication was clear. Andy came very close to being killed. However, he escaped the mission without injury or necessity to bail out of his ship. Andy was mistaken about the Purple Heart. The fact is, if an airman sustains an injury while on a mission, no matter how slight, he is entitled to the Purple Heart.

The Air Medal that Andy mentions was awarded to a pilot upon the completion of five missions. Thereafter, an oak leaf cluster was added for every fifth mission. I suppose Andy felt that winning the Air Medal was "no great accomplishment" because a flier was not required to do anything exceptional.

Andy was proud of his Belgian heritage. He spoke of it among his compatriots. As evidenced in some of his letters, having the opportunity to fly over Ghent was dear to his heart despite the distasteful circumstances. His mission to Bruges would have taken him within thirty miles of his birthplace. The prospect of helping to free his native people from Hitler's grasp must have been thrilling for him.

5-30-44 Honey, you simply mustn't worry about me especially from now on because you have Junior to think about and you must be strong. I'll bet you aren't eating as much as when we were together. Having a baby is going to take all you've got and you must be strong. You come before anything or anyone and I shall always do everything in my power to keep my adorable and beautiful wife happy and in love with me.

5-31-44 Received two letters from you today, mailed on the 16th and 22nd isn't it marvelous?

However. I was alarmed at the contents of the earlier one. Gosh, darling, I would give anything in the world if I could be at your side especially now but prevailing circumstances prohibit this and there is nothing we can do about it. You must be brave or else you will be a nervous wreck in a very short time. As I have reiterated so frequently, don't worry about me. I'll be back with you someday. It's only a matter of time and then we can forget all about these blue and lonely days. You must keep your chin up darling, at all times because you need your rest. I don't worry about myself but I do wonder about you and how you are taking care of yourself. If you don't, that will give me more cause to worry and I won't be able to concentrate on my job as I should thereby jeopardizing my position and giving you cause to worry. So you see my darling, it's a vicious circle. So let's forget about the pessimistic side of it and look for the silver lining for everything happens for the best. Thinking as much of you as I do, I would soon be ready for a psychopathic ward if I allowed myself to become gloomy because it takes a lot of will power and your letters to keep my morale up. Who knows, I may be with you in October, stranger things have happened.

Notice the article in the paper I'm sending concerning Rommel. We did that little job.

Andy affirms that Ginny was "beside herself" with worry even before she received Andy's Purple Heart letter. His inference that his life was in jeopardy on his fifth mission was sure to inflict further anxiety. She used to tell me that she was so thin during her pregnancy, that people thought she had tuberculosis.

6-1-44 Another new month, a new day but the same routine. I feel rather morose tonight probably because I have been thinking of you too much today, and that makes me miss you all the more. I hate to feel this way because a feeling of despondency settles on me and I can't seem to shake it. There seems to be frustration in everything I do and always I think of you and our wonderful memories. ...

Darling, the poem was lovely and makes me envious that I can't express my love so poetically. I shall say the Memorare every time before I fly a mission. Gee honey, I feel improved in spirit just writing to you probably because I imagine I am talking to you.

The Memorare is a prayer of petition that Catholics pray to Our Lady, the Mother of Jesus:

My Sister's Father

Remember, O most gracious Virgin Mary, that never was it known that anyone who flew to thy protection, implored thy help or sought thy intercession, was left unaided. Inspired with this confidence, I fly unto thee, O Virgin of virgins, my Mother; to thee do I come, before thee I stand, sinful and sorrowful; O Mother of the Word Incarnate, despise not my petitions, but in thy mercy hear and answer me. Amen.

6-3-44 Had my first pass today but after a few hours in town, I had enough and came home. We are having a dance tonight, in fact it's in progress and I may amble over and partake of a few drinks and then to bed. It will probably be reminiscent of the Florence brawls and the fun you and I used to have. But as I said before, we will be together again before long and who knows, maybe this time next year, we will be "sweating out" another little Junior. Any definite number, madam? Well, a dozen anyway.

It won't take long to end this fracas once the invasion gets rolling. When Der Fuhur yells "Uncle" we'll all come back for a wonderful homecoming and I shall be once more in yours arms never to leave them.

6-5-44 I received 14 letters today and nine of them were from you.... I was really happy to get so much mail and I was just like a madman screaming and yelling all over the place. Gee, I'm really happy and I feel sorry because you can't feel this way too. Please don't worry darling, I'll come back to you and everything will be wonderful...

I too wish l could be with you come October, but be brave my darling. I know it will be very painful and wish I were there to comfort you but I will be with you in spirit.

June 5th was a stand down for the 416th due to poor weather conditions, but the maintenance crews worked day and night, slapping alternate wide stripes of white and black paint on the wings and fuselages of their A-20s. It was identity "war paint" to protect Allied ships from being shot down by friendly fire. If a plane was not so marked, it was fair game for Allied fighters. "All personnel were called back to base, and no passes were available. Something big was coming.

Off we go into the wild blue yonder,
Climbing high into the sun;
Here they come zooming to meet our thunder,
At'em boys, Giv'er the gun! (Giv'er the gun now!)
Down we dive, spouting our flame from under,
Off with one helluva roar!
We live in fame or go down in flame. Hey!
Nothing'll stop the U.S. Air Force!

The Air Force Song
Robert Crawford

Chapter Eleven
The Invasion

6-8-44 At long last the eventful day has come—the invasion. You can't imagine how happy we all were to hear about it and I could visualize you all back home. I have been over there once since it started. It seems to give me a new lease on life and now we can start counting the days until Hitler's doom. I really feel wonderful and I feel eager to get in there.

Just came back from a USO show here on the base and it wasn't bad at all...

Rather peaceful here tonight, cozy fire and I can devote all my thoughts to you without being interrupted.

My friend in Italy wants to bet a 10 cent cigar that it will be a boy and I countered with an offer to buy him all the drinks if it is.

Andy flew in the first of two afternoon missions on D-Day at 13:00 hours—the target, a major crossroads in Argentown, France behind enemy lines, beyond Omaha Beach. German forces depended on this avenue to transport men and equipment up to the beachheads to meet the enemy.

Of course, today it is common knowledge that General Eisenhower anguished over his crucial decision to go forward with the invasion on June 6th. It all came down to weather forecasting. Operation Overlord had already been stalled by a day, and thousands of military personnel were primed to go at a moment's notice. If they did not go on the 6th, they would be forced to delay the onslaught by another month when the moon and tides would once again be favorable. The best guess was that the weather would hold. But the decision weighed heavily on Eisenhower's heart, realizing the gargantuan consequences of a wrong decision.

The weather did hold, but it was far from ideal. Normally flying at 12,000 feet, the three boxes of A-20s that left Wethersfield at 1300 hours were forced to cross the English Channel under a cloudbank at only 1,700 feet, making them an easy target for anti-aircraft fire. A fighter escort was not an option at this altitude. However, the aviators lay witness to the spectacle of the largest armada ever assembled as they crossed the channel to France and beyond the beach they named Omaha. Happily, no flak was encountered on this earlier mission. The enemy did not expect an invasion on this particular day due to the foreboding weather, so in this respect, the tenuous weather favored the Allied forces. This low-level brand of flying negated the use of the Norden Bombsight, an aid to the bombardiers, which helped to ensure accurate results. Regardless, the men in their Plexiglas cocoons precisely executed their orders and their bombs zeroed in on their intended target. But it was a bittersweet victory because, despite being warned of the invasion, as the planes of the 416th flew over the Argentown skies to deliver their payload, French civilians waved an enthusiastic welcome at the sight of them. There were few survivors.

By the time the second mission of the day was underway at 2007 hours, the enemy had an opportunity to re-group, and these crews had a very different experience than the first. Twenty-five out of thirty-nine planes were hit by flak. Ten men and three aircraft were reported missing and two more crewmembers were wounded.

By the end of D-Day, however, the work of the 416th along with the Jabos (modified fighter-bombers) who preceded them, thwarted the transport of two massive panzer divisions, the 12th S.S. and the *Panzer Lehr*, from Paris to the coast. The Panzers were crucial to abating the Allied assault, but the 12th S.S. never arrived until the morning of the 7th and only fifty per cent of the crippled *Panzer Lehr* made it to the beachhead on the 9th.

6-8-44 Rather blue and disconsolate is my present mood brought on by the prevalent talk of when this will be over and how soon we can again go home. Consequently, my longing for you has trebled and I need you as never before. I fell asleep this afternoon and dreamed about you and one incident which was caused by mother's latest letter, concerning our living there until we find a place of our own which should be rather quickly. And in my dream I was trying to figure out where we would sleep because my room contains only a single bed. When I awakened the problem was still unsolved and so it shall probably remain until l once again am safe in your arms, away from the maelstrom of war, the ever destructive flak and all.

It will seem strange coming home to find an offspring awaiting me. I sincerely hope that Junior has the character of his mother and her good looks. Really would be a handsome kid, of course, the old man's curls wouldn't be a detriment to his appearanc...

The thing I really want to do when I get home is go away for a couple of weeks, just you and I. We could leave the baby with mother and then devote every minute to each other. I'm afraid, darling, that I won't let you out of my sight for an instant. What do you think of my plan darling!

6-9-44 *I'd give anything to see you taking care of Junior; that will be a riot. Know how to put a diaper on, I mean on Junior?*

6-11-44 *I suppose the papers are full of news about the current incidents of the invasion. I imagine a lot of people are already hazarding the idea that the war will soon be over. Apparently, this statement can only be made by some very asinine wits because we still have a long, hard road to travel. Of course the first glimmer of the end can be seen but it won't be easy. Jerry is still pretty tough. But I would rather talk about you. You at least make sense and I love you and I shall never give you any reason to doubt it.*

6-12-44 How is my baby feeling today? I hope you are in as fine shape as I am because I feel very rested and eager to do something. Haven't done a thing the last two days and the unexpected rest was duly appreciated. Today was very nice for a change and I was very domestic and aired my blankets (six) after shaking them...

Last night I lay awake for hours thinking of you and strive as I might, I couldn't make the old lids stay shut. Especially after scanning the pictures that we had taken in the Blue Room the Saturday night that you arrived. Remember how jubilant we were to see each other? Just imagine how happy we will be the next time we meet in a station. I'm afraid we will shock all the people with the ardor of our greeting but then who cares, we're in love and they are just envious.

Long ago and far away
I dreamed a dream one day
And now that dream is here beside me
Long the skies were overcast
But now the clouds have passed
You're here at last!

Long Ago (And Far Away)
Ira Gershwin

Chapter Twelve
A Soldier's Duty

"What he nobly thought, he nobly dared." This quote appeared next to Andy's high school graduation picture in his school paper. Andy was called upon to defend his country and he had answered the call, but it clearly was not his first calling anymore. His heart was calling him to be a husband, and soon, a father. Spurred on by the family life that awaited him, Andy continued to fly his missions to the best of his ability, doing his small part to bring an end to the terrible brutality of war, the pain of separation, and the ever-challenging task of defeating the enemy.

6-13-44 Paid a little visit to France this morning and gave the Jerries something to remember me by. Hope they appreciate the donations. [This was a mission to St. Sauveur Le Vicomte railway junction leaving at 0530 and returning at 0830.]

The boys and myself have just been doing a little hangar flying, reminiscing about our former cadet days. It seems great to be able to laugh about it now but they were rather grueling experiences then.

Gosh when I think of our future, I get all excited. All I want to do now is secure some kind of job so we can live the way we want to without worrying about our source of income all the time. As I said once darling, just what am I going to do? The only thing I know how to do is fly and it really is the only thing that appeals to me. I'm not kidding darling, I'd never attempt to hold down an office job because I don't know anything about it and it is too late in the game to learn anything new. That is one problem that worries me and probably is confronting a few other boys.

6-15-44 I still have my fried eggs in the morning. The mess usually has them a couple of times a week plus our weekly ration of three. One of the boys usually gets a crate from some of the neighboring farmers, and sells us ten of them for three shillings (60 cents).

I get a kick out of you looking over maternity dresses; I'll bet you haven't gained any weight since I last saw you. Your imagination is running rampant.

I anticipated that Detroit would be rather electrified to hear the news of the invasion. But darling, don't worry, the danger is no greater than before. And I'll let you feed me all the steaks and French fries you want because in 24 years I have never had my fill, so you have a job on your hands...

Just wait until we have our own home with little bambinos running around and of course a dog.

6-17-44 I went over to the enlisted men's service club where they had a dance in progress and listened to the five-piece band composed of two of my friends and three GIs. They really are groovy because practically all of them played with bands in civilian life.

I received a letter from mother today and she informs me that you finally got a letter from me. I hope now that your worries have been banished. ...

Darling, doesn't a home in our section of town appeal to you? Then we can be within a short distance of both families and then too it is a new section and the air would be good for Junior. And I'm tired of having twin beds. I never want to see any more of them. Agreed? Darling, I may be way off the beam but it is my firm belief that this party will be home by Christmas. I think Schicklegruber [Hitler] will be washed up by then and then home to you.

6-18-44 Every afternoon when we aren't flying, sack time is in order and snores emanate from every corner. I remember you do that very quantily. You do too!

6-21-44 Churchill is of the opinion that the summer will see the end of this conflict. I have my doubts but sincerely hope he is right.

Two more days and we will have been wed for six months—one half year—it still seems like just yesterday that we walked down the aisle and you did look radiant. How can I ever forget that memorable day? Remember how cold it was and then we didn't know who had the flowers; your brother getting the cop to let us turn on Woodward; my nosebleed at breakfast. It was all over too quickly but when I come home our life will be one big wedding day.

6-22-44 Have been indulging in a little athletics of late. Usually in the evening we get up a volley game and it does wonders for mental strain.

My gunners are now staff sergeants and it remains for me to get promoted. That will mean a few more pounds per month.

The much-publicized pilotless planes were observed by a few of the boys while in London and claim the people just go about their business when the alert is sounded. Guess they are rather diffident towards them by now.

"Germany answered the invasion of France by launching its first V-1 against London on the night of June 12-13. By July 21, 4,059 V-1s had been fired, 3,045 of which reached England. Although the "secret weapon" did little to alter the course of the war in France, it killed 3,875 people and injured 24,960 others, forcing the Allies to divert some airpower to bomb V-1 launching sites."

Andy sent a newspaper clipping to Ginny, most likely from *Stars and Stripes*, describing some of the fallout of one such robot in a London pub. It was written by Judy Barden of the North American Press Alliance. Her story focused on one of the pub's patrons, resolute, never budging from his stool. She explains, " 'He lifted his pint of mild and bitter to his lips.' " After buying Barden a drink, he shared his philosophy with her. " 'I figure it this way. Adolf's gotta be pretty clever to beat them planes after 'im over the channel, then 'e's gotta be pretty clever to get by the ack-ack, then 'e's gotta be cleverer still ter find my street, and I can't think why 'e should sort out my 'ouse, and if 'e does, the Missus and I are usually in the pub anyway, so yer see I'm practically bomb-proof, as yer might say.' "

Please try not to worry about me, my sweet, because I am the fastest and most ardent prayer you have ever seen when I get within sight of Hitler's Festung Europe. And God is being good to me for my guardian angel works overtime warding off the flak and checking my instruments. It's a full time job, I'll grant you and I have no complaints...

Remember that never-to-be-forgotten night when we met again in your home? You took my breath away for you were lovelier than I had ever imagined. My utter surprise when you said "yes" followed by supreme exhilaration. I knew that I had never stopped loving you. Inadvertently, I was very jealous when you came down to Missouri to see someone else and had given you up mainly because of reports from your suitor at that time. He was verbose, wasn't he?

6-23-44 Incidentally, the picture I have of you which was in the paper, has traveled down to Italy to my friend Tom just to back up my boasts about you. It is now safe in my hands again and Tom says I didn't exaggerate one bit.

6-29-44...Today I returned from a two day sojourn in London and I feel pretty good. Not seeing airplanes for even such a short time did wonders. ...

Jack and I made a tour of the city and saw all the famous places such as the Tower of London, Buckingham Palace, Big Ben, Hyde Park and many other places. I wish you could have been with me to enjoy it all...

Oh yes, we have two more of the Smith clique (the Smith Cottages in Florence, South Carolina) *with us now, Allan and Ed Hall are now in my squadron. All the boys that lived at Smiths' are in my outfit, Svenson, York, Henderson, Allan and myself. All we lack now are our wives. See if you can't arrange that will you...*

Honey, you are off the ball; I realize that the papers say we run two missions a day but a lot of times circumstances prohibit this and besides if I even were permitted to run fifty straight, I'd be a wreck believe me. By the time I reach fifty the war might be over. But you may have your wish. I don't suppose it would be too impossible for me to have fifty come October. I'll work on that...

I seem to have acquired that paternal instinct already because little children seem to be my weakness and I can't help thinking that soon we will have one of our own...

Life would be very barren indeed, if I didn't have you to give me encouragement and a soft smile. I know you must be smiling because my wife is brave and will not weep because we are far apart.

7-2-44 Every time one of the boys sees your picture for the first time and discovers you are my wife, they look at me in amazement and ask how I could be so cruel and heartless to ask a girl like you to marry a lug like me. Frankly, I can't figure it out either.

I suppose you are sweating out the heat while I am running around with a nice new jacket on. It has a soft fur collar and lined with soft fleece; also have pants lined the same way.

7-7-44 I haven't written for the past two days because I have been to London again and had a pretty good time...

The buzz bombs were still dropping intermittently and a few uncomfortably close. Stayed at a marvelous hotel. It would put the Taft to shame…

I've been dreaming for the past three years of the kind of car I want when all is at peace and that is a convertible with red leather upholstery. What type do you have in mind?

Say baby, I hope you realize that I am only teasing you about the baby being a boy. If it's a girl, I shall love her just as much. You know the old saying "if at first you don't succeed, try, try again" and sooner or later we are bound to get a boy.

7-10-44 *I'll bet you never guess where I am writing this from. From a nice white bed in the local hospital. Don't get alarmed it's nothing serious, just a case of follicular tonsillitis. I'm to stay here for a couple of days and if the doctor doesn't see any improvement, he plans on removing my tonsils. The poison affects my whole body because all my bones seem to hurt. I am taking sulfa tablets. Hope to get rid of it soon because I have no appetite. I'm the only one in the ward and it's very quiet except for the radio. I can really catch up on my sack time now.*

7-11-44 *Now I have so much time to think. Past, present and future; of the future, I can only say that it will be beautiful and wonderful. To have you always with me is something I haven't as yet experienced but for a few fleeting weeks and then always with the fear of parting in the background. The present finds us miles apart and yearning to be in each other's arms. But our thoughts are always together. The past certainly taught me lessons. Traveling as I did and meeting so many people, going out with different girls. I always found something lacking and then it dawned on me that you were the one person that possessed everything I wanted my wife to have. What a chance I took on losing you. I will admit, I was quite a fool. But now my fair beauty, you are in my power and I shall never let you go. Even if I keep you happy for the rest of your life. So you can't escape, for my love will always hold you. I'm afraid that I shall have a serious contender for your affections when Junior arrives. But I'll just put him or her in his or her place.*

7-14-44 As I write this I remember Fr. Ulhenberg saying that a lot of married couples live together and love each other so much, they even begin to look alike; I can just see you now, curly hair, good-looking and a mustache. Gee, I can't help laughing myself as I visualize your expressions as you read this, and saying to yourself "just as big an egotist as ever."

I haven't received any answer from Fr. Maino as yet and I figure the mail service in this country takes just as long as it does from here to the States.

So you are still wearing your summer clothes; well, I didn't expect you to run around without having them on.

7-15-44 Picture if you can the lowest feeling creature in this wide world and you have me. I can't remember when I have felt more dejected and disgusted and, oh well, I just can't describe the feeling. I'm so doggoned irritable that I blow my top at the slightest thing. This is the disadvantage of loving you, I miss you so much that nothing holds any interest for me. It's getting so I welcome combat as a diversion. It just seems that living with the same fellows all the time, knowing them so well makes their usual line of talk disgusting and childlike. I guess I'm trying to fight the whole world tonight... Right now I feel like going out and tearing things apart. No mail in three days hasn't helped either. I've only flown one mission this month and I'm fed up with lying around. I want to do something but quick... We certainly have a lot of rumors flying around here, some marvelous, others not so good. I'll just wait and see and you can pray harder.

Bravery's Not Dead was the title of an article written by Andy Rooney of *60 Minutes* fame. I found it among a variety of clippings pertaining to World War II that mom had collected over the years, stuck between the pages of her remembrance albums of Andy. The article appeared in an issue of a Detroit newspaper on April 12, 1981. Prompted by the courageous actions of Timothy J. McCarthy, the Secret Service agent who took a bullet for President Reagan, Rooney spoke about what it is to be brave:

During World War II, I saw a lot of brave men and a lot of others who were given medals for bravery who were not.

Among the bravest men I knew were the crews of the B-17 and B-24 bombers who flew day raids over Germany.

<u>It always seemed worse to me for Army Air Corps people than for infantrymen, because when the airmen weren't risking their lives, they lived in fairly civilized circumstances with too much time on their hands in which to contemplate their fate.</u>

Mom underlined this paragraph. Apparently, she agreed with Mr. Rooney.

7-16-44 Everything seemed much better today especially when I received two letters from you and one from Maurine. I can easily say that today has been just about the most sultry day that we have had. Consequently, I have a slight sunburn from playing ball without a shirt. I never believed that the sun could get that warm over here...

Greene and the other boys in the other outfit, are now first lieutenants and here I am the same as a year ago (second lieutenant). *What I have seen around here only makes my pet peeve stronger. The hard working, death facing paddle-feet still get the promotions...*

Yesterday my dream was realized, my most impossible hope came true for I played a record personally autographed by dear little Frankie himself. Isn't that thrilling...?

Today we had a new pest, which covered us practically, known as wheat lice. Little black things, they don't bite but you can feel them crawl.

So you weigh 120, well, all I can say is you had better get on the ball or Junior will be rather puny.

Darling, just keep on praying and maybe some of those wild rumors will come true. I went to Mass and received Communion this morning.

7-17-44 Darling, speaking of our post war plans, I didn't say that I intended to fly for a living after the war but rather that it is about the only thing I know how to do. Even my experience wouldn't mean too much if I would attempt to secure a job with an airline because the boys who have been flying the four engine jobs will have more in their favor. Then too, an airline job would keep us apart more that the army would. What worries me is that if we are to have children, I must have a steady job. I'm not afraid to work but my last preference would be the factory. Never having been married before, I don't quite know how much it would take to keep a family in comfort. The thing that will probably spoil me is the fact that I make about $90 a week now and in civilian life it would probably be half of that. But I suppose we could manage. Are you receiving the allotments regularly darling? Not counting the money you have needed to live on, we should have received a total of $1200 if you have all five months. At least we won't have to start from scratch when I come home.

Darling, I thank God that I have a wife like you who is so sure that everything will work out for the best. I must say it has from the first day I met you.

Ginny writes another letter to her friends, Evelyn and Phil Schaff, still residing at "Smiths" in Florence, South Carolina.

July 18, 1944
2:00 P.M.
Dear Evelyn & Phil:

Remember me? I am that gal that definitely is in the doghouse with both of you for being the world's worst correspondent. Even though my letters have not materialized I have thought of you so many times, and got lonesome for the grand times the four of us used to have. I am glad that my husband is a better letter-writer than I, for I am sure he keeps you informed of our existence. But honestly, kids, writing to Andy every day keeps me pretty busy, and as a result I seem to neglect my friends. So much for that!

Andy writes me whenever he receives a letter from you, Phil, and is always so happy to hear from you. Neither one of us can ever forget the many kindnesses you accorded us, and I am sure someday Junior will be grateful for the many times he rode in such a super car, instead of a bumpy bus. More fun! ...

What is this, Evelyn, that you wrote me about Phil joining Andy soon? Gosh, I hope not, but I suppose it comes to all of them eventually. If Phil does go into combat, I do hope he will be stationed with Andy in the European Theatre. I only wish that I could be with you when, and if he leaves, to lend moral support, for I don't know what I would have done without you when Andy left.

Incidentally, two certain people are celebrating a first wedding anniversary next month, aren't they? What was the date again? I hope Phil is still with you, Evelyn, for that occasion.

I am feeling fine once again and can hardly wait until October arrives. I will be going to the hospital around the 20th I believe. These months have seemed so long, probably because I was so ill at first and was so lonely without Andy, that I can scarcely believe that Junior will be a reality soon and not a fond dream of ours. Still seems too good to be true...

Evelyn, you will be interested to know that I have been sewing for the baby a great deal this summer. I made dresses, sacks, pillowcases, kimonos, and what have you. It really is a lot of fun. Then, I have done rather a good deal of other sewing as well, luncheon sets, guest towels, vanity set and I am now working on a buffet set. All set to go housekeeping someday—soon, I hope. (When Ginny speaks of "sewing", she really means embroidery. It was one of her specialties.)

By the way, Evelyn, how is your housekeeping coming along? How do you manage in such hot weather? I bet you find the cooking situation still a problem, don't you? Have you picked up any more soldiers in the "Chocolate Shoppe"? I think I have just about worn you out with questions.

My little nephew is a doll and will be five months old on the 22nd of this month. They called him "Tommy" and naturally the family thinks him pretty wonderful. He looks exactly like my brother, and needless to say, Leo goes around beaming all the time.

Well, kids, I think I have related all the current news, and hope you will forgive this very belated letter. In the future I promise to be more prompt. Evelyn, if you leave Florence, be sure to send me your New York address so that I can keep in contact with you. I would love hearing from you when you have an opportunity.

Lots of Love,
Ginny

Without fail, Andy does not allow his correspondence to slip, continuing to keep Ginny apprised, and, hopefully, allays her fears.

7-19-44 Here it is time to go to bed and I just returned from a little job and believe me, I'm dead. Have been up since 4:30 this morning and I don't feel very fresh. ...

Sgt. Cochran, a tunnel gunner, was hit by flak and perished on this mission to the Bruz fuel depot. His pilot, F/O [Flight Officer] Byrne left the formation and brought the ship down on a fighter strip in Normandy. They buried Sgt. Cochran in Dlosville, France.

I just can't concentrate on writing. My head feels like it wants to burst. Oh yes, my plane bears your name and it's alongside a luscious redhead. The petty type you know. ...

I'll be glad when the end of this week comes so I can relax in London for a couple of days. I shall probably go on a seven-day leave in a couple of weeks or less. Haven't any idea where I am going but I do want to stay someplace where I can lay on the beach, do a little riding and so on. I can't get too enthused because I know you won't be with me.

7-20-44 *I feel a lot better today after a good night's sleep but I surely felt awful last night. One more mission and I'll have my third cluster.* [This means that Andy was nearing his twentieth mission. His Air Medal represented five missions and for every fifth mission thereafter he received an oak-leaf cluster.]

I finally heard from Fr. Maino and he is somewhere in England. All I have to do now is to locate him...

Hope you are feeling fine honey and take your medicine. Imagine being afraid to go to the doctor for some medicine.

7-21-44 Fr. Maino mentioned in his letter that one of the boys in his outfit saw you and I in New York but lost us in the crowd. Father also anticipates that long-promised steak. I'll be in on that deal myself...

I really have to laugh when I picture you struggling into your clothes. What are you trying to do develop a stomach like mine? I can get rid of mine with a little exercise—can you? If I was at home now, I really would give you a bad time. How about that hot water?

Darling, I have come to the conclusion that you write the most beautiful letters I have ever seen or hope to see. They are superb and they really do wonders for me. How come you never tell me all these things when I'm with you? I want to hear this in person when I next hold you in my arms. I'm afraid though that I won't give you much of an opportunity to talk for you can't very well if I'm kissing you.

In his letter dated July 11, 1944, Fr. Maino writes to Andy:

Dear Andrew:

Your letter was a welcome surprise, and I'm very grateful for all the news it contained. You'll note that our APO is 340—the 403 was correct earlier, but it was changed. You're a little off on your guess as to my arrival in the ETO. As a matter of fact, Sgt. McLeod and a couple of others saw you and the gorgeous Ginny on the street in N.Y.—at a distance, they said, and didn't get the chance to speak to you. So we passed through the POE at the same time. I have since seen Krass and Fricke and they told me of the incident you mentioned. I have not gotten to London, much as I'd like to see the place. We are quite a ways from it, and unlike the AAC [Army Air Corps] can't get passes any more...

So we've had the life of Riley over here. We live in a former convent and boarding school, from which the nuns and their pupils were evacuated at the beginning of the war. For my daily and Sunday masses I have the convent chapel, which also accommodates the civilians from the neighborhood. The congregation is mostly British soldiers plus the civilians and our GIs. I notice a snicker or two from the English, probably provoked by something I say in Yank accent. Of course it would be the same if the circumstances were reversed and we were listening to a British padre in the States.

It must have been a great thrill for you to have looked down on your old home town from the air. Who knows, you may have a chance to look at it from closer range—from the ground I mean. Better keep your Flemish brushed up. The officers here are attending French classes. Hope we get some use out of it. Although I wouldn't be offended if the AGF (American Ground Forces) has them pushed back into Krautland by the time we land over there.

Well Andy, I have no doubt you're getting to Mass and the altar rail as frequently as possible. That's the best guarantee I know for coming through safely. That plus Ginny's prayers and those of your mother and all the others who are remembering you. You and Ginny both have a daily memento in my Mass. Tell her I'm counting heavily on that steak she promised when we are reunited in the vicinity of Charlevoix and Dickerson.

Check into the possibility of flying over here to our location. Till then—or our next meeting, au revoir.

Sincerely yours,
Hubert Maino

7-22-44 Haven't done a thing today and preceding this letter, I was very busily engaged in sewing a 9th Air Force patch on my blouse and a couple of buttons on my shirt. My buttons usually stay on too. Guess I'll make somebody a good husband one of these fine days.

It feels just like winter around here so you can see what I mean by screwy British weather...

My gunners take right good care of me because it seems they are continually getting packages. One evening Rice will bring me a part of his fruitcake and Young will bring some candy. They really are good boys and I am very pleased with them. The three of us usually go out together on passes, something that would be frowned upon by the paddle-feet back in the States.

7-25-44 Returned from my little jaunt to London today and I was rather sorry to leave. Had a pretty good time just looking around the hotel. Of course, I enjoyed the company of my gunner, but still when I see other people dancing, I miss you terribly and I am afraid that I must bore Rice with my continual reminiscing but it's the only way I can ease the pain...

I hear that you are finally showing evidence of Junior. Guess it must be true if you are buying maternity dresses.

Very dreary weather we are having. Sure would like to see the sun shine for a while instead of gray clouds...

It is reassuring to hear that you look and feel so well. Just keep on eating to your heart's content and worry about nothing...

Just keep on praying darling that the Germans keep on cracking and when they collapse, it won't take long with the Japs.

7-26-44 You should see what a sight I am tonight, we just finished playing the gunners five games of volleyball and my left arm is practically devoid of skin and all my nails on my right hand were broken off, more fun. At least I'm tired enough to sleep sound tonight especially after getting up nice and early this morning for a little session in the sky.

7-27-44 Went out this afternoon and had a little fun just like I used to do down in Florence where I used to scare the poor farmers. I really got a kick out of it because it has been some time since I had indulged.

That fellow picking your house in his drunken stupor somehow sounds reminiscent of me. I can just imagine what you would have done if you had been alone. You have more scares around that house imaginary and real than any haunted house. ...

More and more I believe I'll be home by Christmas, I may be way off the beam but I don't believe it can last that long. Then, what a time we will have. Last Christmas was memorable but we will make this Christmas one we will always remember.

7-29-44 [Andy's birthday] *Today we celebrate one of the biggest holidays of the year, a day usually filled with gala fetes and merry making, for on this day twenty-five years ago, a great man was born. His name was uttered by mothers to their little ones as a symbol to live up to. Strong men tremble when they hear his voice and women swoon—no, not Sinatra—me! Anyhoo, here I sit all alone without any revelry and stuff. The last 2 days have been pretty fine though because I have received five letters and the lovely card in that time. The card arrived yesterday and was very well timed. I didn't receive your package but I got one from mother containing chocolate, tuna fish, sardines, cookies and of all things—Spam. Maybe she hasn't heard about the ETO! This is renowned as Spam Heaven.*

I didn't write to you last night because I just wasn't able to concentrate on anything. I had been on a pretty long mission and what with the altitude, I was suffering from a splitting headache. Little remains of it today and I am sure by tomorrow everything will be fine...

Oh yes darling, I have forgotten before but if you want to send me a cable and I hope someone does when the youngster arrives, my cable address is Lt. A.J. Vleghels (service number) *AMBELD London. This is code so don't try to figure out what it means...*

Those sarcastic remarks about my mustache are not welcomed and I will have you know that it is a thing of beauty.

Just think of the tickling sensation darling. Junior will probably be born with one.

Darling if you promise to be especially nice to me, I may consider letting you touch my ribbons for only a light touch but you must make room when the rest of the fairer sex swoons at the sight of me adorned with ribbons and of course, the mustachio…

Incidentally, I have 22 missions and you are getting a workout. Your engines are running pretty smooth and I am trying to take good care of you.

7-30-44 The doc claims the headaches are due to my sinuses. God forbid, I don't want to be afflicted with that. I know what my mother and dad go through.

It's a little after ten and I intend to take a bath when I finish this missive. Remember the times we used to have attempting to get hot water at Smith's? You would have been in fine shape if you would have had the baby then—no hot water.

The last few mornings, I have been up at the cheerful hour of four or five in the morning. You know how that must appeal to me.

I have missed you so very much today and it seems to get worse every day. Someday, I hope I won't have to miss you anymore for you will be with me always.

8-1-44 So Junior is sort of chaffing at the bit. Probably be an energetic little cuss.

Didn't do any flying today but I was quite busy with other irrelevant details.

My leave begins Saturday but that won't hinder me from writing to you every day. I may spend it in London because traveling is limited due the excess of vacationers. I'll still have the buzz bombs to contend with but usually I don't mind them too much.

Gee baby, I sure would like to see you now and see if you have changed very much. But I'll get that privilege when we have the next one. How many do you think we should have— about a dozen? I was just thinking; in a year's time we should have actually saved close to three thousand dollars. Of course, there are the doctor's bills to be considered and your living expenses. I hope you aren't curtailing your buying activities very much just because we are married. I want you to have all you want and then some. Nothing is too good for you darling and I shall always try to have the best for you that includes me too.

When I come home and we get settled, we can begin looking for a house of our own. We were in a comparative heaven in one room, what will it be like in a whole house? Won't we have fun?

8-2-44 Received two letters from you today, one from Maurine and a card from your mother and dad. Convey my thanks to them for their thoughtfulness. Your letter really put me out of this world and I couldn't have received them at a more opportune time for I had just come back from a mission. Yep, the old man has 25 of them now and four oak leaf clusters.

The present advances by our armies is really encouraging especially when only a few days ago we were hitting the same towns our forces have since captured and which at the same time seemed miles from our lines.

I went over to my gunner's hut and played Casino with him and then left them mystified with a few card tricks which I have learned over here.

It seems like the Taft is giving everyone a bad time, first they evict a married couple and now the girls. I can't say much against them though because they really took care of me when everything else seemed hopeless the day you arrived. It was a typical movie scene with the hero running around with a handful of nickels calling everyone from the Ritz down to a flophouse. I sure had a time but the Taft came to my rescue and all was serene when the heroine entered the picture. And they lived happily for four days.

I'm beginning to count the days until that little rascal arrives. I sure hope and pray that it won't cause you too much trouble.

8-3-44 *Shot skeet this afternoon and had a lot of fun. That's one thing I'd like to do after the war. Join a skeet club. I had never fired a shot gun until I hit Advanced and since then have fired quite a few rounds...*

As I sit here I can hear the strains of "Long Ago" emanating from the gunners' barracks and it makes me wish fervently that I could be dancing with you at the moment. Remember our wedding night when we stopped in at the Terrace for a late snack and tired as you were, you still wanted to dance. (The Terrace Room was a popular, posh, nightclub in the Detroit Statler, the hotel where Andy and Ginny spent a brief "honeymoon".) *That was fun and I promise you, we will renew this memory many times in the future. The band that was playing that number was none other than my boy, Glenn Miller and Dinah Shore was singing with him. Really an organization. I would like to see him in person.*

8-4-44 *You are always in my thoughts darling, more so when I am flying over enemy territory and then I pray fervently that God will see fit to see me through safe so that I can come home to you and make you happy. I don't mind so much for myself but the thought of you worrying is more than I can stand. I hope that God will continue to hear my prayers until the day when we can really be jubilant for then will begin the life we both have been dreaming of for so many long months.*

8-8-44 *Here I am living the life of a retired financier with not a care in the world and with you always in my thoughts... Roger and myself are staying in London and living the perfect life of leisure. My only wish is to have you with me. We sleep late, eat heartily and drink merrily. I have French Fries twice a day just to make up for lost time. Since I have stayed at this hotel all my previous trips, we are quite well known and have pretty good service. It really is a lovely day and looking out I can see the throngs of people in Hyde Park and Marble Arch. What a life.* [Andy's squadron leased an apartment about a block behind The Marble Arch Hotel near Hyde Park. It was a clever and thrifty plan, because the men always had a place to stay on their R & R and at a far better rate.]

Everyone is very optimistic about the end of the war and I believe it will be all over with Germany in three months or less. Just thinking about that possibility sends me into ecstasy. . . .

I have seen practically every picture in town and I saw "Cover Girl" again. I saw it for the first time about three hours before we left New York. One of the reasons for seeing it was the song "Long Ago" which is played a few times in the picture. I like the words, "chills run up and down my spine, Alladin's lamp is mine, for you are here beside me."

Met a fellow in the lobby yesterday whom I hadn't seen since I left Nashville. In fact he went with a girl there which I later took over. He's flying P.51s and we really had a hilarious gabfest.

8-9-44 So far the weather has been superb, subsequently, the buzz bombs are practically nil. I am really enjoying this leisure time and it seems strange that someone isn't always after me to do something. Breakfast is served in bed and Roger and I really go for that. Breakfast over, we roll over for a few more minutes of sack time and then a wonderful hot bath.

It makes me feel sick that you can't be here with me. What a time we could have. I hope I find scads of mail from you when I get home.

8-10-44 *Went riding yesterday and Roger and myself almost died laughing. Every time the horse came up, we were going down to meet it. Won't be able to sit down for awhile. It was fun though since I hadn't been on a horse since I left California.*

If only you were here, we could really put on the dog and I could really strut when I brought you into the grill or any other place we went to. You would be by far the most beautiful girl there. I love you so much darling and would want nothing more than to whisper it in your ear. We have been apart for almost five months now but it seems more like five years.

I get so fed up at times, I could scream. Everything seems so futile and I long for the day when I can resume a normal life, which will be the happiest days of my life because you will be with me. I think of you always darling. Adieu sweet.

8-12-44 *Arrived home today and had a most wonderful surprise, ten letters from you and about seven from my family.*

...I'm so glad that you are feeling as well as you do but I believe you are putting up a brave front. Do you think the baby will be worth all the pain and trouble you are going through?

You have my heartfelt sympathy darling; you women have to go through so much pain and discomfort. Wish I could be with you to try and help take your mind off of it.

Say honey, just what are we naming ours? I think Jack, Bill etc., is too common, everyone has a name like that, ours should be different. Who is to be godparents—my dad and your mother?
Incidentally, I'm going to give you a bad time when I come home if you persist in calling a certain man "cutie pie". Let's watch that stuff.

Honey, I wish you would send me a money order for $50 because I sort of ran into difficulties with my finances which were rather depleted by my leave. As it is now, I won't be able to take another pass for a month if I don't have some dough. These English pounds seem to go faster than our dollar bills.

Yesterday I went swimming in Hyde Park and it wasn't bad. Everyone in London flocks to the seaside for their relaxation, therefore trains are pretty crowded.

Now I'm back to the old routine and hope my next 25 missions will be as successful as the past and bring me home to you.

8-13-44 *This morning I was unable to attend Mass due to a little work I had to attend to but I was able to go this afternoon. Later I saw the picture "Gaslight" with Boyer and Bergmann. That gal is really a superb actress. If you haven't already seen it, don't miss it. I really liked it. Think I'll try Boyer's tactics on you, now don't get the wrong idea until you see the picture. Weird noises, strange, noises, the Hermit knows.*

Sure wish I could see Doug, remember when we had supper together at Florence and he always called me "Rabbit"? He was a good Joe. Sure miss him.

I can only surmise that the Doug that Andy mentions was one of his friends from Florence, Lt. Douglas T. Sommers. On August 6th, the 416th received a request from the Commanding General of the IX Bomber Command to attack the Oissel Bridge, the last remaining bridge that spanned the Seine River. Two hundred thousand German troops were trapped in the Falaise Gap due to the relentless easterly Allied advance from Cherbourg led by General Patton. If the 416th could wipe out this bridge, the Germans would be left with no escape route.

A morning mission was attempted, but due to dense cloud-cover, the formation returned to base unable to release its bombs. At 1800 hours, a second attempt was made once the weather had cleared. Following the first failed attempt, the Germans, primed for their return, were well prepared, their anti-aircraft guns readied. Even so, the bomb run was extended to four minutes due to the high priority of the mission. The mission received an excellent rating, the Oissel Bridge demolished, but four planes were lost and every one of the remaining thirty-seven ships had sustained flak damage. "Lt. Sommers tried to crash land his plane on an emergency airstrip but was unsuccessful. His crew was reported as MIA."

Andy's weeklong leave to London began on the 6th. I could find no letters from Andy dated August 6th or 7th. It may have been that he didn't write or that the letter was lost or destroyed by Ginny, because Andy's letter of the 13th implies that she knows what happened to Doug Sommers.

Every soldier had to deal with this reality—a friend, a comrade, gone missing or killed in action. For the most part, however, there was little time to dwell upon the losses. For their own survival, both physically and mentally, the airmen's attention had to remain firmly focused on flying missions and fighting to stay alive.

The CO of the 97th Combat Bomb Wing, Colonel Backus, joined the 416th for the pivotal mission to the Oissel Bridge. The Group was awarded the Distinguished Unit Citation for their gallantry and their superior results. It states in part:

DEEPLY REGRET THE LOSSES IN YESTERDAY AFTERNOON'S MISSION, BUT AT THE SAME TIME, I WISH TO COMMEND YOU HIGHLY FOR THE SUPERB BOMBING ATTACKS CARRIED OUT AGAINST YESTERDAY'S TARGET, THE OISSEL BRIDGE AND UPON THE COMPEIGNE MARIGNY MARSHALLING YARDS ON 5 JULY 1944. YOUR DESTRUCTION OF THESE TARGETS WAS OF GREAT MILITARY VALUE AND IMPORTANCE.
SIGNED
BACKUS

In addition, the 416th received a commendation from the Commanding General of the IX Bomber Command.

8-14-44 *Haven't received a single letter from you in three days now. I wonder what the trouble is this time…*

For the past ten days we have had real summer weather and I took advantage of it today. No jaunts over the continent, but I did go up a couple of times, just joyriding. … Really was a pleasure flying alone. This afternoon I took a sun-bath for a few hours, just like a well-to-do civilian.

Have a brand new ship now and I'll see if I can't christen it like the other one. I'll be very happy when I receive the film then I can take some shots of me and the ship.

8-17-44 *I do hope that by this late date, Junior has stopped acting up. I realize how badly you must feel if your condition in Florence was any indication. Perhaps, cooler weather will alleviate the situation. Don't forget to do everything the doctor tells you…*

The G.I. network claims that the song, "I'll be Seeing You", is about the number one song in the States. Is that true? What else is popular?

I finally got the package containing the films and chocolate. Very thoughtful darling, you give me a million and one reasons why I love you.

Yes, you can send York an announcement… Don't believe you can send one to Sommers. Wish you could.

Got a good look at Paris the other day and we received a most warm reception. I doubt if the Parisians had anything to do with it.

I really feel blue tonight darling and you are the only person in the world that could bring me out of the doldrums..

Received two wonderful letters from you today and one yesterday. As usual, the boost in the old morale was terrific.

The same day, Ginny writes to Evie, now back in New York State:

August 17, 1944
1:00 P.M.
Dearest Evie:

Please don't faint when you see how promptly I am responding to your letter of the 8th. There apparently was some delay en route to me for I only received it this morning. Needless to say, it was grand hearing from you again, and from now on I promise to be prompt in replying to your missives.

Your news that Phil has left did not come as much of a surprise, for when I didn't hear from you I rather surmised the same and kept thinking about you and wished I could have been there to lend moral support if nothing else. It was grand though that he received a leave and was able to go home with you. I bet you had lots of fun...

I was sorry to hear that Phil was not destined for the European Theatre for I was in hopes that he would be joining Andy, for I know how glad Andy would have been to see him. No doubt he is en route to the Pacific.

Andy has completed half of his allotted missions; in fact he completed the twenty-fifth on "August 2" and was getting a leave for a week beginning on "August 5" which he was contemplating spending in London. By this date he should have close to thirty missions. He is supposed to receive a thirty-day leave to return to the States after the completion of fifty missions. But you know the Army and how subject it is to change, but I am still hoping this will come true. Andy now has four oak leaf clusters added to his Air Medal and I like to tease him about all his ribbons. He is rather disgusted that he hasn't received a promotion as yet, but you know how slow that process is, particularly so in the Air Corps.

Oh yes, Andy has named his plane after me and I guess my name is on his plane beside a petty drawing, which I am sure you have seen in the movies. I probably look like a hussy. More fun!

One thing, Evie, about combat is that once they have a sample of it and see what it is all about, they are satisfied and more than eager to return. At least that is how Andy feels and I am sure Phil will too. All Andy talks about besides the baby, is his return home. He is very optimistic about the war situation, and feels confident that the European war will be over very soon, and then he claims it won't be long to clean up the Japs. I surely hope he is right, but the war news certainly is encouraging. Isn't it?

I can well imagine how you must miss Phil, for I still miss Andy as much as the day he left, and I suppose I shall until he returns. We had four wonderful days together though in New York before his departure for England, and I wouldn't trade them for anything in the world. We stayed at the "Taft" which was very nice and really did the town. When I look back on it now, it all seems like a wonderful dream. But the morning he left I was rudely awakened.

You were fortunate in securing your former position, and once you get accustomed to office routine again, you will find that the work is the best tonic for loneliness, for I have found it so. I try to keep as busy as I can, and there always seems to be something to do around the house, then I have been sewing a great deal.

I just can't wait until the baby arrives. I have just about two more months to wait, for I expect to go to the hospital on the 20th of October. It is rather a strange coincidence for just a year on Oct. 13th I will have my ring. I guess Andy has bets with just about everyone in the squadron that the baby will be a boy. You know how fellows are. I can still remember the night we went to the Club dance and Andy had already told everyone it seemed, and I was so embarrassed. Do you remember? Andy still teases me about the "hot water" situation, and I never hear the word mentioned that I don't think of Phil.

My Sister's Father

This month mother and I are going to get the bassinet ready. I am going to make a skirt of white dotted Swiss and have the inside of the hood in blue and pink. I also bought a small, unpainted chest of drawers for the baby's clothes, and Dad is going to paint it white with baby blue handles. These two things will fit nicely in my room. Gosh, I, too, wish we lived closer together so that you might see the baby. But I will send you snapshots from time to time...

I still hang my head in shame when I think of the hole I burned in the table at Smith's.

Please remember me to Phil, and when you have his permanent address, I would appreciate it, for I know Andy will want it, for I believe they have been corresponding. Now don't get too lonesome and write soon for I love hearing from you.

Love,
Ginny

Though Andy makes no mention of it, there was a lapse of bombing missions at this juncture due to inclement weather and the advent of the planned evacuation of Wethersfield, home base to the 416th since they entered the war.

8-18-44 *So, it's strange is it to be hopelessly in love with your husband? What did you expect a year ago, some other joker? If I had you here now, across my knee you would go and you know I can do it.*

That little shaver promises to be expensive, all that money for clothes, what is it, a zoot suit? But then you'll have all this material for the next dozen...

Incidentally baby, I sent a package to you yesterday containing some clothing, personal papers and letters. I shall probably send another in the near future. [Perhaps Andy mailed some of his more superfluous possessions home to lighten his load for the anticipated transport of his bomb group to France the following month.]

8-19-44 *I've been dreaming lately about our own home; you busy in the kitchen making French Fries, and me puttering around the car or garden. We will make all this come true, I know.*

8-20-44 *I have just had a great disillusionment; I was reading a story in the magazine "Cosmopolitan", and was deriving some interest out of it and upon reading the last sentence, the catastrophe strikes me, not discreetly but in very plain letters, "continued in the next issue." Now I'll never know whether Cy married Ivy, Cora or Sybil. It's enough to drive a man to drink. Now there's a pregnant idea.*

I've had a very exciting and eventful day. Arose this morning about seven prepared to embark on another excursion but our wonderful weather put a stop to that. Even the birds were walking. So after breakfast back to the sack, up for dinner consisting of well-aged chicken, peas, mashed potatoes and pineapples. Went to Mass at three, supper at 5:30, played volleyball against the gunners (the officers came through victorious, winning the acclaim of a few degenerates lolling around) whiled away a good hour indulging in the sport of kings, Casino. Then came a momentous decision in my young life; I would take a bath—no, there wasn't any holiday in the offing but my congenial roommates decided it would enhance the air of our hut tremendously. Being very susceptible to the will of the masses, I acquiesced and here I sit, one of the sweet smelling set.

If I seem rather slaphappy tonight, you can blame yourself. I just feel wonderful, simply because I have been thinking of you. Somehow, I've had the feeling all day that I will see you soon. Why if the promise of flak on a mission doesn't frighten me as it used to.

While I was in the midst of my ritual of bathing tonight, I was struck with a wonderful idea; when I come home, I'm going to let you scrub my back. Won't that be a thrill?

This exuberant feeling is strange in one sense because I haven't had a letter from my loving wife in two days. Sure hope it isn't because you aren't feeling up to par.

Honey if you were with me tonight, I'm afraid I wouldn't give you a moment's rest due to the fact that I would be making love to you constantly. Would you mind that?

Ralph Conte, a fellow-pilot of the 669th, relates an event of hair-raising proportions in his memoir, *Attack Bombers--We Need You*. It happened on August 22, 1944 when Sergeant Potter, missing since June 29th, showed up at Wethersfield. His plane had taken a direct hit, sending it into a flat spin. But, miraculously, all three crewmen parachuted out. To make a bad situation, worse, however, the Germans shot at Potter as he descended and he was taken prisoner. He had no idea what had happened to his fellow-crewmen. During the first six weeks of his captivity, Potter became chummy with an Ausie pilot. Together, they planned and successfully executed an escape. Eventually, they made their way to occupied France where they hid, under the protection of a French family. One morning, they awoke to discover that American forces had liberated the town. Following intense interrogation, Potter was allowed to return to England and, soon after, his home in the States.

8-22-44 *Old Blood and Guts Patton is really doing a superb job and naturally the English press does nothing but laud Monty. I can't see what he has accomplished in Normandy that is so spectacular. The Limeys seem to have their hands full just holding on to Caen. Their newsreels are the same way; to their way of thinking, they are winning this single-handed. I wonder where they would be if it weren't for the Yanks...*

I did receive a grand surprise today though. Two packages, one from your family and another from Leo. Convey my most bountiful thanks to them. I'm the envy of the barracks. I feel good knowing so many think of me so much. Hope I can convey my heartfelt thanks in person and especially to a sweet, little girl I happen to be married to...

Once again, Andy repeats his post-war plans for employment, but adds:

Certainly I don't want to slave away in a factory because then all the dreams and hopes my parents ever had would be smashed. My ambition to become an officer had two motives: one, to make my parents proud of me, and the other to prove to myself that I could do it, well with the grace of God, I did achieve my goal. I do believe that the occasion that really boosted my ego and made me the happiest man in this world was marrying you.

I don't believe I ever told you this but when we were in school, I didn't believe you cared much for me and I spent my fervent prayers that you would in time love me. God certainly answered my prayers for that love drew me like a moth is drawn to a flame.

Night and day you are the one,
Only you beneath the moon or under the sun,
Whether near to me or far
It's no matter, darling, where you are,
I think of you, night and day…

Night and day under the hide of me
There's an, oh, such a hungry yearning
Burning inside of me,
And its torment won't be through
Till you let me spend my life making love to you
Day and night, night and day.

Night and Day
Cole Porter

Chapter Thirteen
The Purple Heart

According to the Operations Report for the 669th, the missions that were flown during the month of August of 1944 were "of extreme importance in driving the Germans back toward their own border." The Germans began their retreat from France on August 15th yielding to the relentless pressure of a coordinated Allied attack by air and sea. This enabled the ground troops to advance so swiftly that they outdistanced their logistical support. The air force met the shortfall by air dropping supplies. Disrupting communications and the flow of enemy supply lines, and cutting off an avenue of escape were the main objectives of the 416th at this stage of the war.

After being grounded for a week by poor weather conditions--rain, fog, and a low ceiling, the 416th flew one mission on the 25th and two missions on the 26th when the clouds finally gave way to clearer skies. Mission #129 on the 25th was to Brest, France and the Kerviniou Coastal Defense Battery. An important port to defend, the 416th were joined by the entire IX Bomber Command as well as Naval bombardment from the sea. It was the Group's first experience flying a mission so far away that it would require a prearranged stop for refueling at St. Mawgans on the southern coast of England upon their return. Most missions ran three to four hours, but the mission to Brest took close to five and a-half-hours to complete. Although it was a challenging and grueling mission for the men, they came out of it with zero losses, casualties, or battle damage and scored fair to excellent on their bomb runs. Those who did not participate in the mission were diligently working on their flying skills back at the base. Paris was liberated that day. But there was little time to celebrate. Many more missions awaited the men of the 416th.

The target of the morning mission on the 26th was a fuel depot at Champiegne-Clairox. Accurate bombing touched off horrific explosions and fires. No flak or enemy planes were encountered.

Andy and his crew were assigned to the afternoon operation of the 26th, a mission to Rouen, France where German troops and tons of their equipment stood at a standstill, waiting to be ferried across the Seine. Successful Allied bombing had eradicated all the bridges in the area. This time, the A-20s were armed to drop fragmentation bombs, an invention rarely used by the 416th. The casings of the bombs were scored, causing them to break apart into many fragments upon impact or at tree-level, depending upon how armament set the fuses. The goal was to "immobilize" Von Kluge's retreating army. Six flights [thirty-six planes] approached the target, each flight being assigned its own aiming point. Fortunately for the Germans, with haze and clouds rolling in, only one of the six flights was able to drop its bombs, the lead flight flown by the 671st. Three crews acting as window planes had preceded the formation, dropping strips of tin foil in an effort to confuse enemy radar. In spite of the extra effort, Andy's ship was badly shot up by flak, disabling one engine and taking out his landing gear. He was forced to crash-land in Normandy. He was able to maintain enough control over his skidding ship to prevent any injury to his crew, while he sustained a slight injury. No longer a grid at 12,000 feet, Andy Vleghels, Roger Rice, and Clay Young arrived in France, prematurely, and were warmly welcomed by her citizens. With some expert piloting and more than a little luck, they had survived to fly another day.

The Air Corps recognized Andy's proficiency in a commendation he received on September 10, 1944. It states in part:

It has been brought to the attention of your Commanding Officer, that having encountered severe battle damage caused by intense accurate flak, you excelled as an A-20 pilot on 26 August 1944 on a mission to Rouen, France, that you did, despite extreme difficulties and with the aid of only one engine, navigate your aircraft to a landing strip and did land said aircraft without landing gear and with no injury to personnel.

It is hoped that your fellow pilots will benefit from your experience and that your devoted attachment to duty will serve as an inspiration to your fellow officers.

Your Commanding Officer has been immeasurably pleased with your courageous achievement and desires to commend you highly for your skill.

> *John G. Napier,*
> *Major, Air Corps,*
> *Commanding*

On August 27th, the 416th returned to the Rouen area to finish what they had begun. Six more Groups of the Ninth Bomber Command joined them. Although their bombs had to be released through a thick haze, hundreds of vehicles and tanks were destroyed. It is certain that German troops were killed. Fragmentation bombs cut everything in its path to pieces.

8-27-44 I know I haven't written since last Wednesday but I assure you it was due to circumstances beyond my control. First of all I was on a two-day leave and fly I did upon my return. I spent a couple of days in France. It was rather difficult at times trying to converse with the natives but it worked out pretty well. They really are wonderful people. Young and old alike are very friendly and greeted us at every turn. The little children ask for "bon bon". It really stirs ones emotions when a little child comes along who wishes to shake your hand and say, "Bon jour Monsieur."

I don't believe it would be wise on my part to tell you what I was doing there and someday I will give you all the details.

Darling, I don't know how you will like this but I don't plan on sending you anything for your birthday [September 2nd], mainly because there is nothing to buy over here and besides ration points are needed for everything. The trinkets they do sell are only worth one tenth of the exorbitant price they ask for them. I shall attempt to make it up to you when I come home. You know how much I would like to give you something darling and I hope you will forgive me. Another thing, don't send me anything for Christmas because I would probably be home before it reached me.

I am enclosing a couple of pictures, which I had taken in London.

Gee honey, I hope its cooler now because I know you must be feeling miserable. I know very well that you are attempting to conceal how you feel and I love you all the more for being so brave...

Ronald wouldn't be a bad name, I don't care too much for David. The boys just decided they don't approve of Ronald so I guess I must agree to the consensus of opinion. We do like Sharon but she must have your name instead of Marie and if it's a boy then he'll be blessed with Andre as a middle name. As I *wrote before and you have since voiced my suggestion that your mother and my dad be the godparents. This arrangement would hurt no one and I believe it is only right.*

To change the subject, France is certainly a beautiful country and I saw many sights, some not so beautiful. God was certainly taking care of me, boy, and I can never thank Him enough. You were in my mind vividly during some of my precarious moments but now I am back and in the best of health.

8-30-44 *Today I received two letters from you and as usual they made me very happy. I'm happy to hear that the weather is cooler now so you should feel a little better. . . .*

It looks as though I'll be going to a flak home within the next five days. The doctor is working on it now. I'll be there for seven days and I really should be rested. Horseback riding, swimming, fishing and lots of sleep. Right now I'm a little jumpy...

I wish you could have been with me last night when I saw the picture, "Higher and Higher" with Swoonatra (15). After he finished singing about six of us screamed out, "Oh, Frankie." What an uproar.

8-31-44 *I hate to think of tomorrow and each succeeding day thereafter because the pain of missing you grows with each hour. Pray fervently, darling, that this all ends soon so we may spend the rest of our lives in happiness. The day we can begin building for the future will indeed be a glorious one. Just picture to yourself a nice, cozy home, our children, car, and our friends. Just to be with you right now would be all I ask for now.*

This morning I had three eggs for breakfast and spent the rest of the day in a very leisurely manner. In fact I have spent all my time this way since I returned from France...

Incidentally, how does my family look? Mother never tells me if anything is wrong. I hope Dad isn't working too hard.

9-1-44 *Another day passed with no mail from you and naturally I was very disappointed. I sincerely hope that it is due to faulty mail service and no illness on your part. Perhaps tomorrow I shall be more fortunate.*

My gunners and I are going to a rest home in a couple of days but we won't be together. Later on I may have some other news for you, but at the moment it isn't definite so I won't commit myself...

New York seems so long ago. Remember that last night, when after walking the streets looking in vain for a drink. Later up in our room having cheeseburgers and listening to the radio. The most unforgettable part was making love to you. I can never forget that night in the station. I just couldn't see anyone in that crowded station except you. How happy I was to see you. After an absence of only two weeks, what will it be like when I come home?

9-3-44 Received letters from you yesterday and today and my spirits were in much better shape. Took quite some time reaching here because they were dated the 9th and the 10th. The pictures were cute and I must say you are looking very good. Your face seems a little more full but the loose dress hid most of the facts from me. Afraid to let your husband see how you look?

Tomorrow I leave on my seven-day flak leave and hope the war is over by the time it terminates. The boys are really going great guns over here. Belgium is practically ours. (In fact, Ghent and Liege fell to British and American forces on September 6th.) *I sure would like to get over there and meet the people I know. Really would be quite a reunion.*

Darling, the idea of fifty missions and then home is erroneous. The number is sixty-five. But I'm sure the war with the Germans will be finished before I even come close to completing that number. I only have 28 now, only flew six of them during August. (Earlier in the war, it was "fifty and out", but as the war wore on and casualties mounted, the number of missions was extended to sixty-five before a flyer could complete his tour of duty.)

I received another letter from Fr. Maino and they are finally in combat. Says he still likes you a little bit and looks forward to a reunion with us in Detroit. I haven't flown since last Saturday (the mission to Rouen) and probably won't until the middle of the month…

Just continue to pray darling, irregardless of how wonderful the news may be.

Sept. 5, 1944
My Darling:

Here is my first letter from the flak home and you will have to bear with me if I use V-Mail because I have no air mail stamps to use. But I am sure that typewritten, I will be able to convey all the news and my love for you.

This is a typical English home that you see in the movies. I mean the type belonging to the aristocracy. It has more rooms than you can possibly imagine. At the present moment I am wearing civilian clothes; tweed trousers, striped shirt and blue sweater. This morning I have been shooting skeet, played Ping-Pong and badminton. This morning I was awakened by the valet who served us orange juice in bed. At nine-thirty I ate a leisurely breakfast. I have your picture sitting big as life on my dresser and the usual compliments followed after the boys had spotted it. Really can't blame them because I think that you are rather cute myself.

I really miss you darling, and would like nothing better than to have you here by my side instead of thousands of miles apart but soon I believe you and I will again be in each other's arms and then all the hurt and pain of loneliness will disappear. (Please excuse the errors which are numerous but I just don't seem to have the old touch.)

As I look out of the window, I can see the rolling, verdant hills and the beautiful garden. I made a foolish blunder because I forgot to bring my camera or rather a camera which belongs to one of the other boys. What a dunce I am. I really wish that you were here because I am positive that you would enjoy it very much and it is so quiet here except when the boys hit the keg of beer that is always on hand. What I am going to miss most of all while I am here is no mail. I do hope that upon my return to the base I find a large pile of it from you and I really will be happy.

Darling, you haven't mentioned it of late, but have the allotments been arriving regularly? You should have received seven, I mean six, including August. How is Junior coming along now, hope that he isn't giving you too much trouble.

So my darling, I shall sign off for now and write you more of my experiences tomorrow. Remember I love you dearly and miss you more than mere words can express. You are always on my mind and pray for the day when we can live happily without fear of being parted by a war. Au revoir, sweetheart.

All my love,
Andre

Sept. 7, 1944
Darling:

I shall give you a resume of my day to this late hour and hope that it won't bore you too much. Breakfast and the time thereafter spent riding and laying around and then had the most delicious dinner I have eaten since I left the States: roast beef and French Fried potatoes. I am afraid that I disgraced myself at the table because I ate enormous quantities of both delicacies.

After dinner we went riding for a couple of hours on horses belonging to Lady Margaret Peabody and I really should be writing this letter standing up because certain parts of my anatomy are rather tender and I believe that my kidneys are out of place. When the horse broke into a canter, I couldn't help but roar with laughter visualizing the picture I must have been making—going down as the horse was coming up—I would have given anything to have seen the expression on your face if you could have seen me. It was quite humorous, I assure you. After the ride, we had tea, yes I drank tea with Lady Margaret and then adjourned back to the rest home where I played a game of badminton followed by supper. We then decided to go to the movies in town and the picture was "Now Voyager" with Bette Davis.

Upon returning I indulged in my fifth meal of the day, roast beef sandwiches. So you can see I had a perfectly lovely day and it would have been perfect if you could have been here to enjoy it with me. Living in the country certainly has its advantages but we will have much fun when we are together again. I want you to see the country that I have seen with me as a guide. We will have such wonderful times and my mood is one of exuberance when I think of it. I miss you terribly darling, and I am frequently praying that this war will be over soon and I believe it will. Then we can remember this separation as a bad dream which will never occur again.

I hope that I have oodles of mail when I return to the base. I shall sign off for now with all my love.

Yours always,
Andre

The following letter was typewritten on American Red Cross stationary.

Sept. 10, 1944
My Darling:

The last couple of days have really been hectic ones for me. Yesterday, I don't believe that I sat down for more than a half-hour and that was at meal times. Skeet, badminton, tennis, etc. took up the whole day. In the evening, a bunch of us went into town and went pub crawling as it is so called.

This morning I went to Mass in a chapel located in Lord Wardour's Castle and I wish that you could have seen the altar because it was really beautiful as was the rest of the chapel. The altar was valued at $160,000 back in 1776 and the value must have increased with age. The chapel was originally built in order to escape the persecution at the time. The Sacred Heart was shaped out of solid amethyst. Wonderful paintings, in fact it was a very great piece of art and invaluable.

I hope that I find a veritable deluge of mail from you when I return to the base tomorrow. I have missed you so terribly this past week and no matter what I do, I am always thinking—I wonder if Ginny would like to be doing this, and I can just picture you by my side, but then I wake up to the realization to the cold fact that physically you are thousands of miles away, but in spirit I know that you are with me wherever I am...

Forever yours,
(unsigned)

Sept. 11, 1944
My Darling:

Returned to the old grind this evening and I can't say I'm too happy to be back. I only had some of my mail and shall get the rest tomorrow. I did have a letter from you and my folks. I can't tell you how happy I was to read your letters again.

Oh yes baby, your old man has been awarded the Purple Heart and I am enclosing a copy of the commendation my C.O. (commanding officer) *sent me. If he thinks so much of my ability, I don't see why I am still a shavetail* (second lieutenant.) *I had lunch in London today, at the L'ecue de France and everything was strictly French. An incident occurred while I was standing at the bar, I noticed two officers with the emblem "Belgium" written on their sleeve. I approached them and asked them what part of Belgium they were from and surprising enough they were from my home town—Ghent. The conversation that was carried on from there cannot be described here because I broke into Flemish and all three of us were talking at once. We understood each other perfectly. It really was a thrill. Now I want to see Ghent more than ever. I had been afraid that the people might not understand me but now I am assured that they will, and the two fellows said that I could really expect a reception when I did arrive.*

Darling, it is late and I must write mother. I love you with all my heart sweetheart.

Yours forever,
Andre

The Purple Heart was awarded to Andy in recognition of his courageous efforts on August 26th, the mission to Rouen, France, because he sustained slight injury to himself while carrying out the mission. While he was recuperating, the 416th flew seven missions to the Brest stronghold. Several other Groups of the Ninth Bomber Command were assigned this target as well, and although the 416th had to withhold their bombs on three of the missions, other groups were able to successfully make their drops at alternate times. On the fifth of September, in fact, with the 416th leading the way and numerous bomb groups stacked up behind, one pilot was prompted to quip, "they had to take numbers and get in line to bomb." General Eisenhower had made it clear that the Brest stronghold was to be attacked repeatedly until it was rendered impotent. Surprisingly, heavy anti-aircraft fire was not encountered during this series of bombardments. Considering the priority that was given to the target, conjecture can be raised that the enemy was unable to fortify this site; upon further conjecture, one might conclude that this was due to disruptions in the German supply of munitions or troop movement.

By September 12th most of France and Belgium were in Allied hands. And with German forces receded to the Siegfried Line, it was time for the 416th to move to a new base. No longer would it be practical to fly missions from Wethersfield. A location closer in proximity to the advancing Allied infantry became a logistical necessity. Melun, France outside of Paris was chosen.

Would you like to be the love of my life
for always,
And always
watch over me?
To square my blunders, and share my dreams,
One day with caviar,
Next day a chocolate bar.
Would you like to take the merry go round
I'll lead you?
I'll need you.
Wait and you'll see
I hope in your horoscope there is room
for a dope who adores you,
That would make the only dreams of my life
Come true.
For the love of my life
is you...

Love of My Life
Johnny Mercer & Artie Shaw

Chapter Fourteen
Back to Reality

Mid-September of '44 was a time of increased activity for the 416th due to their impending move to France. In addition to flying their assigned missions, the men had to prepare to disembark from the place they had called home for the past seven months, and move to their new base of operations. Eight-man tents would replace their corrugated huts. Curiously, Andy makes no mention of these plans in his letters. Perhaps he thought it better to enlighten Ginny once he was safely settled in France.

Sept. 12, 1944
My Darling:

I got the remainder of my mail today and it came to fifteen letters and two packages. Eight letters and one box of Sander's candy were from you. Thanks a million, darling. I have the most thoughtful wife in the world.

First of all, finances: I heartily agree that your mother should continue to accept what you give her. I wouldn't want it any other way. We aren't going to live off anyone. Darling, you are mistaken about me receiving my March pay while I was in Florence. That was my February pay of which I took most of for my expenses. I never did draw more than $93 for March, so you should have one more allotment. No wonder our figures disagree so much. Reading your figures, darling, you have done remarkably well. You have only spent $127 so you must be skimping. As I said once before, if there is anything you want, go ahead and buy it. Don't cut down just because you are a married woman. ...We receive nothing extra when the baby arrives. Congress had the bill in discussion but apparently nothing came of it. Majors and up get extra allowances for children. So, sweetheart, don't worry your pretty head about money. I only wanted to know how much we had on hand. I realize Junior is going to be expensive but once you have all the necessary items, his successor won't need so much.

I received a letter from Bill Stephens today and he told me that Mr. Smith [of the Smith Cottages in Florence] got into an argument with a G.I., and rushed the soldier with a club. So in self-defense, the G.I. threw a beer mug at Smith, cutting his throat, which caused his death. It must have been quite a brawl.

Glad you liked the picture, I didn't. My hair was a little short but you should have seen it this past week. Waves all over the place. My hairdresser did a good job.

I was worried that if the baby was too large you would suffer because you are slim. I do hope and pray that God will spare you as much pain as possible. As you say, all this will be forgotten when Junior becomes reality...

I also received a letter from Phil who is now in the So. Pacific. Hasn't flown yet.

Darling, I love you so very much and miss you every moment of the day. It won't be long before we are together again.

Goodnight my darling, more tomorrow.

All my love,
Andre

Sept. 13, 1944
My Darling:

Since my abundance of mail two days ago, I haven't had a letter from you. Still I can't kick too much and I shall probably get some tomorrow. As you can see I am using the stationary you sent me. Thanks a million, darling, it came just at the right time. I am sending you the Stars and Stripes in another envelope and it describes our initial mission to Germany. We'll pound the hell out of them now. I don't believe it can last much longer unless Jerry persists in holding out until we capture all of Germany. I received a letter today written at the cottage by Maurine, Edna, Julia, Charlie and one page in French by Frank. From their description I wish I could be there instead of this place. But when I do get home we will have all that and much more. We have so many things to do and time to make up.

Darling, I'm very glad that you got mother something for her birthday. I don't know what I would do without you. You are thoughtfulness personified. I forgot to tell you but dad's birthday is tomorrow also the day of their 26th wedding anniversary. How does it feel to be 25, married and almost a mother. I'll bet you would have said the person was crazy if they had told you a year ago what was going to happen. I believe I would have felt the same way.

I've missed you very much today, sweetheart, but then a day doesn't pass when I don't. My love for you, darling grows stronger each day and the pain of missing you is always present.

But soon we will be together again and all the dark clouds will disappear.

Goodnight, darling, more tomorrow.

All my love,
Andre

"B26s and A20s Blast Reich 1st Time, Hit Siegfried Line" headlines Andy's reference in the *Stars and Stripes, London Edition*:

"The force of about 150 medium and light bombers returned safely from their initial blow at Germany. Two forces of A-20s attacked rail yards at St. Wendel, 17 miles north of Saarbrucken."

Again, Ralph Conte, 416th veteran and author of *Attack Bombers—We Need You*, notes that their first target twenty-five miles inside Germany generated some "internal excitement" among the crews. "Rather unexpectedly, no flak or fighters bothered the formation. The only thing detrimental to the success of the mission was weather closing in. Of six flights, only two were able to see, and drop their bombs."

Sept. 15, 1944
My Darling:

Oh happy day! I received two letters from you today written on the 1st and the 6th. And then there is mah ideel "Fearless Fosdick" [a character from the Dick Tracey comic] *the ideel of all red blooded American boys.*

Didn't do a speck of work today and spent the afternoon playing "sweat the queen" and having a few friendly drinks. At the present some hot jive is emanating from our wireless.

Was listening to some swell dance music this afternoon and pictured myself dancing with you once again at the Terrace Room or the scintillating room at the Washington Statler. Mouse was a rather intriguing dancer. He was really a master of Terpsichore. What a head he had.

Darling, I told you once if my mail is held up, don't worry. I expect it to be, so please don't think dire things. This whole thing is going to be over in two weeks—I keep telling myself. Definitely we will have fun when we go away for a couple of weeks after I get home. It is rather difficult to say where we can go because I don't know just what the season will be at that time but believe me, we'll go where it is warm. Enough of this cold climate.

What do you mean our baby will have to be good or else we will be disgraced; our baby will be just as good as anyone else's, if not better. If it's a boy, he'll learn a lot of sports and be good at them, I'll see to that. Shame on you!

So darling, adieu until tomorrow. I love you very much and miss you constantly.

Yours forever,
Andre

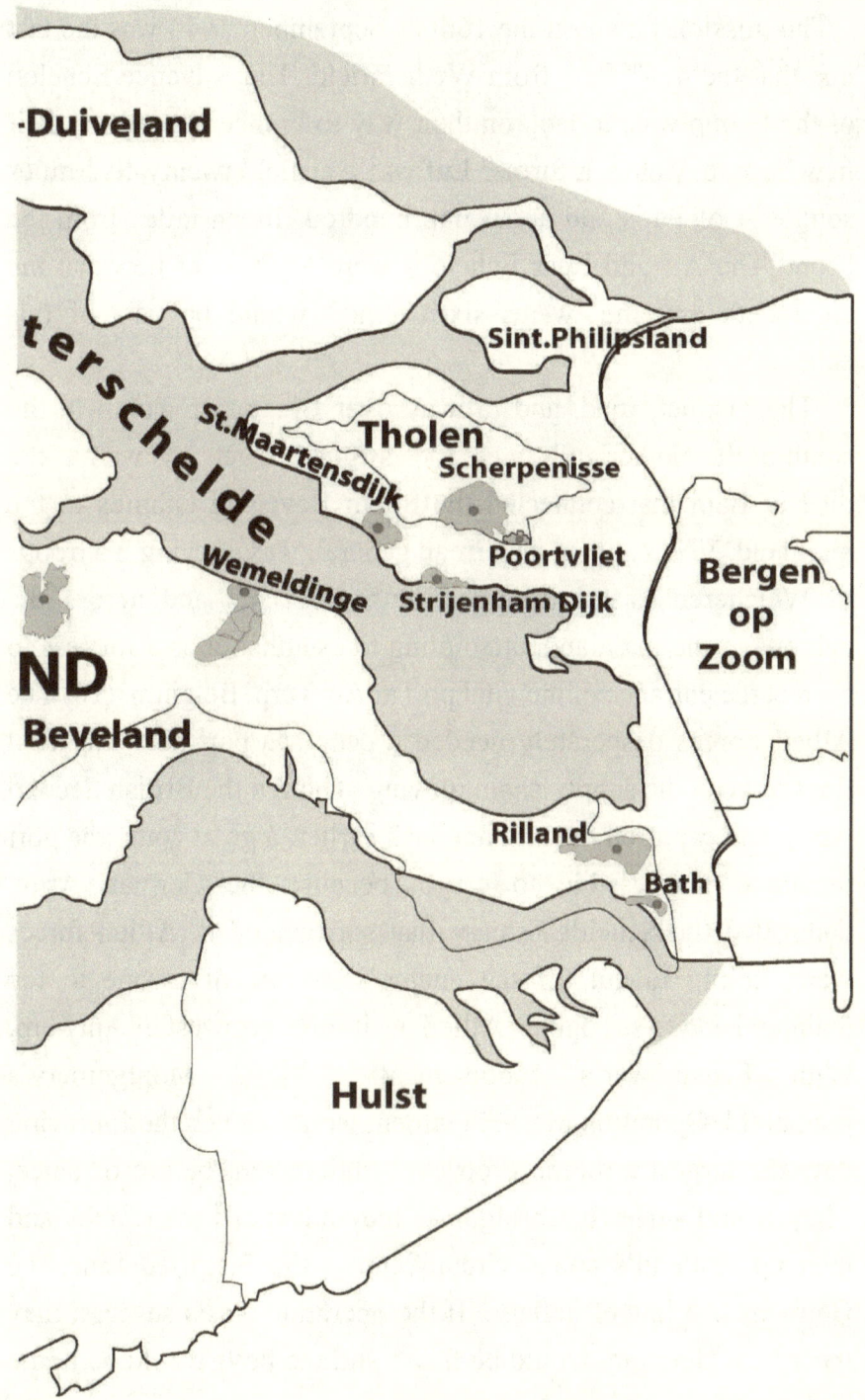

The mission flown on the 16th of September, 1944 was the last one that the 416th flew from Wethersfield. The Advance Echelon of the Group was, in fact, on their way to France headed for their new base in Melun, a former Luftwaffe airfield twenty-five miles southeast of Paris and about one hundred fifteen miles from the Front. The Air and Rear Echelons were to fly over between the eighteenth and the twenty-sixth. Andy would be part of this echelon.

The viaduct, road, and railway over Bergen op Zoom in the south of the Netherlands, were the assigned targets, as well as the dike at Bath that connected the South Beveland Isthmus to the mainland. Von Zangen, a German general, was ferrying his troops to Walcheren Island through South Beveland and across the isthmus to the mainland, attempting to establish it as a fortress to protect the entrance of the vital port at Antwerp, Belgium. (16) The Allied Forces desperately needed a deep sea-port near the front lines to keep the supply chain moving. Though the British Second Army had captured the city ten days earlier, a great coup, the port remained inaccessible to cargo, because the German Army controlled the Scheldt Estuary that surrounded it. Allied forces were aiming to cut off the enemy's avenue of escape to the mainland and to strengthen Allied positions northwest of Antwerp. With Eisenhower's endorsement, General Montgomery's brainchild, Operation Market-Garden, would launch the following day, the largest airborne drop ever undertaken, before or since. They would seize five bridges as they advanced their tanks and men up Holland's spine, circumventing the Siegfried Line, the Germans last line of defense. If the operation was a success, they theorized, Germany would be theirs and the boys would be home by Christmas.

I am certain that Market-Garden was the hope that Andy clung to, the lynchpin that would bring the war in Europe to an imminent and certain end.

So the mission of the sixteenth was intended to soften up the area for the following day's invasion and the 416th was not alone. The 410th Bomb Group and a B-26 formation preempted them, striking the Arnemuiden Dike, a single link between Walcheren Island and the South Beveland Isthmus. In addition, a Marauder Group and a flight of A-26s joined the 416th.

Leading the first box (eighteen planes), Captain Huff and Lt. Kupits, a bombardier navigator of the 669th (Andy's squadron), followed the lower Rhine to its estuary. Andy was in the number six position (lower left) of the lead flight of six planes. Intelligence reports advised them that the anti-aircraft guns that had been in the area were pulled back to the Fatherland. They were wrong. Instead, a heavy stream of flak being fired from both land positions and sea barges greeted the men as they entered the target area to begin their bomb run. It was steady and it was accurate, the enemy sights set on the lead box. Nevertheless, the men held their formation as they were trained to do, concentrating their bombs, and deployed their payload. Andy's flight made the turn, met up with the other two flights from the first box, and headed back to England.

The sky was thick with black plumes of exploding shells, relentless in their search for a target. Several planes were hit, two were seen going down. One was Lt. Clark's and the other was Andy's. Lt. Clark's ship was losing altitude, so he instructed his gunners to bail out, while he managed to crash-land his crippled plane in France. Andy's plane took a direct hit and was seen flaming at the tail and plunging into the water, vertically. It crashed a quarter mile from shore in the southeast corner of the Oosterschelde in the vicinity of the target area. At debriefing, it was reported that two chutes were spotted drifting toward the mainland near Bergen op Zoom. Clark and his crew eventually made it back to base. Andy and his two gunners, Roger Rice and Clay Young, were reported Missing in Action. Captain Huff's flight "scored an excellent on a perfect bomb run."

When it became necessary for the Army Air Corps to notify parents or a spouse that their loved one was Missing in Action (MIA), they did not do so immediately. They allowed some days to pass, because there was always the possibility that, if the crew parachuted into safe territory, as Lt. Clark's gunners had, they would be back at base before too long. On October 3, 1944, Ginny Vleghels and the Vleghels family received telegrams, without ceremony, bearing disturbing news. In one of her letters to her friend, Evie, Ginny elucidates:

October 7, 1944
Dearest Evie:

Although I started a letter to you yesterday, it just didn't materialize, but today when your letter arrived I found courage to respond. I am afraid I haven't very good news, and I still have not recuperated from the shock. Tuesday morning we received a wire stating that Andy is missing in action over "Holland" since "Sept. 16." You can imagine how dreadfully I feel and I believe I have just about cried my eyes out, but that doesn't help much. My last letter from Andy was dated "Sept. 15" the day before this mission. As he wrote me every day, when I didn't hear from him in a week, I knew something had happened. If only I would receive word that he was a prisoner, I would be so thankful. Everyone tells me that "missing in action" is encouraging and that he must be a prisoner or with the underground. I can only hope and pray that this is true, and that I receive word soon.

I have written to several of his friends at the base, hoping that they might give me some additional information, as well as his Commanding Officer, and am eagerly awaiting word from them. One thing I know definitely that he was flying an A-20 and that his gunners were with him, as they are also reported missing. I secured this news by calling the home of one of his gunners in Massachusetts (family of Roger Rice).

Andy had just returned to his base after a seven-day rest at a flak rest camp somewhere in England. He had been sent there after a pretty bad mission over France. Although he made light of it to me, so that I wouldn't worry, he did tell me that he was awarded the Purple Heart for it. However, he sent me a copy of the Commendation he received from his C.O. and it was very plain what had happened. It was on a mission over Rouen, France on "Aug. 26" and his plane had been shot up with flak, one motor destroyed and the landing gear shot out, and yet he landed the plane without any injury to his crew. He was evidently picked up by French people, as he wrote that they were treated very kindly by them. After learning about this mission, I couldn't help being frightened, for I know what a miracle it was that Andy escaped. As far as I can calculate, this mission on Sept. 16 was Andy's 30th.

In one of my most recent letters from Andy he told me that he had heard from Phil, and that he was in the South Pacific but hadn't flown as yet. He always thought so much of Phil and never stopped teasing me about that "hot water" deal.

I do hope that Phil has good luck on all of his missions, and that this horrible war will climax soon. I know how you must feel with Phil where he is, but that I guess it comes with being married to a flier--you have to grin and bear it.

Yes, the days are getting shorter and shorter before the baby's arrival, and I can hardly wait. I do hope, now more than ever, that the baby is a boy for this was Andy's fondest dream. Andy sent me his cable address months ago, so that someone might cable him when the baby arrives, and now this is all impossible. Junior should put in his appearance around the 20th.

And so, Evie, I am afraid this isn't a very cheerful letter, but I will try to do better next time. Please convey my best wishes to Phil and tell him to keep his fingers crossed for Andy. Do write me soon, for without Andy's daily missive I am lost, and say a little prayer that I will have some good news soon.

Love,
Ginny

Among Ginny's keepsakes was the following letter written by one of Andy's comrades, pilot Lt. James G. Miller, a member of the 671st squadron. His plane was positioned in the box directly behind Andy on the mission of the 16th.

Oct. 13, '44
France
Dear Virginia,

I received your letter today asking about Andy. I flew that mission though I was not in a position to see Andy's ship. I'll tell what was reported by those who saw. We were not far from his birthplace when his ship was hit by flak. As it went down, two parachutes were seen to open. That is all I know about the accident from the other pilots. I'm sorry Virginia that I can't give you more definite information. Things happen so fast that we ourselves have to pick up pieces of information among us and patch them together; then sometimes we don't get the whole picture.

I'm very glad to hear from you but am extremely sorry it is under such circumstances. Take care of yourself and the little one. Have faith and all things will come out right.

Sincerely,
Jimmie

An official notification was sent from the Ninth Bomber Command, dated September 23, 1944, one week to the day of the mission to Bergen op Zoom. Evidently, Ginny did not receive it until after the cable of October 3rd.

HEADQUARTERS
IX BOMBER COMMAND
A.P.O. 140

23 September 1944

Mrs. Virginia D. Vleghels
3170 Alter Road
Detroit, Michigan

Dear Mrs. Vleghels:

I deeply regret that your husband, Second Lieutenant Andre J. Vleghels, is missing in action from the operation of 16 September 1944. I am sorry that I can give you no further details. Should additional information become available, you will be notified directly by the War Department or the International Red Cross.

Please accept my sincere sympathy. Andre was a splendid pilot, highly respected by the members of his crew and all those who knew him. His loss is deeply felt by his comrades. His devotion to duty and to our country was unswerving and merited the highest praise.

Again, please accept my deepest sympathy.

Sincerely yours,
SAMUEL E. ANDERSON
Major General, USA
Commanding

Before Andy departed on his mission to Bergen op Zoom, he left two small packages, wrapped with white paper on his writing desk, addressed and ready to mail upon his return. They each contained a rosary for the three women in his life, one for Ginny, one for his mother, Rachel, and one for his sister, Maurine. It's likely Andy purchased the rosaries during his week-long rest in southern England--perhaps when he attended Mass at Lord Wardour's Castle. His CO probably dropped them in the mail. The paper that Andy used to wrap Ginny's rosary was preserved in mom's album of memories, postmarked September 17, 1944.

Don't know why
There's no sun up in the sky
Stormy weather
Since my man and I ain't together
Keeps raining all the time...

When he went away
The blues walked in and met me
If he stays away, old rocking chair will get me
All I do is pray
The lord above will let me
Walk in the sun once more

Stormy Weather
Harold Arlen

Chapter Fifteen
The New Mother

The vague and conflicting information must have left Ginny feeling terribly confused and distraught. Was she to believe that Andy, Roger, and Clay could still be alive or was that just wishful thinking? Of course, it was perfectly plausible that they survived the calamity and were either captured by the Nazis or were picked up by the Dutch, who were protecting them in secrecy. It happened all the time. This was the advent of some very long, dismal days for Ginny and the rest of the Vleghels' family.

And yet, teetering between hope and despair, Ginny was about to become a mother. Time, a mill stone or a savior, stood still for no one. But how was she supposed to feel about the impending birth of their child, not knowing if her husband was dead or alive?

When the labor pains started, Liz called a cab and escorted her daughter to the hospital. It was October 13, 1944, exactly one year to the day that Andy and Ginny had celebrated their engagement. A few days later, Ginny reaches out to Evie, a friend who could appreciate her circumstance.

October 17, 1944
Dear Evie:

Surprise—I am writing this letter from a hospital bed, so please excuse the writing, but I am still rather weak. Mother brought your letter to me yesterday and I surely was happy to hear from you so soon.

I came to the hospital last Friday afternoon, Oct. 13, and the baby was born 11:55 that night. No, it isn't a boy, but the cutest little girl you ever saw, and I wouldn't trade her for anything in the wide world. It's funny but I always felt that I would go to the hospital a week early, and I wanted it so, for on Oct. 13, Andy and I were engaged just a year. Wasn't that a coincidence?

I am going to name the baby Sharon Virginia. Andy and I had decided upon that name; I was going to call her Sharon Marie but Andy wanted it Sharon Virginia. The baby weighed six pounds, ten ounces and looks like a little doll. I can hardly believe she is reality for we dreamed of our baby for such a long time. She has very tiny features and I think she looks like Andy, at least I am hoping she will. She has lots of black hair and deep blue eyes. Her eyebrows and eye-lashes are very light, so I believe her hair will be light. It just has to be curly like Andy's and not straight like mine.

If only Andy would know about her; remember how thrilled he was about the baby? I am so lonesome for him; it would even help if I could write to him. He has been missing now just a month yesterday and yet to me it seems like years. But, I feel like you do that he must be either a prisoner or being protected by the Underground. He just has to be for he wanted this baby so much. Just keep on praying that I will receive some good news soon.

I received a grand letter from Steve [Bill Stephens] *also, and he too was most encouraging. He is writing for me to several officers that he knows in Andy's squadron to secure any further information that might be available. Steve is still an instructor at Florence, but anticipates being sent across soon. I wouldn't be too surprised if Steve joined Phil.*

Also received a letter from the wife of Andy's gunners and her husband is also missing, so that means that Andy and both of his gunners are together.

So, Evie, my hand is getting rather shaky, so I think I will sign off. I am feeling fine and should be going home about the 23rd. Give Phil my fondest regards and tell him I managed to survive without his "hot water". Wish you could both see the baby, but let's hope that someday we can all have a grand reunion. Do write soon and please keep Andy in your prayers.

Lots of love,
Ginny

In the nineteen forties, it was usual for new mothers to remain in the hospital for as long as ten days. The wisdom of the day dictated that bed rest was the best medicine. In reality, it weakened the patient. The war taught the medical profession that patients regained their strength faster when ambulated early in their recovery.

Liz gladly helped with Sharon in any way that she could, full throttle. But she had her own way of doing things. The diapers must be boiled, and then boiled again, in large pots atop the gas range to ensure that they were thoroughly disinfected. Mom always said that there was no arguing with her mother on these matters. At the same time, I am certain that Ginny, weakened by childbirth and her horrific news, welcomed the help. She could not have survived well, nor given a newborn the care required, without the solid support of her family.

October 30, 1944
Dearest Evie:

Your welcome letter arrived today, and as always I was cheered up after reading it. I still haven't broken myself of the habit of watching for mail from Andy, but these days I am forever disappointed. If only soon I would have some good news. These days of waiting seem endless as you can well realize having Phil overseas now.

Yes, I am now home from the hospital and am feeling fine. It surely is good to be home, and I am fortunate having mother to help me so much with the baby, for I am still rather weak. Gosh, Evie, I surely wish you could see Sharon. She gets cuter every day and it is so much fun taking care of her. I honestly don't know how I would get through these lonely days without her. If only Andy might see her, he would be so proud, even though she isn't a boy. I have so many lovely things that I received at showers and as gifts for her. I love dressing her for when I am all finished she looks like a doll.

It surely is a shame that we live so far apart, but I am sure in the future we will get together, pray God Phil and you and the Vleghels family, just like old times, but this time Sharon will be a reality.

I was surprised to hear that Phil was moved again, but glad to learn that he liked his new base better. Tell him to be sure and take good care of himself.

As yet, I have had no further news except a letter which I received from Lt. Jim Miller. You probably remember him from Florence. I am so mixed up about the whole situation concerning Andy but will quote you what Jim wrote me. "We were not far from his birthplace when his ship was hit by flak. As it went down two parachutes were seen to open. That is all I know about the accident from the other pilots." Andy's birthplace was Ghent, Belgium. After I read these words, I spent the rest of the day crying, for sometimes I can't seem to stop. Of course, this news, as you know, is not definite, but I pray with all my heart that Andy is safe.

And so, Evie, this is about all the news for today. I appreciate more than words can tell your daily remembrance of Andy in your prayers. Sharon sends her love as do I.

Ginny

Ginny never mentions it in her letters, but the Vleghels family was thrilled with Andy's daughter and Ginny visited with them regularly. It was all so convoluted—the miracle of a new baby coupled with the ever-present anxiety of Andy's whereabouts. Sharon was the connection to Andy; the blood that flowed through her veins flowed through his. One of my favorite photographs depicts Ginny holding her baby bundle alongside Maurine as they stood on the Vleghels' front porch, the Stars and Stripes unfurled behind them.

Ruth, Bettie, and Jane, Ginny's closest friends and bridesmaids, paid frequent visits to the Egan household, sitting around the kitchen table, sipping fresh-brewed coffee, and cooing over Sharon. Life for Ginny was starkly different than it had been just one year before--so many life-altering experiences in such a short span of days.

November 13, 1944
Dearest Evie:

It was so grand hearing from you again; you can't possibly imagine what your letters mean to me these days. Your news concerning your cousins was surely encouraging to me. I am so happy for your aunt and certainly hope that she has good news of her other son soon.

Like you I am confident that if I have patience and faith that I shall receive news of Andy soon. It seems to me that if the worse had occurred, I would have known by this date, for Andy will be missing two months on the 16th. Perhaps as an anniversary present I will have word that he is well and safe.

I haven't received replies to my letters addressed to Lt. York and Lt. Svenson, and have a feeling that they too are missing.

I have been corresponding with the wife of one of Andy's gunners, and from her letters she seems to be a grand person. She is a receptionist in a Doctor's office and welcomes her work as a temporary escape from worry. Sharon is getting fatter and cuter every day. Of course I am not prejudiced! I love giving her her daily bath and she even smiles at me occasionally. There's nothing like a baby, for they are the most marvelous gifts in the world. She still has my dark hair but she looks exactly like Andy.

He would be so proud of her if only he might see her. She keeps me plenty busy but, naturally, I try to keep busy every minute. Today she is just a month; time does pass quickly in spite of all the worry of these days.

...You may be sure as soon as I get some snaps of Sharon, you shall have some immediately. After all, you and Phil were the first ones to know of her prospective arrival. Will you ever forget how Andy told all the boys and how embarrassed I was?

So, Evie dear, I shall leave you until later. Perhaps my next missive will relate good news of Andy. Sharon sends her love to you and Phil. Write when you have a spare minute.

Lots of love,
Ginny

November 29, 1944
My Dearest Evie:

Your lovely gift for Sharon arrived yesterday, and I can't find the words to adequately express my thanks to you and Phil. Whenever she wears the dainty little dress, or I wrap her in the shawl, I shall always think of two very dear friends of the Vleghels.

As yet, I have received no further news of Andy. Perhaps by the middle of December, which is three months since he has been missing, I will have good news. I realize that it takes at least three months to be notified that he is a German prisoner. But then, now I feel more confident, that if he had been wounded, etc. we would know that by now.

I received a letter from Ruth York this week informing me that Bob is also missing. Do you remember the Yorks? They lived in the first cabin in our section. I am sure you will recall them. I wrote Bob York hoping that he could give me some information concerning Andy, but he went down on Sept. 29, and never received my letter. Ruth said that he went down in Julich, Germany as a result of anti-aircraft fire. Our forces (9th Army) are now in Julich so perhaps some information may be found regarding Bob. I surely hope so.

Sharon has a slight cold, but otherwise is as good as gold. I don't know where she got the cold, but I guess infants pick them up easily. The Doctor only laughed when I told him she had a cold and said he didn't "believe it was much of a cold." She changes each day and I believe she is going to keep her blue eyes. ... She is beginning to notice everything and yesterday I pinned a rattle to her bassinet, and she loves to look at it. Her favorite amusement is her bath and I have more fun giving it to her. Tell Phil I have plenty of "hot water" now keeping her clean. Do you remember, Evie, what a hearty appetite Andy had? Well, Sharon is following in his footsteps for she eats and eats! She loves orange juice but is not so fond of cod liver oil. Believe it or not, she already has a double chin.

How is Phil these days and how many missions has he flown? I always remember him in my prayers each night. Give him my fondest regards. And how are you, Evie? I hope you are not working too hard. How did the paint job turn out?

As I hear Sharon crying, I guess I better sign off for now. Sharon sends her love and sincere thanks to you and Phil. Write when you have a minute, but I understand how it is when you write Phil every day.

Lots of love,
Ginny

The attack on the Julich Marshalling Yard on the afternoon of September 29, 1944, was intended to prevent sorely needed enemy supplies and troops from reaching the front lines. However, it was fiercely defended, and the 416th sustained heavy casualties. Five ships and crews were lost that day, including Lt. Robert York.

December 4, 1944
My Dearest Evie:

What do you mean by apologizing for not writing sooner? I understand perfectly, for I know how I used to be when I wrote to Andy every night. How I miss those nightly letters! Any feature of the day was important then, for I knew I could write Andy about it. What bothers me so much is the fact that I can't write him about Sharon, for there are a thousand things I could tell him. He was so very eager for her arrival, and I can't dwell on this too much, for it really hurts terribly. So Evie, dear, write whenever you can and know that I understand perfectly.

The only other news I have received about Andy since my last missive to you was a letter from the War Department informing us of where the boys were last seen, etc. Andy had been on a bombing mission to some island in the Netherlands, and to my understanding must have been returning—it was about 6:00 P.M.—which is still light over there. His plane sustained damage and went down over a bay one-quarter mile from shore. Two parachutes were seen floating towards a town in Holland. This is about all the facts we have. The letter also stated that Special Forces search for our missing airmen continually by land, sea, and air. I know that on Sept. 16 the vicinity where Andy went down was Occupied, so he must be a German prisoner. Then too, he was just two miles from Antwerp. ...in Antwerp, Belgium Andy has relatives, and being of Belgian descent, he can speak the language. I was quite encouraged by this news for I felt Andy had a good chance being so close to shore. The families of Andy's two gunners received the same letter, so they must be together.

I was glad to hear that Phil is getting along so well. I know how you feel about his flying, but I guess he is like Andy and doesn't mention his missions, because he doesn't want to worry you. Andy never told me much about his missions. In fact, when he received the "Purple Heart" for one of his missions, he very casually mentioned it as if it were nothing. Yet, I knew without his telling me what he must have gone through and it made me just sick. . . .

Sharon is fine and I put your dress on her today. She looks adorable in it and it fits perfectly. How I wish you could see her in it! Everyone says she looks like Andy, and I believe she is going to have blonde hair, for it seems to be coming in light.

This is about all the news for now, Evie. Say "hello" to Phil and tell him for me to be very careful. Keep praying hard for Andy that I may have good news soon. Write me when you have the time.

Lots of Love,
Ginny

Ginny failed to realize that, although reports indicated that Andy's ship crashed a quarter mile from shore, it did not mean that he or his crew landed so close to the mainland. At least two of the men bailed out and it would anybody's guess where they came down. They could be miles apart. Nevertheless, scarce as it was, the evidence did enkindle hope.

January 3, 1945
My dearest Evie:

Thank you so much for the lovely Christmas card. It brought back many happy memories that we shared. I hope you had as happy a Christmas as possible with Phil being away.

I haven't been too well and of all things, fainted on Christmas Day while at my brother's home. I was so embarrassed afterwards, for I frightened my family as well as Andy's folks.

Then I had a nervous chill. It really is a bad case of nerves, and I am feeling better now. Andy and I were both so happy last Christmas just having been married, that after thinking of Andy and not knowing where he is now, a nervous reaction set in. But perhaps soon I shall have good news of him. . . .

But to date no further news and it will be four months on the 16th that Andy has been missing. However, from following the newspapers daily, it seems to take on an average of from six to seven months to receive news that captured airmen are prisoners. Of course there are always exceptions. Then too, Andy may be with the Underground and Heaven only knows when I shall find this out. The relatives of his two gunners have received the same reports as I, so apparently the three boys are together. I feel now that if something had happened to one of them, one of us would know by this date, since it was Occupied territory where they went down. Don't you think so?

According to news reporters and the papers, the War Department is going to release 60,000 reports including casualties, wounded men and prisoners, so please remember Andy especially in your prayers these days. Perhaps I shall learn that he is a prisoner. It seems like all my life has taken place these long dreary months of waiting. And yet, just a year ago you and I were so deliciously happy and carefree.

I received bad news from Ruth York about a month ago to the effect that Bob York had been killed the day he was reported missing. He was missing over Germany on Sept. 29, and Ruth received the second telegram on November 25. When I received her letter I felt just terrible, because I thought Bob was such a grand fellow, and Andy and I spent many happy times with the Yorks.

How is Phil these days? I hope well and getting along first-rate with his missions. Give him my best regards. How many missions has he flown?

Sharon is a wonderful baby and I'll never know how I would get along without her. Two weeks ago, she weighed 12 ½ lbs. She is changing every day. I can't decide if she is going to have dark or blonde hair, but it seems to be coming in dark. Her eyes are still deep blue. Santa was grand to her and she received many lovely gifts.

And so Evie dear, this is adieu until later. I am eager to hear from you again, so be sure to write me when you get an opportunity. Sharon sends you a kiss and as for me

All my love,
Ginny

Observing these initial letters from my mother to her faithful friend, Evie, I am struck by the metamorphosis of her closings. As time dragged on and no decisive news about Andy was forthcoming, Ginny's correspondence became more and more endearing. She uses the phrase "this is adieu"—a phrase that Andy used many times in his letters to her. But her letter writing days to her beloved were over, snatched away in an instant. My heart aches for all the pain that my mother felt during these grueling months of speculation. The specter of war cast a pall of doubt during her first six months of separation, but never as acutely as the mind-numbing anxiety that existed after October 3, 1944.

Do not desert me in the days of ordeal,
in the time of my helplessness against the proud.

Ecclesiastes 51:10

Chapter Sixteen
Unknown Territory

Ginny was on a journey—destination unknown. She was not in control. She was but a passenger on a terrifying ride fraught with tenuous climbs and harrowing plummets, peppered with unexpected twists and turns. She had weathered the initial plunge to the bottom. But what would the next day bring, the next hour? Maybe encouraging news would come in a news article, or a broadcast, or a telephone call--or maybe not. I suspect she welcomed the smallest scrap of information to fortify her spirit, to give her hope that she and Andy could live out their dreams and all that they had planned.

January 24, 1945
My dearest Evie:

Please forgive this belated reply to your last letter. I believe our letters must have crossed and arrived at this destination about the same time.

I have some further news about Andy, which is most encouraging. We received a letter from the Adjutant General's office in Washington dated Jan. 13th, and it stated that no further information had been given to their office regarding Andy and his crew. However, last Thursday evening I received a phone call from the family of Roger Rice, one of Andy's gunners. They live in Somerville, Mass. His sister told me that they had received a telegram that day stating that Roger had been killed "Sept. 16". Well, I don't have to tell you how terrible I felt; in fact, I told Roger's sister that I would call her back later. I had been hoping and praying that the three of them were together. So, Evie, from this latest news I feel that Andy and his other gunner must be together, either prisoner or with the Underground. As I told you before, Jim Miller wrote me that when Andy's plane went down, two parachutes were seen to leave his ship. Then, the letter from Washington also stated, "that two parachutes emerged from the disabled craft." Perhaps, if they are prisoners, this information will come through soon. Did I tell you previously that Andy went down only ten miles from "Antwerp, Belgium" where he has relatives living? Who knows, perhaps he was able to reach them. Oh yes, I called the wife of Andy's other gunner to inquire if she had any further word. But she had none, so we both feel that our husbands must be together.

The War in Europe looks so much brighter now, and perhaps it will climax one of these days. I was told that if I learn that Andy is a prisoner of war, through the Red Cross I may cable him about the baby. Won't that be wonderful? I worry so much about Andy, and yet it must be even worse for him not knowing about the baby.

Has your aunt heard any more about her son who was missing? I sincerely hope she has received good news by now.

Sharon is fine and you would never believe she is mine, for she is just like a butterball. She surely takes after Andy for that and has his ravenous appetite. I started her on pabulum last week and she doesn't like it any too well. . . .

Leo and Pat (Ginny's brother and sister-in-law) *bought a home and moved in just before Christmas. It really is a dollhouse. Leo met Phil at my home when he and Andy flew home. Remember how lonesome we were and how sick I was? My family still teases me about how they gave Andy the works that night. Guess we were better off in South Carolina.*

So Phil is in the Philippines? Do you know whether or not he is flying an "A-20"? I am sure he will be eager to hear the latest report on Andy. Tell him Sharon sends him a big kiss and as far as me, my fondest regards.

So this is all the news for now Evie dear; don't forget to write me at your leisure. The minute I have any good news I shall let you know. In the meantime, keep praying hard.

Lots of Love,
Ginny

Two parachutes, two parachutes, two parachutes… it implied that one of the three did not make it out of the ship with a parachute. Word of Roger's death was a double-edged sword. One family's worst nightmare bore another family's fervent prayer, wafting the cinders of hope's fire.

At this juncture in the war, the last great German offensive, the Battle of the Bulge, was finally quashed in little more than a month's time when the British First Airborne and the American 82nd Division met in the Ardennes Forest. They closed the gap and helped to ensure victory in Europe.

February 19, 1945
My dearest Evie:

Doesn't the War look marvelous in Europe as well as the Pacific? Really, I don't see how the Germans can hold out much longer.

No further news of Andy, and as the days go on, I am inclined to believe that Andy may be in the Underground. Either that or the Germans certainly are slow reporting his capture. His gunner's wife has received no additional word, so it is almost positive that Andy and his gunner [Clay Young] *must be together. Really, Evie, sometimes I wonder if I have a single brain left, trying to figure out where Andy is; one day I think he is in the Underground and the next that he is a prisoner. I travel around in a circle and always arrive at no conclusion. But perhaps soon I shall have the answer.*

I am writing this letter on the kitchen table and Sharon is lying on the table kicking and playing. How I wish you could see her. She has Andy's grin and I love to make her laugh. . . . I gave her prunes for the first time yesterday and she loves them. Oh yes, last week I put her in her highchair for the first time. Andy's folks gave it to her for Christmas. When I am working in the kitchen, she just sits and follows every move I make. She loves colors. Really, when she laughs she is Andy in person.

I suppose you are kept mighty busy these days, but work is the best remedy that I know of. So, Evie dear, this is about all the news for the moment. Keep Andy in your daily prayers. Sharon sends you a big kiss.

Loads of Love,
Ginny

P.S. I just got this snap of our wedding and thought you might like it. It's not very clear but will give you some idea of the wedding party.

April 2, 1945
My dearest Evie:

Do forgive this belated reply to your last letter, but this is really the first opportunity I have had for correspondence. I appreciate your card from Oklahoma and your trip sounded like fun, although a little on the dangerous side. I imagine the change did you worlds of good.

I have been at my brother's home since March 14 keeping house for him and taking care of Tommy. My sister-in-law had her baby on the 14th, another boy called "Dennis Michael Egan." Really Irish to say the least. I had Sharon with me and I really had my hands full as Tommy is just 13 months. But it was a nice experience and the change did me good, for I couldn't dwell on Andy too much. They have such a darling new home that it was lots of fun keeping house. I haven't done as much cooking since we were at "Florence." I stayed with Pat until she was able to get around and came home last Wednesday. Then, of all things, Sharon took sick. She got a high fever suddenly and when the doctor came he thought she was coming down with a cold. However, yesterday her fever went down but she broke out in a rash. From all appearances it looks like measles. Imagine getting them so young! Today she seems to feel alright but the rash is still there. She seems so tiny to have anything like this. This is the first time she has been sick, so naturally it frightened me.

Still no further news of Andy. I guess the good lord is trying my patience. However, the War looks so wonderful that I believe it is a matter of days before it will be over. I was so excited last week when those false peace rumors were circulating. I have been following closely the German position in Holland and it has been all occupied territory with the exception of a small portion by the British. But today's news was grand—the Germans were reported fleeing and Montgomery's forces were advancing. So perhaps if Andy is with the Underground I'll have news soon. Then, of course, if he was captured perhaps the Germans moved him. Here I go again in circles! Please keep

Andy in your daily prayers especially now for I feel he needs them.

Phil is really going to town with his missions. I am so glad that he is getting along so nicely. ...

So Evie dear, this is about all the news for now. I'll wire you the moment I have news of Andy, and in the meantime pray hard for I just feel I am going to have news soon.

> Loads of Love,
> Ginny

May 4, 1945
Dearest Evie:

I don't really believe that this is going to be a very cheerful letter, for I am so terribly worried about Andy, but I did want you to know that I haven't forgotten you.

The reason for my anxiety is the fact that Andy's second gunner was reported killed also. I received a phone call from his wife's family just two weeks ago today—April 20. The shock of this news was terrible and has upset me a great deal, for I felt that this gunner and Andy were together. I can't seem to understand what could have happened and why it took seven months to come through. The only conclusion that I can arrive at is that this gunner may have been wounded when he bailed out and died of wounds. It just doesn't seem logical or make sense. Really every minute I look for news and am afraid of what *it might be. Still, I believe if anything had happened to Andy, we would have been notified at the same time.*

I look for the end in Europe any minute. In fact, I just heard a special broadcast announcing the German surrender in Holland, etc. so I guess the end will be this weekend. I am so relieved that Holland is finally free, for now if Andy has been with the Dutch Underground, I shall receive word.

Sharon is fine and now has two teeth. I took her to the doctor's last night for her first shots and she was so good. In fact I think the whole thing hurt me more than she.

How is Phil these days? How many missions has he flown? I hope they haven't been too rough.

And so, Evie dear, this is adieu for the present. I know you remember Andy daily in your prayers but pray especially hard for him now that I may receive word of his safety, for I don't know how much longer I can stand the suspense.

Lots of Love,
Ginny

VE Day came and went and, still, no word of Andy. With headlines proclaiming victory in Europe, Ginny must have been conflicted about how to feel. While America and all of Europe were steeped in delirious celebration, she was left in limbo. Exhilaration was tempered by her unsettled state. Would these torturous days ever end?

June 21, 1945
My dearest Evie:

I am afraid I owe you an apology for such a tardy response to your last letter. I think of you each day, and delay writing hoping the next day will bring me good news of Andy. But at the present moment I know nothing more. One thing I do know and we are basing all our hopes on this fact. I learned from the "Dutch Council" here that no mail has been permitted out of Holland since the people were liberated, and that was approximately two weeks before the war was ended. The reason for this is because of an epidemic caused by the floods. I have been hoping and praying that Andy has been hidden by the Hollanders all these months. I know in my heart he must be somewhere, and I won't give up until there is absolutely no hope left. Then too, Andy's relatives in Belgium are starting a search for him so we should have some reports soon.

Then too, I have heard just this week of cases where letters have been en route for six to eight weeks from liberated American prisoners and are just arriving now. Naturally, the mail situation must be terrific.

How is Phil, and how many missions has he flown? I had a letter from Steve this week from Luzon and he mentioned that he sees Phil every day. Also that he has flown quite a number of missions with him.

I hope you are not working too hard these days. Is the weather warm in New York?

Sharon is just fine and her two top teeth came through this week. She tries hard to stand and is beginning to creep. Her eyes are still hazel but her hair is blonde like Andy's. The older she gets the more she resembles Andy, and if only he might see her he would be so proud, but I am confident before much longer my prayers will be answered.

At long last I have a snapshot of Sharon taken when she was six months. I just received them this week and are the first snaps I have of her. The film situation here is terrible, so I can only send you one. I wish I had a duplicate for Phil, but I thought you could send it on to him. I am sending Steve one with a notation that he is to share it with Phil. As soon as I am fortunate enough to get more films, I shall send you some at once.

And so, Evie dear, I shall sign off until later. I know you are keeping Andy in your prayers. Give my fondest regards to Phil and tell him for me to be careful. Write me soon for I am so lonesome for you.

Lots of Love,
Ginny

The "floods" that Ginny refers to in her letter were the result of a Nazi strategy of placing obstacles in the way of the advancing Allied armies. Just as the Germans had flooded the farmland of Normandy prior to the D-Day invasion, likewise, they ordered the Dutch to open their sluices, a lock system of sorts which controlled the water level inside their dikes. In addition, Allied bombers targeted dikes to prevent the German

Army from escaping. Consequently, land was rendered useless for growing crops and the people were forced to navigate by boat in order to travel from place to place.

July 8, 1945
Evie Dearest:

Your nice long letter just arrived and I can't tell you how wonderful it was hearing from you again. I think of you so often, and whenever I reminisce about South Carolina, you and Phil are always in my thoughts. What I wouldn't give for those happy carefree days. The four of us had such grand times together. Whenever I feel particularly lonely or discouraged, I would give anything just to see you and talk to you. Then too, I would give anything in the world if you might see Sharon, but then I know sometime in the future all of my dreams will come true.

The news about Phil's promotion to Captain is marvelous, and I am so very happy for you both. I know he deserves it and I can well imagine your pride in him. Please extend to him my heartfelt congratulations and best wishes for his continued success. "Seventy missions" seem enormous to me, for Andy had about 33 when he went down. [Usually pilots could return home after the completion of sixty-five missions, unless they re-upped.] *It would be perfect if the Army would permit him to come home now, but if not, the fall isn't too far away, although I know only too well how you feel. ...*

I am so glad that you liked the snap of Sharon, and I hope to send you more very soon. I thank God every day for her, for I really don't know how I would get through the days without her. If you only could see her, you would at once note her striking resemblance to Andy. Naturally this makes me so happy. ...She has the nicest disposition and always laughing. Her appetite, as I told you before, is as ravenous as Andy's. He would enjoy seeing her eat so much. I am training her now and that is quite a task. More fun. Her hair is getting quite thick like Andy's, color I mean; so far I don't see any evidence of curls.

Still no definite news of Andy, but I don't believe it will be much longer and he will be home with us. One thing which renewed all my hopes and gave me encouragement was an article that appeared in our "Detroit News" just recently. It was about a gunner who had been shot down over Holland on September 26 (just ten days after Andy) and had been living with the Dutch Underground for eight months. He went down over the North Sea. After reading it, it was so similar to Andy's case that I almost thought I was dreaming. It gave his address and I was able to contact him by phone, and I had a long conversation with him. He was just grand to talk with, and after I explained Andy's case, he answered all my questions and gave me so much data about Holland. He was in Northern Holland, while Andy went down in Southern Holland. He told me that Andy had a much better chance of hiding out where he went down than he had as he was close to the German lines. He said that the people might have put him on a boat and moved him way back. He knew where Oosterschelde Bay was where Andy's plane fell, and assured me that it would have been recovered by either the Germans or the Dutch people months ago. His plane went into the North Sea and was recovered. This is what struck me—he *wasn't liberated until "May 29" and just returned to the States about a week ago. It took him one month to come home. I inquired if he was able to write, he said he wrote one letter to his mother, and when I was speaking to him his mother had not as yet received it. So, he further stated that Andy might not know yet that the War is over. Then too, when coming out of hiding one has to be very cautious. After talking with him, from the very spot Andy is, I felt better than I have in months. Oh yes, a point I forgot, he was picked up by Dutch fishermen, after bailing out over water. He was unconscious and suffered from a fractured skull. He said the people were wonderful to him and nursed him back to health. He was a gunner on the ship and is only 20 years old. Now I am more confident than ever that is where Andy has been. So don't be surprised if I send you a wire soon with the glorious news of Andy's safety.*

Before I forget—I love the name of Phil's plane—and I know how happy you must be with the title. Yes, Andy named his plane "Ginny" and I have never gotten over the thrill of it.

Thank you so much for the lovely picture of you and your father. You look just grand and your outfit is sweet. You look thinner to me. Have you lost weight?

And so, Evie dear, this is about all the news for the present. Sharon just awakened from her nap, and I have her sitting on the floor beside my desk, playing.

Wish you could be here with me. Give Phil my fond wishes and Sharon sends her love to you both.

Loads of Love,
Ginny

July 26, 1945
Dearest Evie:

Since Sharon is taking a nap, this is an opportune time to answer your latest letter. She is getting so big and I believe she is going to be quite a chatterbox. She says da-da, ma-ma, bye-bye, very plainly. She has her two dolls, one was my own and the other mother bought for her. She will sit for hours, either in her play-pen, or in her bed, and play and chatter to them. She will let you take any of her toys and possessions except for her two dolls, and puts up quite a racket when anyone takes them. She has six teeth, four at the bottom and two at the top. Her grin is exactly like Andy's, and I really don't know how I could ever manage without her.

The weather here has been exceptionally hot during the past week. I haven't been in swimming as yet, but hope to before the season is over. It seems I just hate to leave the house for fear I will miss some news, but I suppose I should get out more than I do.

I wrote to the Adjutant General's office in Washington again and received a reply Saturday. However, they could furnish me with no news. I inquired if they could give me some details regarding Andy's gunners, but they stated that they did not have such data available at that office. I have also written to the "Netherlands Embassy" in Washington and they were most gracious. In fact, I sent them a current picture of Andy and gave them a complete description, which they are passing on to the Netherlands authorities. I have placed a great deal of confidence and faith in their ability to trace Andy and pray that I won't be disappointed.

We are anxiously awaiting news from Andy's aunt in Belgium and it should come through very soon. She should be in "Bergen op Zoom, Holland" at the present time, if she was able to get transportation there. Andy's mother asked for her to cable any news she might have, so I am praying that surely she will find Andy. Honestly, Evie, some days I think I am losing my mind with this constant worry. Lately I am beginning to think Andy might be in a hospital suffering from loss of memory, etc., but I suppose I am allowing my imagination to run riot. If only I might search for him myself, I just know I would find him, but that definitely is impossible. Andy's birthday is Sunday, the 29th and I am praying that I will hear from him by then. On the 28th he will be commissioned two years.

It hardly seems possible that Phil has been over a year already, but I know to you, it must seem much longer.

And so, Evie dear, this is about all the news for the present. Sharon sends her love to you both.

Love,
Ginny

July 31, 1945
Dearest Evie:

I guess Andy won't be coming home. I received a telegram yesterday, the day after his 26th birthday. "It has been officially established from reports received in the War Department that your husband, Second Lt. Andre J. Vleghels was killed in action September 16, 1944 in Holland etc."

Still can't believe it is true.

Ginny

Ginny's declaration, bereft of any emotion, seems to reflect her state of shock. Andy's killed in action (KIA) status was based upon official rote reports that inundated the War Department on a daily basis. It is likely that their source of information came from German records, confiscated when Bergen op Zoom was liberated. Once again, no details were given. There were no tangible details to be had, no body found. Reports left room for doubt and therefore, room for hope in their ambiguity. What Ginny needed was hard evidence. Like a victim, drowning, she grasped for floating debris. She floundered, her resolve fading, to keep her head clear of the rising tide. Adrift, she was left to wonder when she would be rescued from her ever-consuming quandary. That was the rub. Did she wish to be rescued? Or was it better to exist in this purgatory, however agonizing, just a little while longer? Decidedly, Andy's fate was beyond her control. But what was the truth? Either his remains would be located, or one day soon he would come walking through her door--or the worst of outcomes, neither would happen.

You have folded up my life,
like a weaver who severs the last thread.
Like a swallow I utter shrill cries;
I moan like a dove.

Isaiah 38:12, 14

Chapter Seventeen
The Vigil

Buoyed by their love of Andy, Ginny and the Vleghels family were like-minded and dogged in their resolve to remain optimistic. They would not permit themselves to believe that the Army had it right. Rachel, Maurice, and Maurine kept a keen eye turned toward military photographs, scouring newsprint and movie newsreels that featured the boys returning home from combat or being released from POW (prisoner of war) camps. Their dear Dré had to be among the living. He just had to be.

Father Maino responds to a letter that Ginny apparently wrote to inform him of her shattering telegram of July 30, 1945. He writes with a heavy heart as he penned this missive to Ginny. It remains a truly inspired letter that I shall cherish, always.

Straubing, Germany
9 August 1945

Dear Ginny:

Words just cannot express the grief I felt at receiving the news about Andy. I cannot, however, say honestly that it was a shock, because every one of the innumerable times that I paused at Mass to make a memento for you and Andy in these last few months, especially, I'd been dubious. As the months dragged by, and Holland was liberated, and VE Day came without word of him, I began to feel that some such word would come as you have received. God rest his gallant soul. My Mass today will be for him. And another will soon follow to be offered for your consolation, your intentions and for Sharon. I realize the futility of mere words in the face of a loss so overwhelming, but still there are certain facts that will bear emphasis. You have every right to be tremendously proud of Andy, because he was a truly Christ-like sacrifice.

He died that others might live. Generations to come will owe him their liberty and their peace. You get to realize that they are more than empty phrases when you talk to so many, as I have recently, Poles and Ukrainians, priests and others, who were released after five and a half years in Dachau. The last few weeks of the war, as we advanced in Germany, the roads were choked with thousands of liberated slave laborers, streaming back out of the combat zone. Many of them were just about out of their minds with joy. After months of the grim and bloody business—all of us then realized—and many remarked—that *these scenes made the war seem worthwhile. As I've told you before—woman's part in this business is much harder than ours. In all probability Andy went out suddenly and painlessly. And I can tell you from my own knowledge, that in the excitement of action there is no fear—in fact, no time even to think. So in reality you are the real heroine in this business. You had all the worry and suspense and now you have the loss. You have laid upon us all, your fellow Americans, a debt that we can acknowledge, but never hope to repay. But your Faith assures you, not only of the grace and courage to bear up bravely now—but of the adequate recompense that will be yours—when you and Andy are reunited in a happier world.*

As I recall now my brief look in on your little household in South Carolina, it seems to me to have been a great blessing from God that you and Andy married. Though worldly prudence might have counseled otherwise, you undoubtedly did the better thing. You achieved your Divine vocation of Motherhood—Sharon is your joy and crown. But right now I'm thinking about Andy—and you. Your own experience has undoubtedly been witness to the fact that a perfect marriage, like yours, makes people better. So being married to you for a few months not only gave Andy intense happiness, but probably made him a better boy—with a better chance of getting to heaven—and having a higher place once he got there. And the same is true of you. You have profited spiritually by your opportunities to be unselfish as wife and mother. I have no doubt that you have a more beautiful soul right now than you had when you were only "Miss Egan".

Please let me hear from you very soon to the effect that you are being cheerful. You have always been very brave. You know you can count on my prayers, as on my admiration.

Faithfully yours,
Hubert Maino

P.S. I'm writing today to Supreme Headquarters to learn what I can as to burial, etc. There's just a faint chance I might pick up some information or visit the locality, and perhaps pass on details to you that you might not otherwise learn. Will let you know. H.M.

On the last two missions that Andy piloted, he earned the Purple Heart. The letter that follows preceded the arrival of his second Purple Heart. It also reflects Andy's promotion to First Lieutenant, the promotion that had eluded him for so long. Following the mission to Bergen op Zoom, it finally came.

August 11, 1945
My dear Mrs. Vleghels:

At the request of the President, I write to inform you that the Purple Heart has been awarded posthumously to your husband, First Lieutenant Andre J. Vlegehls, Air Corps, who sacrificed his life in defense of his country.

Little that we can do or say will console you for the death of your loved one. We profoundly appreciate the greatness of your loss, for in a very real sense the loss suffered by any of us in this battle for our country, is a loss shared by all of us. When the medal, which you will shortly receive, reaches you, I want you to know that with it goes my sincerest sympathy, and the hope that time and the victory of our cause will finally lighten the burden of your grief.

Sincerely yours,
Henry L. Emerson

Father's letter of sympathy and the proclamation of the Purple Heart must have flown in the face of Ginny's steadfast beliefs. But in spite of mounting evidence, in truth, no one had located Andy's remains--not the War Department, not the Tracing Bureau for the International Red Cross. The door was not completely shut on this case, and until it was, Ginny would persist in her persuasion, though paling, that Andy survived the fray. Traces of her former self emerge in her next letter to Evie.

Aug. 24, 1945
Dearest Evie:

Thank you so much for your grand letter, it meant so much to me. I am trying to get over the shock, still find it hard to believe. Still have absolutely no facts from the Government—they sent a confirmation letter following wire, but no facts in it.

Andy's aunt wrote yesterday that they have absolutely no records in Holland, but was unable to visit "Bergen op Zoom." Cannot secure a pass for at least another two months to visit that spot.

So you see Evie dear, I still can't give up.

Sharon sends a big kiss. Remember me to Phil. I hope he will be with you very soon.

Love,
Ginny

In September, nearing the first anniversary of Andy's disappearance, Ginny receives a response from her faithful friend, Father Maino.
Straubing, Germany

12 Sept. 1945
Dear Ginny:

Many thanks for the photograph of Sharon Virginia. She is certainly a beautiful child. You are surely blessed a hundred fold in such a treasure. She seems to me to favor her father's side of the house, although I may revise this opinion on closer inspection. It may not be too long before I shall be able to do so in person, as it appears now that we may leave here to begin the home bound journey sometime next month. At any rate I should be in Detroit before Christmas.

It has been pretty pleasant over here this summer. The climate in Southern Germany is milder than yours. There is much sunshine in the daytime, but nights are invariably cool. None of those stifling heat waves of the Middle West.

Don't trouble to answer this if you're not in the mood. I'll understand perfectly. I have said several masses lately for Andy—and for you—and I have supreme confidence in the power of prayer—that yours and those of your friends will sustain you, and make you cheerful and courageous.

With all good wishes, and kindest regards,

Sincerely,
Hubert Maino

October, the month that Andy had dubbed "our lucky month" was on the horizon. On the thirteenth, the family would light a candle upon Sharon's first birthday cake. Yet another dichotomy presented itself--celebrating life, but life without Andy. A year had come and gone since Ginny and Andy became engaged, a year landscaped by manic highs and depressive lows.

Seven days later, on the twentieth, there was a remembrance of a different sort, a memorial mass for Andy with only a hollow, flag-draped coffin.

October 21, 1945
Dearest Evie:

I am hoping by the time that this letter reaches you that Phil is either home, or will be shortly. How well I can imagine how excited and happy you must be. I am so glad for you that you expect him to be discharged. That will be a grand and glorious feeling, won't it?

My Sister's Father

First of all, Evie dear, I want to thank you so much for your lovely birthday gift for Sharon. It is just darling and just what she needed, for she has outgrown all of hers.

She had a lovely birthday and everyone was so kind in remembering her. All of my friends and relatives dropped in with remembrances for her. Really, it was just like Christmas for her. Mother baked her a three-layer birthday cake with "Happy Birthday" in pink lettering on it with one candle in the middle. Sharon just was so excited and seemed to know it was her first birthday. As I watched her, in her appearance and manner so like Andy, I would have given anything in the world if he could just have seen her, but still I felt his presence in a thousand ways.

Yesterday at St. Philip Neri Church, our parish, a Solemn High Memorial Mass was celebrated for Andy, and as I look back on yesterday, I wondered how I lived through the day, but God gave me the strength. You see, both Andy and I graduated from St Philips, we were married there and Sharon was baptized there.

The friends and relatives that paid tribute to Andy were a great consolation to me. The students of St. Philips sang the Mass and attended in great numbers. Then, Fr. Clancy, the priest that married us, celebrated the Mass. But, I am greatly relieved that this ordeal is over, for I had been dreading it. I am enclosing a remembrance of the Mass together with one of the clippings that appeared in the Sunday paper. And so, Evie dear, this is adieu until later... Write soon, for I enjoy your letters so much. Sharon sends you a big kiss, as for me

> *Lots of Love,*
> *Ginny*

Underscoring Andy's dual loyalties to God and country, Christ's "Agony in the Garden" is depicted on the cover of Andy's remembrance card with the words "Thy Will Be Done" inscribed beneath along with a commemorative banner, a gold star centered on a field of white bordered by the colors of "Old Glory"—the proper designation for a fallen soldier. These were, indeed, days of agony. Andy's Memorial Mass, though, not a Requiem, was a first step toward acceptance, an acknowledgement that maybe he was, in fact, dead.

A reflection of her religious beliefs, Ginny included a poem entitled, *"Safely Home"*. It reads, in part:
Then you must not grieve so sorely,
For I love you dearly still;
Try to look beyond earth's shadows,
Pray to trust our Father's Will...

As the sun continued to set each evening and another day passed, Ginny's life was blessed with Sharon to nurture and to love. Andy's child was her salvation, her constant joy. His words, written months earlier, now seemed prophetic, "Now when Junior is born, you will have someone to remind you of me."

With no response from Evie, Ginny writes again a few weeks later, this time, trading her pen for a typewriter.

November 15, 1945
My dearest Evie:

How are you these days? Since I haven't heard from you in so long, I decided to dash off another letter. I rather imagine Phil must be home by this late date, and that is the reason I haven't heard from you.

Sharon and I are both fine, and Sharon is getting to be quite a young lady, although she still is not walking. I guess she is quite heavy to walk at a year, but I am hoping that she will be walking by Christmas. She just talks and talks all day long and loves music and to have the radio on. She was born with Andy's love of music and reminds me so much of him, for you know how he loved music, mostly jazz. She does so many cute things now and each day does something new and different. Her hair, although blonde, has no semblance of a curl thus far, but I surely do my best to coax it along. She just has to have Andy's curly hair.

I have been contemplating of late of returning to secretarial work, and have been shopping around. It is going to be more difficult to return to work than I first realized and leave Sharon, but I am afraid that I must make the break sometime. I know that she will be perfectly content and happy with mother and, in that respect, I realize I am very fortunate. But, if I don't find anything at present satisfactory, I believe I shall wait until at least the spring.

A letter I had written to Steve (a friend of Andy's from cadet training days) *on July 31, 1945, giving him the details regarding Andy was just returned to me yesterday. That was absolutely quite a shock, but there was no notation on the envelope. Do you know anything concerning Steve? I know that he was flying with Phil so hope that you can give me some good news regarding him. I hope and pray that it won't be bad, but that you will tell me that he returned to the States safely. All our boys can't be lost.*

Ruth York, Bob York's wife wrote me this week from Clintonville, Wisconsin, where she is employed selling war bonds. I believe that I told you that Bob lost his life two weeks after Andy. I am sure that you remember Bob and Ruth, for they lived in Cabin 1 in Florence. Ruth stated in her letter that Bob wrote her on September 16, 1944 that Andy didn't come back that day, but sounded so hopeful that Ruth was positive that Andy was somewhere safe. What could have happened to him? She also told me that Swede (they lived next door to Andy and I) was a prisoner and also Whipperman. (Do you remember him?)

I also received a letter from the Adjutant General's Office stating that I was to be awarded the Silver Oak-Leaf Cluster to the Air Medal, which has been posthumously awarded to Andy. This ceremony is to take place in Downtown Detroit on November 29. How I dread it—yet somehow I guess I will get through this too.

I am enclosing some clippings from our local papers regarding Andy, which I knew you and Phil would like to keep. Also am mailing you a copy of Andy's last picture, which I had made for you. He had it done in London for me on August 25, 1944, the day before he was shot down the first time, in France.

And so Evie dear, this is adieu until later. Please write when you have a spare minute for your letters mean a great deal to me. My love to Phil if he is with you. As always Sharon sends all of her love.

Lovingly,
Ginny

"Clippings from our local papers." Ginny eschews the word, obituary, to describe the articles. Maybe it was too final a word to use just yet. One day soon the paper might have to print a retraction, and her life would be as it should be.

Even as she languished over Andy's whereabouts, she was able to look beyond her immediate circumstances and personal pain to inquire about the safety of other boys. It was a kinship wrought from raw feelings of loss and a sobering schooling in the price of war.

By August of 1945, Egon Fricke, one of Andy's acquaintances had returned to his parents and his home in Detroit. Egon first met Ginny three years earlier when Ralph Krass, Ginny's beau at the time, and he dropped by the Egan household. Ginny mentions this brief encounter in one of her early letters to Andy: "*Ralph and Egon Fricke both received furloughs together after maneuvers in Tennessee... I believe you know Egon, don't you? He is a grand fellow and lots of fun."*

Ralph and Egon had served together with the 182nd Field Artillery and eventually became attached to Patton's Third Army in Europe. Father Maino was their chaplain throughout the war. A German transplant, Egon sometimes served as a translator for his battery. He, along with his mother, Bertha, and younger sister, Edith, had emigrated from Germany to America in 1912 when he was two years of age. With the First World War brewing, the children's father, Johannes Kloppenbörger, preceded them to America, sending for them later. Bertha divorced Johannes soon after their arrival and later married Herman Fricke when the children were still very young.

Whether Egon contacted Ginny at this time is unclear, but based upon family oral tradition, I know that he eventually came-a-calling. Prodding Ginny along, it was Egon who gave her the continual encouragement she needed to return to her secretarial work. He was working for an insurance company and he used his influence and gregarious personality to arrange interviews for her. He felt it was important for Ginny to move beyond the confines of her parents' home, and effectively, move forward with her life.

Perhaps it was no accident that Evie's letters to Ginny took a hiatus following her November letter. Both their lives had been rerouted in startling different ways during those early post-war months. Phil and Evie were reunited back in Hicksville, New York (although Ginny had not received confirmation of this fact from Evie) while Ginny was left to forge ahead in a new direction, a gaping hole where Andy once stood.

My Sister's Father

With Andy's fate still in question, Ginny had to tough out another wedding anniversary and another Christmas without her beloved. She made it a habit to pin Andy's Air Corp insignia, wings, superimposed by a propeller, on Sharon's dainty dresses.

On February 26, 1946, Ginny, unwilling to forsake her pursuit of the truth, types two letters of inquiry, identical in content; one is sent to the Adjutant General's Office and the other to Major James L. Prenn, Assistant to the Quartermaster General, both in Washington D.C. She writes:

Dear Sir:

I am writing to you in regard to my husband, Lt. Andre J. Vleghels (serial number), who was reported "missing in Action over Holland on September 16, 1944." Then, subsequently on July 30, 1945, I received a telegram from the War Department stating that "from reports received my husband was killed in action on September 16, 1944." To the present time I have not received any details regarding his death or burial. I am addressing this missive to your attention with the fervent hope that perhaps you might assist me in securing at least some details regarding his death. Even the most minute detail would be appreciated by me.

He was the pilot of an A-20 Boston Havoc based in England and his two gunners, Roger Rice and Clay E. Young were also reported killed, but absolutely no facts were received regarding any of the three. If there is any further information you desire relative to this case, I will be very happy to forward same to you.

Sincerely hoping that you may be able to assist me, I am

Yours very truly,
Mrs. Andre J. Vleghels

It appears from this letter that Ginny was settling into the possibility that Andy was not coming home to her and Sharon. Or maybe she was simply patronizing the War Department, playing along with their supposition that evidence, though never stated, was sufficient to establish the fact of death.

A prompt acknowledgement came in a letter dated 9 March 1946 from the Office of the Quartermaster General:

Dear Mrs. Vleghels:

Your letter concerning your husband, the late First Lieutenant Andre J. Vleghels, has been received by this office.

I regret that I must inform you that to date, no information has been received concerning the burial of the remains of your husband, or of the late Staff Sergeant Roger W. Rice. Information, not yet verified by the American Graves Registration Services in Europe, has been received from the German Government through the legation at Bern, Switzerland, indicating that the remains of the late Staff Sergeant Clay E. Young are buried in the Prisoner of War Cemetery at Bergen op Zoom, Holland. An investigation is now being made in order to locate and identify the remains of these three men and to reinter them in an established military cemetery. When this investigation is completed, you will be informed.

A copy of your letter has been forwarded to the office of the Adjutant General for reply to you concerning the circumstances surrounding the death of your husband, as that office has jurisdiction over the release of information of this nature.

FOR THE QUARTERMASTER GENERAL:

> *Sincerely yours,*
> *JAMES L. PRENN*
> *Major, QMC*
> *Assistant*

It had now been one year, six months and counting since Andy had gone missing. How much longer could Ginny endure this mental torture? The burden was great, with just a sliver of hope remaining.

My mother never told me what happened the day the letter arrived at her doorstep bearing the ghastly news, and I never pressed her for answers. She did confide that it was the International Red Cross who ultimately came through with definitive information. The stationary bore the heading of the Netherlands Embassy in Washington D.C. dated May 1, 1946:

Dear Mrs. Vleghels,

Further to Baron von Boetzelaer's letter No. 74 of January 7, 1946, I beg to inform you that the Minister of Foreign Affairs has stated in a letter which I just received that the Netherlands authorities have at last found the grave of your husband.

It appears that on September 25, 1944 in the vicinity of the small town of Scherpenisse, province of Zeeland, the body of a pilot was found. According to the identification-tag this pilot was your husband, as the numbers and the name on the tag correspond with those which you transmitted to me some time ago. On September 26 your husband was buried in the Public Cemetery of Scherpenisse, south of the Dutch Reformed Church. The grave is indicated by a wooden cross on which his name is written.

I deeply regret that I have to transmit to you this sorrowful confirmation of what you probably already expected.

Yours very sincerely,
E.L.C. Schiff,
Second Secretary of Embassy

Maurine told me of the day she was called down to her high school principal's office. Her memory, intercepted now by nearly six decades, is jumbled. But one detail remains explicit—as the principal, Sr. Marie Bride, softly and compassionately, related to Maurine that her parents had received word verifying that her brother was killed in action, her eyes became fixed on the wall behind sister. Hanging there was the much idolized flag-raising at Iwo Jima. Sister went on to inform Maurine that her parents were with her brother's widow, Virginia, and that Maurine was asked to return home. Feeling abandoned and confused, Maurine gathered up her books and rode her bicycle to her home, a mile away. A next-door neighbor, Mrs. Bodeman, was watching for Maurine, and called her over to the fence. She wanted to reassure her that her parents would be coming home in a little while.

Maurine never understood why her parents did not stop by school that day to pick her up on their way to be with Virginia. Maybe it was a misguided attempt to protect Maurine from the ensuing hysteria or simply the urgency that they felt to be with Andy's widow, following months of interminable torment.

Ginny's parents were with her and Sharon when the Vleghels arrived. I expect that Grandma Egan sheltered Sharon, her little charge, from the turmoil as the shock waves passed through them. In her elder years and in one of her more lucid moments, Grandma Egan confided to me that she "felt so sorry for Virginia when Andy died. She just went crazy."

Nineteen months of pent-up hopes were sucked out of them all at once, finally and completely, leaving them writhing in pain from the vacuum it created. How does one calm the hysterical or console the disconsolate when you, yourself, are destroyed?

Their hearts were crushed. Their world collapsed.

In Flanders fields the poppies blow
Between the crosses, row on row
That mark our place; and in the sky
The larks, still bravely singing, fly
Scarce heard amid the guns below.

We are the dead. Short days ago
We lived, felt dawn, saw sunset glow,
Loved and were loved, and now we lie
In Flanders fields.

In Flanders Fields
John McCrae

Chapter 18
The Aftermath

Apparently, Ginny took action and wrote to the embassy relatively soon after receiving their notification, because on June 12, 1946, another notice from the Acting Director of the Netherlands National Tracing Bureau (part of the Netherlands Red Cross), J. van de Vosse, arrived. He states:

My Sister's Father

Referring to yours of May 1946, I beg to inform you, that I made inquiries regarding the place of interment of 2nd Lt. Andre J. Vleghels (serial number).

Lt. Andre J. Vleghels was buried on the cemetery of Scherpenisse in Holland on 26th September 1944 and it has been ascertained now that the mortal remains of a/n person have been transferred and buried again in Plot GG Row 10, Grave 237, at the U.S. Military Cemetery Hamm in Luxembourg. Hamm is located approximately 2 1/2 miles east of Luxembourg City.

I am, Madam,

Yours very truly,
J. van de Vosse
Act. Director

It was not until the 18th of September that Ginny received an official confirmation from the War Department, Memorial Division. Responding to her inquiry, it simply restated Andy's grave designation in Hamm.

The tale I recall hearing from mom as I grew up was that Andy's body was discovered by a farmer, fifty meters behind his home, and that he buried him in a public cemetery in a small town in Holland. I had the impression, then, that the Dutchman accomplished this task single-handedly. This farmer wrote a letter to her, she said. But this is a bit of a departure, I think, from what actually happened. The "farmer" who discovered Andy's remains would not have been able to speak English, though his words could have been translated. I have come to believe that the letter my mother had ascribed to the Dutchman was actually written by someone working for the International Red Cross. She must have received it in May or June of 1946, around the time she initially learned of the discovery of Andy's grave and his re-interment in Luxembourg. It may have even accompanied the notice sent by J. van de Vosse of the Netherlands Tracing Bureau.

Carefully preserved in one of two binders that Ginny had relegated to a shelf in her closet, the letter is hand-written, penned on a simple sheet of loose–leaf paper. The cursive is nearly perfect, much like the standard one sees on bulletin boards in elementary classrooms. I surmise that the grim facts were transcribed from records secured in the town hall of Scherpenisse. It is evident that its author is unfamiliar with things American. The letter is unsigned and bears no heading, date, or salutation. It reads:

In answer upon your request August 29, 1945, (a request most likely addressed to the International Red Cross) *I am now able to let you know that on Monday, September 25, 1944, about 8:00 ' clock at the sea dike on the Ooster-Schelde Bay, under the evacuated village of Scherpenisse, was washed the remains of an English or American flyer.*

On the body was found the following identifications: On a little plaque was written this: Andre' J. Vleghels, Nr. O (serial number). T. 42-3 B. T. 44. What was left on his person was 1 American dollar, 2 English halfcrowns, 1 Eng. florin, 1 Eng. shilling, 1 Eng. pence, 1 Eng. threepence, 1 Eng. farthing, one nail file, one R.K. [Roman Catholic] *rosary, one medal and chain, a small whistle, a key, and a handkerchief. All of this is kept by the secretary of the village of Scherpenisse and Tholen. On September 26, 1944 the remains were buried in a general cemetery in a respectable coffin in the village of Scherpenisse. We presume that the flyer during a bombardment upon the Zd. Beveland-North Brabant, on September 16, 1944, came down with a parachute in the Ooster-Schelde.*

In December of 1944, A.L.G. van Doorn, the Secretary of Scherpenisse, personally delivered Andy's effects enumerated in this communication to the office of Civil Affairs in the city of Tholen. Eventually, they found their way back to his grieving widow. The last, seemingly ordinary, remnants of Ginny's betrothed became irreplaceable mementos, the very same keepsakes that I had stumbled upon, safe in her dresser drawer, the morning that she died.

Ginny expresses her sentiments about Andy's personal effects in a letter that she wrote to Dick Schmitt in 1995. Dick, the son of one of Ginny's closer friends, was living in Brussels at the time. Upon hearing Andy's story from his mother and realizing that Hamm was only a two-hour road trip away, Dick wrote to Ginny inquiring about Andy's final resting-place.

In a reciprocal spirit, Ginny, touched by Dick's kindness and interest, writes back. "On his body was found a Sterling Silver Rosary (which I had given him as a wedding gift) and a scapular medal around his neck. These were returned to me. They are my most precious possessions."

How ironic and unfortunate it is that Ginny could write these words to a family friend, but could not utter them to her own children. Certainly letters, by their very nature, are a safer means of communication, since the sender does not have to face the recipient. Perhaps mom feared that candor would compromise our regard for her; that we would question her love for Egon, her second husband and father to us all, if she ever dared to reveal the sequestered love that she still harbored for Andy. It was a miscalculation that she made throughout her life—that to expose the underbelly of her humanity was to expose weakness and something less than perfect.

Do not abandon your heart to grief,
drive it away, bear your end in mind.

Ecclesiastes 38:20-21

Chapter 19
Moving Forward

On January 10, 1948 Ginny Vleghels and Egon Fricke became husband and wife. Ginny vowed, once again, to honor, cherish, and obey, until death do us part. This time, she wore a simple suit, flared at the knees and topped off by a wide-brimmed hat adorned with colorful silk flowers.

Egon received his First Holy Communion that day. He was a baptized Catholic, but since his mother had divorced and remarried, he was not reared in the Catholic tradition. However, it was vital to Ginny that they practice the same religion and follow the guidelines of the Church.

This time, Father Maino was called upon to witness the union at Saint Ambrose Church. In rapid succession, revered occasions had brought the Egan and Vleghels families together to celebrate a sacrament--the promises of a marriage, the consecration of a baptism, a mass in memoriam, and now, the nuptials of a second union, milestones that traced joy and sorrow and gave witness to the stuff of life.

Still a bachelor at the age of thirty-six, Egon Fricke patiently petitioned Ginny for a date for more than a year before she, tentative, surrendered her fears and ventured beyond her insular haven. She once confessed that her decision to remarry was the most difficult one of her life. Love and acceptance of Sharon were her suitor's measure. That was a non-negotiable prerequisite. Nothing less would suffice. Ginny was staunchly uncompromising when it came to the welfare of Andy's daughter.

Ginny chose well. Egon never betrayed the trust he was given. He embraced Sharon as his own and never wavered. No one could have guessed that he was not her natural father.

Egon's disarming good nature and genuine demeanor quickly won over the affections of Maurice, Rachel, and Maurine Vleghels, his German heritage notwithstanding. Maurine recalls that a party was held in the Egan's basement to celebrate the engagement. Considering the high esteem and deep love they held for Andre, the Vleghels' approval was a resounding vote of confidence for Ginny's choice. In a very real sense, Ginny was letting go of the life she had envisioned with Andy. She had to extricate herself from the past in order to live in the present.

Getting off to a fresh start, Ginny and Egon purchased a newly built home, one in a maze of post-war suburbs rapidly springing up across the country, housing en masse. Egon happily assumed the privileges and responsibilities of fatherhood. He was a warm and principled man who was more than ready and willing to foster a family of his own.

Writing on club stationary, on a day in May following her wedding, Ginny resurrects her correspondence with Evie:

My Sister's Father

Dear Phil & Evie:

Do you remember me? I am really ashamed of myself for not writing, and so much has transpired since we last corresponded that I should start from the beginning. To begin with, on January 10, I was married to Egon Fricke, the boy that I had told you about previously, and after our marriage, we took a trip to Phoenix, Arizona where Egon's folks live. Mother took care of Sharon for me and we had a grand trip. We bought a new Colonial home in Grosse Pointe Woods and it is lovely and I am very happy. My husband, as I told you, is a Golf Professional and manages Lakepointe Country Club. Sharon is fine and is so big. Egon is a wonderful father to her and she just idolizes him.

I have thought of you often and wondered how you all were. How is Linda [Phil and Evie's daughter]*? Please send me a snap of her, for I don't even know what she looks like. I imagine you are in your new home by now. Is Phil still doing carpenter work?*

And so, Evie dear, this will have to be brief for now for I am writing this at the club, and hope that you will let me hear from you soon. Sharon sends you a big kiss and my love to Linda and Phil.

Lots of Love,
Ginny

In the fall, Sharon was enrolled in *The Grosse Pointe School for Little Folks*, a preschool. It was rather forward thinking for the era, but I think Ginny was anxious to socialize Sharon with other children, since she had been living within the protective confines of an adult milieu. Mom used to remark what a smooth transition Sharon made to her new surroundings. However, with so many things changing in her young life, all at once, it had to be somewhat disconcerting.

Sharon gave her school mixed reviews. She questioned the integrity of a school that assigned no homework. To her way of thinking, a real school meant homework. Once her teacher became aware of the problem and assigned homework, Sharon was content.

In time, Fricke replaced Vleghels on Sharon's school papers with no discussion. It proved a practical exchange, but it turns out that Egon never legally adopted Andy's daughter. Sharon's maiden name remains Vleghels. I am guessing that the decision to leave Vleghels legally intact was not incidental. But it could just as easily have been a pragmatic solution. Although Ginny's second marriage would not preclude Sharon's eligibility for compensation as Andy's daughter, it might have simplified matters as far as the government was concerned. Either way, it remains a fitting tribute to the man who helped to give Sharon life, but was never able to cradle her in his arms or bounce her on his knee.

I was born the week before Christmas in 1948, eleven months after my parents married. Mom said it was the best Christmas she ever had. I think I understand why—her fractured family had been made whole. At age twenty-nine, Ginny had been emancipated from the ever-impinging confines of the Egan family. She did, of course, appreciate all the support that they had offered during her time of tribulation, but when she made the decision to remarry, her mother tried to dissuade her. Elizabeth had grown very attached to Sharon, and she did not surrender her without a struggle. She wanted to continue to keep Sharon with her for a time, but Ginny would not have it. One of the very first practices that she did away within her household was Liz's ritual of warming Sharon's undergarments by the register. Mom always gave Sharon due credit for adjusting very well to her new life. I would wager that Egon's love for Sharon helped to ease that transition. Sharon was his "cheetie pie", Sharon's pronunciation of sweetie pie.

Over the course of five years, Ginny had fought many battles. Finally, she and her husband could celebrate Christmas with their daughters in their new home, creating their own family traditions.

How mom loved to reminisce about that first Christmas Eve on Linville Avenue. As her story goes--snow had begun to fall when a troupe of carolers arrived at our door. Their voices filled the air with sounds of good cheer, goodwill toward men. It was a veritable page out of Alcott's *Little Women*. That evening, as we gathered around our Christmas tree, Egon sang a prayerful, *Silent Night*. I was a babe in arms, and peace on earth had truly descended upon the four of us. It was a treasured moment of serenity, a picture-perfect vignette. It had been a long time coming. Some goodness was beginning to melt away the frozen pain of a horrific loss. Prevailing sadness gave way to satisfaction and contentment.

*Love takes off masks
that we fear we cannot live without
and know we cannot live within.*

James Arthur Baldwin

Chapter 20
Touchstones

In August of 1954, the last of Ginny and Egon's children was born—a son, Michael Egon. Not unlike Andy's musings while awaiting the birth of his child, dad was excited to have a son to rear with whom he could share his athletic prowess. He began tossing a ball to him when Mike was still a toddler in a stroller. I was five and a half then. Sharon was nearly ten.

I believe it was somewhere along this timeline, between the age of five and seven, that I had my first encounter with Andy Vleghels, and I started down a path that would take me more than fifty years to navigate. It began one afternoon when I wandered into my parents' bedroom and, quite by accident, made an astonishing discovery. I was poking my nose between some framed photographs atop their bureau. A colored one depicted my dad out on the golf course. But there was a picture right up in front that puzzled me. I had never seen it before. A soldier stared back at me. I stood up on tiptoe and craned my neck to get a closer look. He had a kind look about him and the hint of a smirk at the corner of his mouth beneath his military brim. But who he could be, I certainly could not guess. I was completely immersed, studying my new-found mystery man when mom entered the room behind me.

Startled, but unabashed, I asked mom about the man in the picture. She softly told me, her voice, cracking with emotion, that the man was a friend of my father's. She quickly added that he had died in the war.

I felt sad for my dad, that he had lost a friend to combat. He must have been very important to him, I thought. How sad it was that my dad's life could go on, while this fellow's ended at a young age. I accepted my mother's explanation, as a child would tend to do, although I suspected that there was more to the story. Logic cast a shadow of doubt in my mind. Even if this man was a friend of my dad's, I reasoned, it seemed to me that he really did not warrant such a high place of distinction. The bureau was a place for family photographs. The following day I went to revisit the man in the picture, but he was gone.

Then, when I was about seven, mom was able to tell me the rest of the story. Perhaps she had rehearsed in her mind--just how she would broach such a delicate subject with her young daughter. She waited until we were alone. It was my turn to dry the supper dishes; mom was washing. As she stood over the kitchen sink, carefully setting each washed plate in the drying rack, mom began. She probably started out by saying, "I have something to tell you," to give me fair warning that she had some important news to share. The last time this happened, she told me that she was going to have a baby. Though I did not jump to that conclusion, she had my full attention. Slowly and carefully, she explained to me that she had been married once before, but that her husband had been killed in the war. She went on to say that her first husband was also Sharon's father.

At first, I felt strangely excited at the revelation—at the surprise of an out-of-the-ordinary occurrence that involved our ordinary family. Nothing outstanding ever happened to us. But an instant later, realizing mom's loss, I wrapped my arms around her middle and pressed my head against her. I told her I was sorry. I know I had some questions for her regarding Sharon, but it is difficult to recall, exactly. Time has a way of blurring our memories--words fade to gray, while emotions remain vivid.

What I do recall is that my prevailing instinct was to console Sharon. She was my most immediate concern. I did not know what it was like to have a husband, but I did know what it was like to receive the love of a father. Imagine, losing your father!

I raced down the steps to our recreation room in the basement. Sharon sat, intent, poised in front of the TV screen, ready for some evening sit-coms. She was eleven. Of course, she was completely unaware of the conversation that had just ensued. But in my eagerness to express my sympathy, I blurted out that I was so sorry about her dad; mom had told me. Sharon stared at me for a second as she tried to absorb my words; then shrugged it off. I made an awkward attempt to hug her, but she stiffened, thwarting my advance. She looked passed me in her dismissal and refocused her attention back to her TV program. I felt shut out. But mom had explained that my dad was the only dad that Sharon had ever known. So maybe it all made sense.

Now I understood, at least, why we had a third set of grandparents in our family, Grandma and Grandpa Vleghels. I also understood why, when we posed in front of their camera, they wanted a snap of Sharon by herself. Sharon was the daughter of the son they had lost. They had a special connection. She was their consolation. At last, the true identity of the man in the picture was now known to me--the first piece of the puzzle that would take decades to complete.

My mother's disclosure became an epiphany for me and the beginning of many touchstones. Until that moment, suspended in time, my world had been quite idyllic, free of adult concerns. For the first time, I learned that life could be unpredictably sad. But it did not scare me. Although I knew that my mother had suffered a great loss, she had survived it. She seemed strong. It made me feel safe.

I can remember boasting to my best friend down the street about my mother's first husband who had died in the war. I told Andy's story with a sense of pride. I did not comprehend the historical significance, but I did know that Andy had done what he was asked to do. And he had paid for it with his life.

What I did not know then was that mom's original story was tainted. She told me that Andy had fought and died in the Korean War—an intentional disconnect with reality. Perhaps altering the facts, even slightly, gave her the emotional distance she felt she needed. Opening a wound, so visceral, must have terrified her.

The compassion that I felt for my mother and my sister that day has never left me. A seed took root. During the years when I was growing into adulthood and beyond, I tended to make allowances for my mother whenever she was cross or unreasonable, because she had suffered so much tragedy early in her life.

In the bottom two drawers on the left side of my mother's dresser, stacks of papers and snapshots relating to Andy were stockpiled in disarray. Sharon and I were both aware of them, though I do not know just how. Most likely, one of us was snooping; mom discovered it and reprimanded us. We had crossed a line and invaded our mother's privacy. But, her repeated attempts to thwart our curiosity, only served to heighten it. So, every now and again, each of us would sneak in at different times to view the forbidden evidence of a life once lived--reminders of Andy buried at the bottom of the dresser. Separately, we would burrow through the paper trail and snaps, hoping to uncover some new information. But it was all for naught. We were children and we could not make sense of any of it. The more that was withheld, the more I wanted to know.

I remember the day that my mother told me that Grandpa Vleghels was sick with cancer. He was not going to get well. My family visited him one day in his home. It made me very sad to see him so weak. I was going to miss his sweet ways. His belly, swollen from the cancer, frightened me. He sat in a chair, quiet, head down. I sat at the end of the sofa across from him. I did not want to be rude and stare. It was disturbing to see such a loving man suffer. He died in 1959 at the age of sixty-two. Maurine believes that he died of a broken heart. He and Andy were buddies.

In the years that followed, Sharon married and moved to Indianapolis where her husband, Dick, had accepted a job for Eli Lilly, a pharmaceutical company headquartered there. Sharon, a nursing graduate, accepted a job at a local hospital. Two years later, in 1968, Jeff and I married. Over the course of the next four years, my parents became grandparents four times over.

Years passed before talk of Andy resurfaced. It was 1979 when our children were in elementary school, ages eight and nine. Pa-Pa and Grams had invited them to attend a ceremony at our War Memorial to commemorate the local war dead on Memorial Day, or Decoration Day as it used to be known. Afterwards, Scott and Michelle came home asking why Grams was crying. I retold the story of their grandmother's first husband. I saw no reason to protect them from the truth. To me, secrecy meant bondage; truth meant freedom.

Then one Christmas, soon after, I decided to have an artist sketch a drawing of my parents' home, using a photograph I had taken as a model. Following the example of meaningful gift-giving laid down by my mother, I thought it would please my parents to have a special rendering of the home they had worked so hard to create. But first I needed to retrieve the picture from their photo album.

I waited until mom was at work one Saturday. Dad served as my accomplice. He led me to the bedroom that had become a spare, no longer having children to house. He opened the closet door and pointed to the shelf of photo albums lined up like soldiers, then returned to his room to resume his afternoon nap.

It was anyone's guess which album held the desired photo, so I randomly pulled one down and began to turn its pages. There they were in front of me—page upon page of pictures under plastic, Andy and Ginny resurrected from the dresser tomb, a pictorial testament of their abbreviated life together. I was mesmerized.

The photograph that impressed me above all others showed Andy standing next to a plane with the name, Ginny, and a "pin-up" painted on one side of the ship's nose. Andy had a grin on his face that stretched from ear to ear. That's what really killed me. He looked so damn happy and proud. I never knew that Andy had honored mom in this way. It broke my heart to see it. Now, more than ever, I could appreciate the depth of mom's loss—a part of her had been severed. At the same time, I felt frustrated and disappointed, once again, that mom was unable to share these tender memories with her family.

It was as if time rewound, and I was a young child again, snooping. But now I was a married woman and a mother. I turned the page to find a collection of obituaries. Some used the photograph I had seen on my parents' bureau, others used a hatless picture, revealing Andy's neatly shorn thick, blonde locks. It was the very one that Andy had taken in London a few weeks before he perished.

Riveted, I read every word of the eight obituaries. "Army Declares Local Pilot Killed Near His Birthplace," November 15, 1945, stated that Lt. Andre J. Vleghels died in a raid over Holland, thirty miles from his birthplace in Ghent, Belgium. The yellowed newsprint verified mom's story for the first time. It took my breath away. Another obituary reported: "He is survived by his wife, Mrs. Virginia Vleghels of Alter Road, his one year old daughter, Sharon Virginia, born shortly after he was reported missing, his parents, Mr. and Mrs. Maurice Vleghels of Britain Avenue, and a sister, Maurine Vleghels."

My heart sank. I wept, quietly. Even as a blanket of great sadness fell over me, I felt thankful, amazed that I had been given a chance to catch a glimpse into the lives of Lt. and Mrs. Andre Vleghels. It actually felt good to be enveloped by grief. There was a certain satisfaction to be gained from the truth. The cold, hard facts were no longer shrouded in mystery. The experience left an imprint upon my soul.

I am not certain if I said anything about my discovery to dad before leaving the house, picture in hand. Most likely, in an attempt to spare his feelings, I did not. I am certain, however, that later, I told mom how moved I was when I came upon the snap of Andy and his plane with her name on it. Once again, the picture went missing. I have never seen it since. Sometimes, I wonder if I dreamed it.

In 1994, we threw mom a surprise seventy-fifth birthday party. Something told me that she might not make it to her eightieth, so I offered to host the celebration. For the second time, mom had borne the loneliness of widowhood. It had been nine years since our father's death. Though there remained a void that only a spouse could fill, I was hoping that a celebration with family and friends would bring her some happiness.

As is often the custom for such occasions, my family pooled their photos to create a collage of memorable moments in our mother's life. I searched out my favorite photograph of Mom and Andy; it was classic World War II. A professional photographer had taken the picture in the "Blue Room" of a New York City hotel on the night of their reunion. It was Saturday, March 25 of 1944. They are seated at a table covered in white linen. Ginny, wearing a suit and dainty hat is smiling, demurely; Andy, hatless, looking gallant and proud in his dress greens. There were celebratory drinks before them, and twin Army Air Corps wings pinned to their jackets. It was the last picture of them as a couple. I could not imagine leaving it out, so I tacked it up with the rest of Ginny's life-mosaic.

When mom noticed the image of herself and Andy, a lifetime ago, she pursed her lips and diverted her eyes as she always did when trying to contain her feelings. I like to think that a part of her was pleased. Andy's sister, Maurine, seemed touched by the courtesy, happy that her brother was not forgotten. She never understood why Ginny had constructed a wall of silence when it came to Andy.

For me, the party and seeing Maurine became a stimulus to keep Andy's memory alive. Soon after, I decided to contact the cemetery in Luxembourg to inquire about his final resting-place. Not being computer savvy, my husband, Jeff, came to my aid to send a FAX to the American Military Cemetery in Luxembourg. It seemed like magic to me when we received a reply the following day. The American Battle Monuments Commission (ABMC) respectfully informed us that Andre's grave now had a different designation than the original. Back in the spring of 1960 when the rebuilding of the cemetery was completed, Andre's remains were relocated. They assured us that the re-interment was carried out with the utmost respect and decorum in accordance with military guidelines. They would be forwarding a color lithograph of the cemetery and an individual photo of Andre's grave to his widow, Virginia Fricke. I was ecstatic!

Once the package arrived from the ABMC, mom learned that she could mail in a check for thirty dollars whenever she chose, and the commission would place an arrangement of fresh flowers at the base of Andy's cross. Fifty years following his death, she could finally honor Andy in a more personal way. She had never been able to make the trip to Luxembourg. Part of her yearned to. She had hoped to go with Maurine, but the trip never materialized. Thousands of miles separated them, still. But now, Mom, Maurine, and Sharon could take turns commemorating significant days in the life of Andre Vleghels. It gladdened my heart. It was a start. The seed that took root at age seven was beginning to bear fruit.

A year later, as mom's seventy-sixth birthday approached, I decided it was time to take the next step. Somehow, it came to me. I would search out a book about World War II that would "speak" to her. I thought it was important for mom to deal with Andy's loss on an emotional level, a dimension of herself that she continually stifled. I desperately wanted her to move beyond the "grin and bear it" philosophy of the forties. If mom could vicariously return to the war years through the written word and read about her peers whose experiences were similar to hers and Andy's, I postulated, maybe she could work through her latent feelings of loss that had been trapped in her psyche for decades. Ultimately, my hope was for Ginny to arrive at a resting place and find a peace that she had never known since the day she learned that the love of her life had gone missing.

As my eyes scanned the shelves relegated to the Second World War at my neighborhood bookseller, an adrenaline rush came over me. My heart was racing. This Andy fascination, smoldering since my youth, was igniting a passion in me. Almost immediately, I spotted a book jacket, facing out. It featured a photograph of eleven aviators donned in flight suits. The caption read: THE STORY OF THE LAST AMERICAN BOMBER SHOT DOWN OVER GERMANY IN WORLD WAR II. Turning to the copyright page, I noted that the first printing was a mere five months earlier. It felt like destiny.

Turning to the inside flap, I read further:

My Sister's Father

"On April 21, 1945, the twelve-member crew of the Black Cat *set off on one of the last missions in the European Theater of WWII. Ten never came back. This is the story of that crew—where they came from, how they trained, what it was like to fly a B-24 through enemy flak, and who was waiting for them to come home."*

I bought two copies of *Wings of Morning* by historian, Thomas Childers, inscribed mom's copy, and presented it to her on her seventy-sixth birthday. I suppose she had mixed feelings about receiving such a gift. She confided to me later that, although it was a difficult account to read, she was glad that she had read it. She said she knew what it was like to be the woman who received her loved one's Purple Heart in the mail, posthumously. Head bowed and stifling sobs, she continued, "I didn't want the Purple Heart, I wanted my husband"--a mere ten words that took more than five decades to speak. I could not fully appreciate the significance of her statement at the time. Later, I came to see it as a real breakthrough. It was the closest she ever came to verbalizing her feelings about losing Andy to war.

A surprising coincidence was realized when I read my copy of the book. It turned out that one of the crewmembers lost on the *Black Cat* was George Noe, a friend of Andy's from his neighborhood. It was George's family who had housed Andy and Maurice during Maurine's bout with scarlet fever.

In the last years of her life, mom and I spoke on the phone almost daily. In one such conversation, on the advent of a visit to Sharon's, mom admitted that she felt guilty about withholding information from Sharon when it came to Andy.

"Well," I said, "It's not too late. You are both still alive!"

"Yes", she retorted, "But you know Sharon. She's always very busy."

Sensing that she was just looking for a way out, I rallied, "I am sure that if you told Sharon that you wanted to talk to her about Andy, she would make the time."

When mom returned home, she reported to me, "I talked to Sharon about Andy." She seemed proud of her accomplishment. Sharon told me later that once mom broached the subject with her, they retired to the privacy of her living room. There, for four hours, Ginny unraveled the story of Andy Vleghels and how it came to be that her former high school beau became her husband during wartime. She answered Sharon's questions, but never ventured beyond the facts, omitting, even now, anything of a personal or emotional nature. Her feelings about this chapter of her life remained guarded. Nevertheless, it was a brave step for Ginny after decades of stowing her memories.

Less than three weeks before Ginny died, July fourth weekend of 1998, we went together to the bookstore to pick up a copy of *Lost in the Victory*, a compilation of personal accounts written by orphans of World War II. Once again, it was Dick Schmitt who thoughtfully sent Ginny an article about the book, the American War Orphans Network (AWON), and its founder, Ann Mix. Dick thought Sharon might be interested in reading it.

A couple of days later, I stopped by at Mom's. She had devoured the book in a day, and now, with her arms wrapped around it as she stood in her driveway, she offered to let me read it. Raising her voice to compete with the whir of my running engine, the cadence and inflection of her speech punctuated her words, revealing a sense of urgency. Mom was animated and surprisingly enthusiastic about the book. I could not figure it out. Wasn't this the same woman who dodged talk of her painful past at every turn?

My bewilderment was dispelled when mom went on to say that she was anxious for Sharon to read the book because then she would understand that, by comparison to some mothers, at least, she had not fared so bad in her struggles to raise her orphaned child.

"One mother became an alcoholic," mom proclaimed.

Ginny had held herself to a very strict accounting for Sharon's upbringing. Most likely, she felt an added pressure to make Andy proud when it came to matters of raising their daughter, though her self-imposed proclivity was to hold her offspring to the same high standard that she had come to expect of herself. Andy, himself, sheds light on Ginny's perception of her parental duty when he admonishes her in what turned out to be his last letter to her: "What do you mean our baby will have to be good or else we will be disgraced; our baby will be just as good as anyone else's if not better. If it's a boy he'll learn a lot of sports and be good at them, I'll see to that. Shame on you!"

Actually, she had done relatively well, mom seemed to imply, in spite of her shortfalls. The weight of her conscience was lifted. She said there was one accounting in the anthology that reminded her so much of Andy. Not a trace of angst permeated her demeanor, only joy. She had found salvation in the testimony of orphans. She could throw off the mantle of guilt that had plagued her. Its void left room for peace.

Mom cautioned me that I would have to read the book right away and return it to her the following day so that she could mail it off to Sharon. I declined, knowing I could not get to it that soon, and dismissed mom's impatience as being nothing more than usual. She always wanted things done yesterday.

Mom's final gift to Sharon arrived a few days before her death. The inscription was dated July 16, 1998. It read: "Dear Sharon: Until we meet again. May the Lord hold you in the palm of His hand."

I was aghast when I read these words, months later. They seemed so final. Sharon lived but six hours away. Mom was referring to heaven. She sensed the end was near. It was a fitting farewell to Andy's daughter.

Andy's daughter—I believe that is always how mom saw Sharon. She harbored a bias toward her, so subtle, that it remained undetected by me until I began to unearth the past and reflect upon it, layer by layer. Logic dictates that whenever significant events were celebrated in Sharon's life, mom's thoughts would turn, naturally, to Andy. First Communion, graduations, marriage, first job, first home, first child were milestones in the life of their daughter, special occasions when Andy would be intensely missed. Ginny's words would not expose her feelings; her tears were the evidence. How could I ever object to or censure, in any way, her intimate connection to Andy—I could not.

In 1966 mom gave Sharon and Dick six thousand dollars to begin their new life together. The money was unspent compensation for Andy's death awarded by the U. S. Government, money that Ginny had held in escrow for Sharon. Ginny could have used the funds however she wished, but she chose to offer it to Sharon and Dick on their wedding day. Sharon recalls that mom took great delight and pride in presenting her with this remarkable gift. It was a gift that exacted a high cost--a gift that together, Ginny and Andy, had made possible through unspeakable sacrifice known only to them.

Separations were tough for Ginny where Sharon was concerned. It began when Sharon entered college, less than an hour away, and continued after her marriage and subsequent move to Indiana. Whenever it came time to part, Ginny would break into heaving sobs. Sharon was part of Andy, his body and blood, and as long as mom had Sharon, she had a little bit of Andy right here on earth. It must have been hard to let go of her, considering what happened when she let go of Andy. I do not think it was possible for mom to separate her feelings for Sharon from her feelings for Andy. It was a triune bond, unspoken and, still, unbreakable.

Maurice, Maurine, Andre Vleghels and friends—Army Training Camp, Fort Leonard Wood, Missouri, 1941

2Lt. Andre Vleghels flanked by his gunners, S/Sgt. Roger Rice (L) and S/Sgt. Clay Young (R).

"Ginny and Andy"—Saturday night in the
Blue Room, New York City, March 25, 1944.

(L-R) Hut mates P. MacManus, A.J. Vleghels, W.H. Land, J. Madenfort, H.B. Clark, Whethersfield, England, 1944.

Andy and Ginny Vleghels and wedding party,
December 23, 1943

Ginny Egan's official engagement photo, the one that Andy always kept with him throughout his military service during The Second World War.

Newlyweds, Andy and Ginny, Army
Barracks, Florence, South Carolina.

My Sister's Father

Sharon, Ginny, Maurine on the steps of the Vleghels' home, Detroit, Michigan.

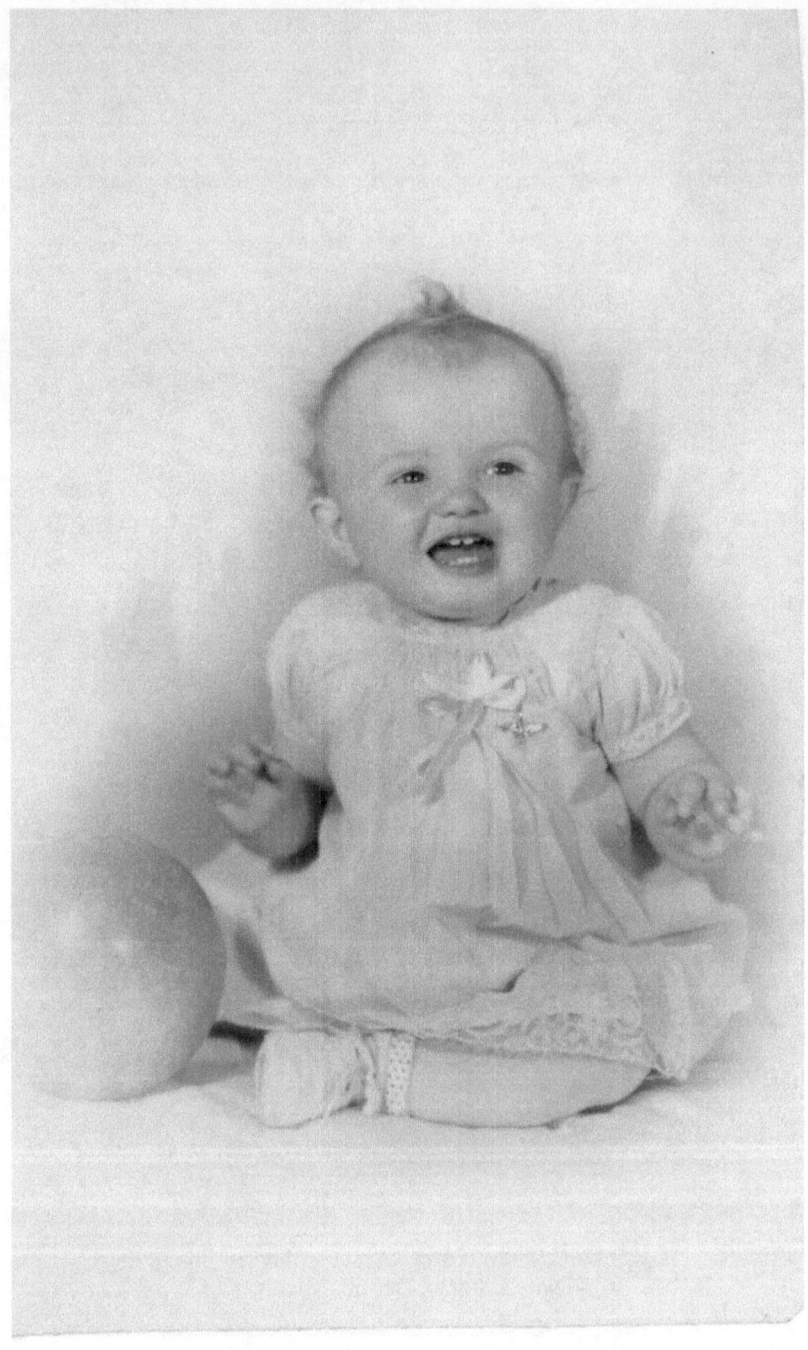

Sharon at six months old wearing Andy's flying pin over her heart.

PART II

Believe in what you feel inside,
And give your dreams the wings to fly.
You have everything you need,
If you just believe.

Trains move quickly to their journey's end.
Destinations are where we begin again.
Ships go sailing far across the sea.
Trust in starlight, to get where they need to be.

Believe
Josh Groban

My Sister's Father

To you from failing hands we throw
The torch; be yours to hold it high.
If ye break faith with us who die
We shall not sleep, though poppies grow
In Flanders fields.

In Flanders Fields
John McCrae

Chapter One
The Search

A confluence of events crystallized my determination to set out on my search. The week following my mother's death, my family and I went to see the newly-released film, *Saving Private Ryan*. While the discovery of Andy's missive at my mother's bedside left me wanting to know him, Spielberg's D-Day depiction of American soldiers clawing their way onto Omaha Beach under a relentless barrage of enemy fire, left me in awe of the sheer brutality of war. My reaction was visceral. It energized me. Like a rising tide, my passion swelled. Ambition seeped into my soul. It set me on a course to discover all that I could about the mystery man of long ago, determined to know him. Beyond that, I felt compelled to do something to honor Andy and Ginny and all that they had sacrificed, as hundreds of thousands of others had, on the cusp of adulthood and a life of possibilities.

When I reflect upon it, I had been preparing for this journey most of my life. My own life challenges tutored me in the importance of recognizing my feelings and dealing with them. With both of my parents gone, I felt free to pursue my dream—a dream that had only recently settled into my consciousness and, now, could finally be realized.

Although my mother had been tight-lipped about Andy, she had left behind a blueprint—all her memorabilia, carefully preserved. I needed to do a little digging, but the clues were there. For one who is drawn to jigsaws and intrigue, I found myself to be well-suited to my task. And whatever I was lacking, I could learn along the way.

At the start of 1999, I began in earnest with an e-mail to The American War Orphan's Network. I was looking for a contact person for the 416th, Andy's Bomb Group. They responded the same day with the name, Dolph Whitten, the veteran who was the impetus for the bomb group's newsletter and subsequent reunions. Dolph had been at it for thirty years.

When I contacted the Whitten residence, I was graciously greeted by Marie, Dolph's widow. Dolph had recently died. I could hear the grief in the timber of her voice. They had been happily married for fifty-nine years. Marie was cordial, and after patiently listening to my story, she said she would be happy to send a copy of the group's annual newsletter to me. In fact, Dolph's secretary was in the process of preparing it for mailing. She mentioned that there was a reunion coming up in May, to be held in North Carolina. Billy Brewer and his family would be hosting the event. She encouraged me to give Billy a call and that I would be most welcome to attend.

As promised, the newsletter arrived in early February. Basically, it was a running list, single-spaced, of more than a hundred and forty members of the 416th. Deceptively innocuous, the newsletter contained valuable information for me, because it included each veteran's address, phone number, squadron, and military assignment, followed by a brief message. The names filled more than six sheets. Thumbing through the pages, I highlighted the names of the pilots belonging to the 669th, Andy's squadron. It seemed the logical place to start.

When it came time to take the next step, I had to muster a little nerve as I punched in the appropriate numbers on my phone key pad. The uncertainty of what I might discover, or the disappointment if I came up empty, nagged at me. But I had to try. My first few calls were met by the familiar sound of message machines clicking on and the recording that followed. Frustrated, I set the list aside to begin anew the following day.

I decided to call Ed Renth back. He lived in Texas. It was the morning of February 5, 1999. This time, when the phone rang, a man answered.

"Is this is Ed Renth?"

"Yes."

"My name is Debby Smith," I began, "and I am calling because my mother's first husband was a pilot in your squadron in World War II. But he was killed in the war,"--familiar words that resonated in me from childhood days.

I found it to be unduly cumbersome to refer to Andy this way--my mother's first husband. It was the truth to be sure. Andy was not my father; he was Sharon's. Regardless, he was a man denied to me as well, my mother's lost love. His death affected us all, a death that was magnified by silence. I felt compelled to resurrect him, to become acquainted with him, to reclaim him. It seemed a pity that he walked among us, but we knew him not.

I heard a racket in the background that I could not identify, so I began to speaker louder.

"His name was Andy Vleghels. I wanted to know if you remember him."

There was an awkward pause and I was not sure that Ed could hear me very well, but I pressed on, hoping to jar his memory. I chose a fact that I thought would be unique to Andy.

"It was kind of ironic because he was shot down near his birthplace, Ghent, Belgium."

The voice responded, "We had a guy in our outfit from Belgium, but his name was Vleghels."

Somewhat exasperated, I said, "That's who I'm talking about. Andy Vleghels!"

"Oh, I thought you said Bleghels."

Then the tears came. Try as I might, I could not hold them back. All of a sudden the "story" of Andy Vleghels became real in a way that it had never been for me. His comrade on the other end of the line was telling me he was real. Like a fuzzy photograph, Ed's words abruptly brought the picture into focus and I was jolted by its clarity.

Ed moved to another room, away from the vacuuming, the noise now identified. Feeling quite embarrassed for blubbering over the phone to a perfect stranger, I apologized for my tears as I tried to explain the unexplainable.

"Did you know him very well?"

"No, the only reason I knew him at all was because one time his crew and mine went on R&R together."

"What was he like?" I continued.

"The only thing I can tell you is that he was a family man and I was a bachelor, so we didn't see much of each other on our pass."

Ed went on to say that the men who would know Andy best, other than his gunners, were his hut-mates. They were the ones who had day-to-day contact.

He had not been on Andy's final mission to Bergen op Zoom, but he had asked Andy to bring his footlocker across for him to their new base in France.

It was difficult, still, for Ed to hear me; said his wife had been trying to convince him to get a hearing aid. But before we hung up, I thanked him and told him that I would write, explaining things in more detail. I wasted no time in sending off a four-page letter to Ed Renth. Hoping a picture might jolt his recollection of his brief acquaintance with Andy, I enclosed a photo-copy of Andy and his crew. My search had officially begun.

My good fortune in contacting Ed proved to be a false start. Subsequent calls, and there were many, did not yield similar results. Over and over I was told by Andy's comrades that they did not remember an Andre Vleghels. No, they did not go on the mission to Bergen op Zoom. They were on their way to France.

The results of my phone survey should not have been surprising, really, since Andy was a replacement and had only served with the 416th for four months and one week. Furthermore, only thirty-six planes flew to Bergen op Zoom manned by thirty-six pilots and seventy-two gunners, a hundred and eight men. That was approximately one twelfth of the 416th.

Beyond this calculation, these vets were now approaching their eighties. They fought in a war a generation ago. Bottom line, it meant that I was searching for a comrade who not only flew Andy's final mission, but could recall details of it. Most of these men flew sixty-five missions. The chances that I could find even one who was still alive, and could recollect a single mission amongst all others, were slim to none.

The veterans I spoke with always said good-bye with the wish that they could help me somehow. I could hear their frustration. Often, I would deflect my disappointment by asking them questions about their experiences: "What was it like to fly an A-20? What was the usual altitude? How long were most of their missions? What was a milk run?"

Ed sent me a substantial packet of material along with a seven-page letter. In it, he described the day-to-day living conditions at their base in Wethersfield. He much preferred the tents of France over the huts of England, because the men always had plenty of fuel to keep warm. That also meant that they could "bathe" more frequently, a "sponge-bath" really--they heated water on their tent stoves and filled up their helmets. At Wethersfield, the men had to make an appointment to use one of six bath tubs located in a separate building if they liked warm water. Otherwise, they had to be content with a cold shower or bath in the ablutions hut.

Ed wrote about the orientation they received from the Brits when the 416th first arrived at their air base. Biscuits took on a whole new meaning. Each man was issued three cloth bags with string closures. They were instructed to fill them with straw and lay the "biscuits" across their cots to serve as mattresses. Toilet paper proved a puzzle. It came in two varieties, waxed and sand.

Ed made no attempt to elucidate. Despite these examples of British "ingenuity", it was Ed's perception that the American soldier influenced English culture more than the other way around.

Regarding Andy, Ed had this to say: "When I saw Andre's picture I immediately knew who I was looking at. Yes, we had gone to London on R&R with our gunners, together one time. Our squadron had leased an apartment about one block behind the Marble Arch Hotel near Hyde Park. I don't know whose idea that was, but it was cheaper than hotel rooms and we never had a problem finding a place to stay. ... As I told you, I certainly remember Andre—I didn't know him as Andy, but I recall him telling me about his family and that his parents and he came from Belgium to the U.S. We did do some sight-seeing in London together, but he was a family man and I was an unpredictable bachelor who was trying to experience everything before fate, or whatever, cut things short. So, we were not close friends, but I liked him and I know he was respected for his flying ability."

Ed also included parts of the actual Operation's Report for the 669th. Each of the four squadrons had its own account of every mission flown. The print of the micro-film copy was miniscule and tedious to read. SECRET was typed at the bottom of each page. The record documented Andy's crash-landing in France, as well as his final mission. The entry for September 16, 1944 states:

The last mission flown by the Group from its base in England was flown on the 16th. The target was the viaduct, railroad, and road over Bergen op Zoom in Holland. The attack was launched to strengthen Allied positions northwest of Antwerp, to eliminate a German avenue of escape, and to soften the area for the great airborne attack to follow on the next day. Capt. Huff and Capt. Morton led the two boxes. (A box was a formation of eighteen planes or three flights; six planes comprised each flight). *Capt. Huff's flight scored an excellent on a perfect bomb run despite intense, accurate, heavy flak fire at the target. Capt. Morton chose to hold his bombs when he was forced to alter his course to avoid a collision with another flight rather than release them too short a bomb run and miss the target. Lt. A.J. Vleghels' plane was hit on the bomb run and was thought to have gone down in the southeastern corner of the Oosterschelde Bay. One engine was burning badly. Two chutes were seen drifting toward land. His gunners were S/Sgt. Roger W. Rice and S/Sgt. Clay E. Young. Lt. H.B. Clark's plane was hit on the propeller dome causing oil to leak out. The pilot left the formation, feathered the prop, and continued on through flak, centered on his plane which was losing altitude on its single engine. When he neared Antwerp, he instructed his gunners to bail out. They did so successfully and returned to the base a day later. Lt. Clark, expecting the plane's one engine to fail soon, headed toward the beachhead. When he attempted to land, he discovered that his hydraulic system was out. He crash-landed the plane near Caen, escaping unscathed himself.*

Quite a harrowing mission, though fairly typical, I surmised, when the lead box encounters heavy flak—engines smoking, landing-gear failing, planes floundering, men parachuting. There was one notable difference for us, however. Our family member was one of the "survivors" floating down from the sky until his feet smacked the water's surface and the gaping jaws of the Oosterschelde swallowed him whole.

When I read this first-hand, confidential account of Andy's final minutes, I experienced the same mix of conflicting emotions as I had in my younger days. The initial exhilaration of learning something new was quickly deflated by the grim realization that Andy and Roger and Clay were all dead.

Within days of receiving Ed's correspondence, I was off to Indianapolis for a couple of days to visit my sister, Sharon, and her husband, Dick. Part of my plan was to make copies of Andy's letters, which were now, rightly, in Sharon's possession. But when I started to sort through the stacks of airmail, I soon realized that my goal was overambitious. It took hours just to arrange them, all one hundred and fifty, in sequential order. Itching to discover any new tidbit, I stopped frequently to read passages that whetted my appetite. There was not a one-pager among them. I think the shortest missive was three sheets long.

Sharon declined to help organize the letters. Instead, she busied herself in her bedroom, but told me to let her know when I found something of interest. I read aloud whenever I came upon a tasty morsel.

We laughed at Andy's adoring descriptions of our mother-- pure perfection, in his eyes. And it was touching to learn that he had taken an active role in deciding the name his offspring; Sharon Virginia, if it was a girl and Andre, as a middle name if it was a boy. How nice, I thought, for Sharon to know that.

I read through the evening hours and into early morning until my eyes ached and the faded blue cursive grew blurry. Reluctantly, I set war's testimony aside and retired for the night.

Sharon generously offered to let me take Andy's missives home with me so that I could copy them at my leisure. I zipped them into plastic bags for protection and secured them in a large fabric tote to carry on the plane. My cargo, irreplaceable, was far too precious to entrust to baggage. As I safeguarded my secret stash beneath the seat in front of me, I had to smile. Here I was, a middle-aged, principled, law-abiding woman, feeling a bit like a courier smuggling contra-band.

Upon my return home, whenever I could make time at the end of the day, I would slip into a cocoon of blankets and pillows, secure and comfortable, and begin to read Andy's prolific epistles to his sweetheart. They filled two shoeboxes.

I felt so lucky to finally have the chance to become acquainted with Andy, to learn first-hand how he wooed my mother and what it was like to go to war. Admittedly, it was a form of voyeurism, and I, its willing participant. But the content of the letters was neither incriminating nor explicit. It simply filled in the blank pages of my mother's life for me and allowed me to become acquainted with the man who had eluded me all of my life.

The early letters were fun—filled with Andy's Air Corps training stories. Like the morning sun illuminating a darkened room, Andy's persona gradually emerged from his correspondence, bringing to light the many facets of his character--a nice mix, I concluded, of integrity, stability, tenderness, perfectionism, sociability, intelligence, and wit. I think I would have enjoyed his company. But, later, when I read about their plans for the future, pregnant with promise, and their clandestine parting in New York City, crinkled balls of tissues piled up on my bed. I knew how the story ended.

Continuing down the newsletter list, I made a phone call to Bill Fields, a gunner with the 669th. He had a miraculous story to tell. The lone survivor of his crew on a mission to Frevent, he was captured by the Germans after he, quite literally, fell out of his disintegrating plane. As a POW for nine months, he marched hundreds of miles on very little food until liberation, mercifully, came.

Bill promised to send me a photo of Andy. Although he was fighting all sorts of ailments due to age that caused him to tire easily, he remained true to his word. I studied the snapshot. The door to the hut was swung open and I could see the number ten painted above it. The smallest detail took on importance. Andy stood, bare-chested, taller than the rest, his arms dangling, relaxed at his sides, sandwiched among four of his hut-mates. The lieutenant-pilots were lined up alongside their Quonset hut, posing for the lens of Lieutenant Scott Street. Street later told me that he took a number of pictures that day, focusing on some of the more popular lads of the 669th. Bill identified them as: Patrick MacManus, Andre Vleghels, Willard Land, Madenfort, and H.B. Clark. Besides Andy, LT Clark also became a casualty of war. Though he survived the flak on the mission to Bergen op Zoom, he piled up his A-26 at the end of an icy, haze-covered runway on January 2, 1945.

Judging by the shadows cast in the photo, the day was sunny; and the men were soaking it up. Their garb ranged from shirtless to undershirts to full uniform. Save for the outline of their ribs, one could barely discern the topless men from the white-shirted ones. Lily-white skin attested to the overcast skies of England. Madenfort, shirtless, was definitely more toned than Andy. I suppose, since Andy spent much of his leisure time pushing a pen rather than pumping iron, he did not have well-defined biceps to sport.

Bill jotted down a few facts about each veteran, except for Madenfort. MacManus died around 1997. He had forged a career in television and radio, announcing sports events in Biloxi, Mississippi. Land hailed from Texas, and made his living from crude. He owned a sprawling ranch not far from Lyndon Johnson. He was the only one of the five still living.

My measured success from my initial inquiries set me to ponder what more I might unearth if I continued to dig. I began to seriously consider attending the reunion. It seemed like an opportunity worth pursuing, and if I put it off, I was afraid that I might live to regret it. Besides, it might be fascinating to mingle with Andy's compatriots, the men who lived and worked alongside him. Even if I was unable to learn any new information about Andy or his final mission, it would be an honor to meet the men of the 416th. I decided to call Billy Brewer to learn more.

Billy, in his non-threatening, laid-back southern drawl coaxed me into attending the reunion. I did not want to intrude upon the kinship of comrades, but he assured me that I would be most welcome. In fact, he said, there was a couple planning to attend who were family of Roland Enman. They were on a similar mission as mine, looking for information about a brother, lost. I decided to head to Kinston, North Carolina.

Before I left, a sizable piece of the puzzle arrived at my door. I had learned from the American War Orphan's Network that I could request Andy's Individual Deceased Personnel File, a politically correct term for his mortuary record, from the U.S. Total Army Personnel Command located in Alexandria,

Virginia. Andy's Army Air Corps records no longer existed. They went up in smoke back in the seventies along with thousands of others when an unfortunate fire set them ablaze in the building where they were housed in St. Louis, Missouri. Consequently, I had to settle for his mortuary file. I was notified in early March that they had received my request and that I could expect delivery in approximately six weeks.

A month later, a thick manila envelope arrived at my door. When I noted the return address, my heart began to race. I was in the midst of preparing dinner, so I ran to the kitchen and ripped open the envelope. Feverishly, I flipped through the pages, manic with curiosity. Skipping the superfluous, I hunted for the meat of it. I was looking for new information. What would I learn about how Andy died or the condition of his body? The most recent data was at the front of the record.

I came upon the "Report of Investigation Area Search." Next to cause of death, it said, "plane crash." Whoa--real specific. I moved on. I read the typed-in responses to the questionnaire:

How did crash occur?—ENEMY FIRE; Anti-aircraft?--YES
Did the plane explode in the air?—NO; on the ground?—NO
Did the plane burn in the air?—NO; on the ground?--NO
What was the civilian opinion regarding destination of the plane?—ENGLAND
Had bombs been released prior to crash?—YES
Number of planes in formation prior to crash—SIX (6)
State precise time and date of plane crash—16 SEPT. 1944, 1600 HOURS, DAY
Were parachutes seen?—NO

Were the remains found near the wreckage?—NO—SEVEN (7) KILOMETERS NORTH NW OF CRASH
Was a casket used?—YES Type of casket—WOOD (CIVILIAN); How marked?—IDENTIFICATION TAG NAILED TO UPPER RIGHT HAND CORNER
Were personal effects found at the time of death?—YES Where?—ON BODY By whom?—J. de Graaf
Is it possible on surface investigation to obtain from civilian sources the condition of the remains?—UNRECOGNIZABLE How is the grave marked?—WOODEN CROSS

These were some of the grim particulars of the seven-page, fill-in-the-blank style report. I began to read the accompanying narrative. The type was very faint--only a skeletal outline of the letters was visible. The second paragraph began:

When the police came, they identified the body as Andre J. Vleghels. They found on the body a small picture of a woman...

The news stopped me cold and I began sobbing. The handwritten account that mom had safeguarded in her album did not mention the picture. I felt deeply moved and unbearably sad. My immediate curiosity satisfied, I put the file aside to be taken up after dinner when I had regained my composure.

Later, upon further scrutiny, I read four signed statements by most of the key participants in the recovery and burial of Lt. Andre J. Vleghels. Two of the affidavits, dated March 1, 1946, were co-signed by Jules E. Franklin, 2nd Lt., QMC (Infantry) Operations Officer.

J. de Graaf, acting police officer of Scherpenisse, testified:

My Sister's Father

This is to certify that I, J. de Graaf, residing at Ryhsstraatweg 423, Scherpenisse, saw on the 16th of September, 1944 at 1600 hours a four-motored bomber crash into the Oosterschelde. This plane was shot down by German anti-aircraft. There were six (6) planes in the formation prior to the crash. It was impossible to reach the scene of the crash, as it was in the sea entirely covered over with water.

On the 25 of September, 1944 I was called to the Strijenham Dyke by D. van't Hof, a water mill worker, who had found a body. ...The body was that of Andre J. Vleghels who I identified by the means of his identification tags, which were around his neck. ...I gave one (1) identification tag and these personal effects to the Civil Affairs, 330, in Tholen, Holland.

I then obtained a casket from B. Suurland, residing at Lage Markt 171, Scherpenisse, Holland. He also made a cross with the deceased man's name upon it; he copied the name from the identification tag I had retained. I then nailed the identification tag on the upper right-hand corner of the casket.

I buried the deceased at the Algemeens Begraafplaats te Scherpenisse on the 26 of September, 1944.

I believe this man was from the bomber which crashed on the 16 of September, 1944.

An A-20 Havoc has only two engines. But in the narrative summary, Pfc. Robert E. Lawson speaks to the inconsistency of the "four-motored bomber" that de Graaf identifies: "J. de Graaf is an old man, and in my viewpoint he could have been easily mistaken as to the number of motors on the plane."

The testimony given by D. van' t Hof, the water mill worker, and B. Suurland, the carpenter, corroborated de Graaf's account. D. van' t Hof specified that he discovered the body at 0800 hours. "He was lying half-submerged in water. I pulled him to dry land and immediately notified the police."

These new details brought life to Andy's story. The players were identified. A picture was beginning to emerge. No matter how gruesome the particulars, it was the truth I was after.

The final affidavit was signed by the Secretary of Scherpenisse. He stated, "I, A.L.G. van Doorn, in the month of December, 1944 personally took Andre J. Vleghels', A.S.N., one (1) identification tag and personal effects to the Civil Affairs in Tholen, Holland." Personal effects--the sterling rosary, the scapular medal; they made all the difference for Ginny Vleghels.

As we express our gratitude, we must never forget, that the highest appreciation is not to utter words but to live by them.

John Fitzgerald Kennedy

Chapter Two
The Reunion

The first leg of my flight to Kinston took me as far as Charlotte, North Carolina. When I arrived at the gate to catch my transfer, a smallish, turbo-prop plane, I began to study some of the more senior passengers. I assumed that some of the passengers must be headed to the reunion, since Kinston would not be the most frequented city on the map. I zeroed in on a few who looked the part--men in their seventies, dressed like gentlemen in their sport coats and dress pants, a hallmark of their generation. On the way up the tarmac, I mustered the nerve to approach them and ask if they might be members of the 416th. I met Lowell Geffinger and his wife, Ruth, along with Royal Everts and his companion. They were friendly and accepting and surprised to learn that someone in her fifties was attending a WW II reunion.

As the plane labored off the runway, I tried to imagine it as an A-20. Eyeballing it, my rough estimate was that the two might not be too disparate in size. I peered out at the prop through my

Plexiglas window, intent, as the engine began to drive it, the spinning blades became a blur. Like a film in reverse, the trees and buildings grew smaller as we ascended. I waited for the pilot to announce our altitude so that I could have some idea of what Andy would have seen at 12,000 feet. The land faded to patchwork.

Once we landed in Kinston, a representative of the Brewer family, namely Charlie, was there at the curb to shuttle us to our hotel. That was just the beginning of my first encounter with Southern hospitality. And it was most impressive. The reunion turned out to be one of the finest examples I have seen of what a family can accomplish when all of its members work together toward a single goal, which, in this case, was to transport, accommodate, entertain, and feed about two hundred people for four days--truly remarkable.

My camera became my constant companion in my attempt to document my felicitous meeting of Andy's comrades—an opportunity, I realized, that would not be possible for many more years. As I framed the vets in my view-finder, again and again, a twinge of regret crept into my consciousness, reminding me of the life treasures that Andy had missed. These men of the 416th, well into their seventies and beyond, had the good fortune to live long lives. They had proud tales to tell to their children and grandchildren and a spouse to grow old beside. But it was not my place to question fate and I believed that Andy was always present, in the mystical sense, through the years.

The next morning I had the thrill of meeting Ed Renth. I had been asking about him since my arrival, but no one had seen him. He was my first, and at this point, only connection to Andy's life in the military. As I approached the hotel dining room, a man seated at a table overlooking the lobby, stood up and waved. I had seen pictures of the younger version, so I was fairly confident that it was Ed. Someone must have prompted him, because he had no idea what I looked like, only that I was about thirty years younger than most of them, tall, and brunette.

Ed rather resembled Little Orphan Annie's savior, Daddy Warbucks. He stood about six feet and carried himself with a gentleman's reserve and a soldier's call to attention—standing tall, chest out. Delighted to finally meet, we opened our arms to receive each other. Ed graciously invited me to join him and Bill Kinney for breakfast, explaining to Bill by way of introduction why I had decided to attend the reunion. Following some preliminary questions to clarify my quest, Ed said that he did not understand why I was pursuing my search now, since my mother was deceased. Wouldn't it have made more sense to have done it earlier while she was living? I struggled to reduce a very complex, emotional issue into a couple of intelligible sentences. My stomach knotted up and my tears began. Clearly, Ed did not understand. My lame attempt to articulate my rationale had failed, miserably.

Ed had struck a sensitive chord in me that really went straight to the heart of the matter—given my mother's reticence to discuss her loss, I never felt that I was free to delve into Andy's history while she was alive. It simply was not an option in my mind. Intuitively, I knew that any effort on my part to ultimately feel better by resurrecting Andy, would, at the same time, inflict further pain on my mother. Most likely, rekindling old wounds would have triggered nightmares that she had attempted to quell. She had suffered enough mental and emotional torment.

And now, my pent up frustration and sorrow came crashing down on me with the question that Ed had posed. I could barely speak. The honest truth was that there was no clear-cut, rational answer that would suffice. Decades of concealment had obscured a reality that I was only beginning to unravel.

That afternoon, there was an excursion available to the Seymour Johnson Air Force Base in Goldsboro, about an hour's road trip. My itinerary stated that we could begin boarding the buses at 1:30 PM, scheduled to depart at 1:40 PM. I arrived at the designated area slightly after 1:30 and to my horror, saw the first of two buses pulling away from the curb. I began to run, shouting and waving my arms, in an attempt to "catch" the bus. Fortunately, my wailing proved effective. As I stepped onto the bus, breathless, we all had to laugh. I noticed an empty seat next to Ed, and with his permission, I plopped down, vowing to be early the next time. I should have anticipated that former military men would adhere to a precise time-table. Disciplines instilled by the military decades ago, remained.

When we arrived at Seymour Johnson, two young soldiers, one male and one female, dressed in camouflage, heartily greeted the aged warriors of the 416th. They even provided a handout comparing the appointments of the A-20G Havoc to their own F-15E Strike Eagle. The differences were stark. But the most staggering statistic laid claim that one F-15E could destroy a target deploying precision guided munitions equivalent to 108 B-17s dropping 648 bombs to achieve the same result!

Once inside the hanger, a representative group from the 335th Fighter Squadron welcomed their trailblazer counterparts and related some of their proud history. Patient and unhurried, the young men introduced themselves and graciously offered to answer any questions their guests might have. After responding to general questions, they dispersed to key positions and invited us to have a look around. No cocky attitudes were in evidence. The airmen of the nineties seemed humbled by the opportunity to host "Mace's Aces" of the forties.

Decades beyond their glory days, the men of the 416th gingerly ascended the hard stand to the cockpit of an F-15E Strike Eagle, eager to learn from Peterson, seated there, all the intricacies of the cutting-edge technology available to the modern pilot. I felt truly gratified to behold the genuine enthusiasm, keen interest, and mutual respect that the young airmen and the World War II fly boys demonstrated toward each other. The men of the 416th Bomb Group had helped to save the world over a half century before, and the men of the 4th Fighter Wing were standing guard, taking America into the twenty-first century.

As I panned the hanger looking for photo-ops, the dove in me could not help but dream that, one day, all this fire power would not be necessary. But the pragmatist in me doubted it.

Back at the hotel, one evening in the "hospitality room", a place to gather, fraternize, and share war stories, I pulled out some official papers that had been included in Andy's mortuary record. So far, my inquiries among the vets had turned up no one who knew Andy well; some remembered him in their ranks, but had been assigned to different squadrons. Willard Land, the only man still alive to have shared quarters with Andy, was not in attendance. No one had specific recall about the mission to Bergen op Zoom. In an attempt to lighten my disappointment, I decided to have some fun with Ed Renth and Bill Trip.

According to the documents in my possession, money had changed hands among Ed, Andy, and a fellow by the name of Jack Smith. Three days after Andy had been declared MIA, the office of Effects Quartermaster sent a memo to the C.O. of the 669th stating that Ed Renth and Jack Smith were debtors to Andre Vleghels and that they were required to send a check in the amount of sixty dollars and eighty dollars, respectively, to be credited to Lt. Vleghel's account. A Captain Weisman, Adjutant, writing for the C.O., responds in kind to the Effects Quartermaster explaining that a mistake has been made and that Lt. Vleghels is, in fact, the debtor not the creditor. He further states that "since travelers checks received for the account of Lt. Vleghels are not negotiable by this office, the sum of $9.74 is all that is available with which to pay indebtedness of aforesaid officer. However, should Lts. Renth and Smith desire to represent their claims, the enclosed invoices should be amended to include the following signed statements:

I certify that this invoice is true and correct, that no part thereof is a gambling debt, and that payment thereof has never been received."

Ed and Jack signed said declarations, each requiring a formal witness, Bill Trip being one, Leo Poundstone, the other. Ed and Bill identified their signatures as genuine, but had no memory of signing the papers.

In keeping with the policy of the Effects Quartermaster, if Lt. Vleghels was not reported to be a prisoner of war after six months had expired, action would be taken on a pro rata basis to the extent of the available funds. Unbelievably and like clockwork, in a memo dated 16 March, 1945, precisely six months after Andy was reported MIA, the Effects Quartermaster issued checks to 1Lt. Jack F. Smith and 1Lt. Edward J. Renth in the amount of $4.87. There were nine pieces of official papers documenting the dispersal of nine dollars and seventy-four cents! I did not know whether to be outraged or impressed. Either way, it seemed the epitome of Army minutia. The only thing left to do was laugh. And laugh we did, Ed and Bill and me.

Lowell Geffinger, one of the men I had met at the airport, approached me, anxious for me to witness something that he had discovered. He led me over to a table where other vets were poring over their scrapbooks and the Operations History of the 670th Squadron. Lowell pointed to the passage he wanted me to read. It told of the mission to Bergen op Zoom. "On this mission, Lt. Hall sighted a barge which was throwing flak at our planes, and, diving down to strafe it, left it in flames. He received slight damage to his own plane."

Lowell wanted me to know that Lt. Hall's actions had avenged the deaths of Andy and Clay and Roger. I nodded politely and thanked Lowell for showing me the account. While I recognized the valor of Lt. Hall, in my heart, it brought me no degree of satisfaction to know that other families would be mourning the loss of their husbands, sons, and fathers. They were in a "kill or be killed" situation. It was war.

Saturday evening brought the banquet. We all dressed for the occasion and gathered for food and fellowship. Ed informed me that these soirees had grown subdued with the years. In times past, there had been dancing and a lot more drinking.

During dessert, some of the men stood at their places and recalled some memorable event from their tour of duty. They had, after all, been a part of the single most significant event of the twentieth century. Farmers and factory workers and West Point grads fought side-by-side on foreign soil for a just cause. They never doubted that victory would be theirs. But it really was not until they made the pilgrimage to their reunions, like tributaries to a river, that they discovered story after harrowing story that existed outside the limited radius of their bomb sites. In some cases, crewmembers were reunited, never knowing if the other had survived the war.

Once the testimonials worked their way around the room, one of the veterans walked up to the podium to formally address us. Following his service in the military, Robert Bower finished up his college degree. After graduating from Princeton Seminary, he became a minister. Not even his comrades could have guessed at the fire that burned within the man. He was tall and handsome, quiet and unassuming in his demeanor--the kind of person who does not impose himself upon others, though little escapes his attention.

Looking far younger than his years, he faced us now and began in a brogue. He held us, spellbound, as his story rolled off his tongue.

His squadron was heading back from a mission, relaxed, the setting sun before them, so brilliant that its penetrating light forced them to squint. Bower was flying in tight formation, his right wing tucked in behind Captain Rooney's left wing.

Inexplicably, and with no apparent sign of impending danger, Bower heard a command in his earphones, "Bower, move out!"

He did as he was ordered. One of their own had invaded the space that Bower had just vacated, overtaking them.

"Realizing what was happening, I immediately pulled back my throttles, pulled up the nose, and seemed to be suspended in space as I watched the tragedy evolve." An A-26 struck the tip of Rooney's left wing. Rooney looked to his left. His eyes met Bower's, thinking it was he who had hit him. Bower clearly saw Rooney's smile of relief when he realized that Bower had not caused the collision.

Encroaching further and further into Rooney's airspace, the misguided aircraft listed to the right. Rooney's left prop ripped through the rear bomb-bay of the invading plane piloted by Lt. Anderson.

To avoid a larger catastrophe, the box was ordered to remain in formation. Bower ignored the directive, desperately trying to save Rooney. With a diving left turn he followed him down. He hit his mike, pleading with Rooney to jump. "Rooney, for God's sake, jump, jump, go, go!" But he did not. Perhaps he recognized the futility.

Bower wondered if Rooney's canopy had jammed or if Captain Slaughter, a passenger and guest from a ground outfit, had panicked.

Kirk, Rooney's bombardier-navigator, decided to bail at 5,000 feet. It was later reported that Rooney was heard to have said, "Go ahead. Good luck!" Bower saw Kirk's chute blossom and thought, "What a lovely sight!"

But the doomed ships fell off to the right, hopelessly entangled as they whirled into a flat spin to the ground. A massive explosion incinerated the crews.

Rooney had just completed his sixty-fifth mission, his ticket home to America and his fiancé. His tent mates, awaiting his return, had prepared a celebratory send-off for him.

It has been theorized that Anderson had been blinded by the sun's rays bouncing off of Rooney's ship. Six American flyers perished on a beautiful Sunday afternoon, 21 March, 1945, seven weeks before the war in Europe ended.

Bower's heartfelt tale represented so many other tales of the Second World War that begged to ask the question—why did I survive and they did not? Tell me, Lord.

In the 2003 edition of the 416th newsletter, Robert Bower shared:

Still vertical and every day is thanksgiving! I thank God I survived and yet, feel heartache for those who didn't! So, I make the most of every day—once for me and once for those who were not so fortunate.

*Remember that all through history
the way of truth and love has always won.
There have been tyrants and murderers
and for a time they seem invincible
but in the end, they always fall—think of it—ALWAYS.*

Mahatma Gandhi

Chapter Three
For Posterity

At the reunion I learned that Frank Basford, a former gunner from the 669th squadron, had single-handedly spearheaded a campaign to procure memorial plaques to honor their comrades both living and dead who doggedly fought to help save the world from tyranny. There were seven in all, one at Wethersfield in England, home to their air base, and six others scattered throughout the states. The nearest location to me was in Dayton, Ohio on the grounds of the Wright Patterson Air Force Museum, the largest and most complete air museums in the nation. But, for me, the créme de la créme was a very rare A-20 Havoc, and according to veteran, Wayne Downing, one of a handful left in the world. Dayton is a four-hour drive from our home. Without hesitation, my husband, Jeff, graciously agreed to make a day-trip of it over the Memorial Day Weekend.

With the experience of the reunion still settling into my bones, even the eighty degree weather and Jeff's sporty convertible could not temper my melancholy the morning we set out for the museum. Within the span of a few months, I had been inundated with mounds of emotionally-charged information. That information, coupled with the reading of Andy's letters and Ginny's letters to Evie, left me reeling. I could not contain it all, and so, it spilled over in a stream of tears. Not even the wind against my face could dry them. I simply could not stop crying.

I believe it was the onset of true grief for me. Until now, I never had a sense of who Andy was, and therefore, I could only sympathize with my mother's loss; now, I could empathize. I understood all along that if I risked knowing Andy, losing him would follow.

Jeff and I found Basford's plaque pretty quickly. Cast in bronze, the 416th was recognized as being the first A-20 combat group in the ETO and the first A-26 combat group in the world. It was only one of many memorials in the mosaic, some grand in scale, others not. But all served as a reminder to those who followed, that the veterans of the Second World War were part of a defining moment in world history. Their unfaltering dedication preserved our freedoms and dispelled the evil of tyranny.

As we stepped into the portico of the museum, dazzling streams of natural light blinded us and flooded the space pouring in from the glass ceiling overhead. A bronze of Icarus, its centerpiece, bathed in the light, stood atop a bolder striking a valiant pose with his right winged-arm thrust toward the heavens. The sheer brilliance of the sight wrestled me from my stupor.

I had a vague recollection that Icarus was the mythical fellow who flew too close to the sun, but I was not entirely sure why he was chosen as a centerpiece for the museum. Certainly, men drafted into war are typically young and possess an invincible quality. Was it meant to be a cautionary tale in opposition to war? I wondered.

Later I learned that according to Greek mythology, Icarus was the son of Daedalus, inventor of the labyrinth. Daedalus, however, lost favor with King Minos and the two were imprisoned within the walls of the labyrinth. Being a clever architect and sculptor, Daedalus fashioned wings of wax and feathers for himself and his son to make their escape. But he cautioned his son not to fly too close to the sun or the wax would melt and he would perish. Icarus, exalted by the thrill of flight, chose to ignore his father's warning and fell into the sea where he drowned. "Icarus' body was carried ashore by the current to an island without a name." I was struck by the parallels to Andy's demise.

We headed straight-away for the aircraft of World War II. With quickened steps we raced passed plane after plane, hunting down the A-20. It was Jeff who hit pay-dirt. The A-20 was parked directly below a majestic American flag.

I had seen pictures of the A-20 Havoc. Andy had sent Ginny a large color fold-out of his ship. Seeing it now, did not alter my initial impression that it was rather homely. But I felt sure that it must have been a thing of beauty to ground troops and occupied nations when formations of them decimated bridges, rail yards, and fuel depots.

I took a few minutes to soak it all in. It felt good to see a clone of Andy's aircraft. Inspecting it up close, touching it, brought me closer to Andy and the war that took him. Moving around the plane, I snapped off a series of shots from every conceivable angle, wondering how Andy and Roger and Clay attempted their frantic escape from their disintegrating plane. Roger and Clay would have had to fall through a hatch in the belly of the plane directly below the turret. Andy's extrication would have required him to pull a red handle to release the cockpit canopy, stand on his seat, step onto the wing, slide toward the tail to avoid the propellers, and pull his ripcord, all the while dodging falling debris as their ship plummeted to the sea. It seemed impossible to execute.

I would have loved to have been able to climb into the cockpit, settle in behind the controls, and vicariously "stand in Andy's shoes", but that was not possible. I tried to envision Andy piloting his A-20 as he gained speed down the runway at Wethersfield and lift off to join up with his flight and head into combat.

[Beneath the left side of the windshield was painted the name, Lt. Jones Dobrowski, below the name, three long rows of bombs, and below the bombs, "Little Joe"; guess Dobrowski did not have a sweetheart. The tip of the nose was adorned with skull and crossbones. Two .50 caliber guns protruded from the ocular orbits of the skull and two from the top ends of the crossbones. The ship bore the markings of the 389th Bombardment Squadron which operated in the Southwest Pacific during the war. The serial number, 43-21475, appeared under the side window to the pilot's left and the last six digits were repeated in larger numbers on the tail fin. The 43 referred to the year the ship rolled off the assembly line.]

According to the accompanying placard, the A-20G was the first series assembled with a solid nose. The Army built 2,850 of them at a cost of $74,131 each. It stood 17 feet, 7 inches high and 48 feet long, which meant that seven A-20s, end to end, could span a football field.

Continuing on, we came face to face with the enemy--an 88mm flak gun. Flak was an American term used to describe the shells that the Nazis launched at enemy air forces. Its origin comes from the German phrase, Flieger Abwehr-Kanone (Flier Defense Cannon). I was surprised to learn that the Flak 36 88mm Multipurpose Gun had a vertical range of 34,073 feet, well beyond the altitudes of not only the A-20 at 12,00 feet, but also the heavy bombers like the B-17 and the B-24 which cruised around 22,000 feet.

Oversized display boards documented the course of the war. It was mind-boggling, really, that the designers of the museum were able to succinctly consolidate the volumes of information available to them into comparatively few paragraphs. On the subject of flak, they had this to say: "By the late spring of 1944, German flak claimed more AAF bombers than were claimed by Luftwaffe fighters. Throughout the summer of 1944, flak was to be the major worry of daylight bomber crews."

Intermingled among the copy of the displays were dramatic photographs of the Allied Air Force at work. I was thrilled to find an aerial view of an A-20 bombing raid of railroad yards over Louganis, Belgium. The casual observer never heard of an A-20. More often than not, the more prolific Flying Fortresses (B-17), Liberators (B-24) or the Spitfires and Mustangs who escorted them grabbed all the attention.

As it turned out, the 416th entered the European Theater at a crucial time. Once again, I read a placard: "Bombing operations in March 1944 marked another turning point in the air war over Europe, for the Luftwaffe lost the advantage it had maintained so successfully since the fall of 1943. It still retained the capability for striking back at AAF bomber formations in force, but was able to do so only periodically because of a shortage of skilled fighter pilots. Although German production of fighters increased rapidly through September 1944, their effectiveness was reduced as the quality of their pilots decreased and as reserves of aviation fuel depleted." I remembered Maurine's words—Andy had told his family that he wanted to join the Air Corps because America needed pilots. I felt comforted knowing that people like Andy had truly made a difference.

In war, there are no unwounded soldiers.

Jose' Narosky

Chapter Four
Digging Deeper

My correspondence with some of the veterans of the 416th expanded after the reunion. I had met the acquaintance of a few from Andy's squadron who never seemed to tire of satiating my ever-growing curiosity. Every time I opened a letter from a vet, it was like Christmas morning. What surprises awaited me? What new piece of the puzzle would be filled in? Good or bad, just knowing was so much better than not knowing. These letters were such a gift, a slice of history, our family's as well as our nation's.

Patiently, and complete with diagrams, Wayne Downing detailed how missions were flown and clarified the nuances of the initial point, the target, and the aiming point. He meticulously described the location of another of Basford's plaques, this one located in the shadow of the Tomb of the Unknowns in Arlington National Cemetery under a cherry tree. Toward the waning days of summer in 1999, I visited the spot with my son, Scott, and daughter-in-law, Denise.

[The cherry tree conjured up thoughts of President George Washington and the legend of him chopping down a cherry tree.

I had prepared a presentation for my elementary school class that had impressed mom. She would ask me to perform George's tale for company, dollar bill in hand. A man of integrity, he told the truth regardless of the consequences. Truth and honor were the objects of my search.]

I eventually caught up with Willard Land by phone, the only living pilot from Andy's hut. A few words into our conversation convinced me that Land was a character. I detected a swagger in his Texan drawl as he peppered our repartee with, "Well let me tell ya what it was like, darlin'." Most importantly, he remembered Andy. However, I sensed his resistance to discuss him. He said he never got too close to replacements. It seemed that, too often, they didn't make it. I was exasperated. I finally track down the only man, still alive, who shared a hut with Andy, and this is the response I get?

I maintained my composure and broached the subject of the mission to Bergen op Zoom. The mission stood out in Land's memory because his ship was crippled by flak that day. He was flying in the #4 position of the lead flight of the first box with the lead plane above him, Vleghels on his left wing and Clark on his right. As he told it, they approached the target from the north along the lower Rhine (in truth, the Scheldt Estuary), the proverbial "back door", in an attempt to evade known anti-aircraft batteries. Allied intelligence had assured them that they would encounter little resistance. (The German Army was on its heels at the moment and making their escape back to the Fatherland. The port at Antwerp, Belgium had recently been overrun by Allied Forces and taken intact. It was a vital port to defend and secure.) They were dead wrong. Land recalled that as they reached their initial point, the beginning of the bomb run, "all hell broke loose." According to his log, the Germans were throwing up 105mm shells, not the usual 88mm munitions. "The shock of the large shells exploding"—he remembered that. His flight successfully deployed their bombs, but as they turned to join up with the other flights in their box and return to their home base, several planes were hit, including Land's.

Land noticed Andy's plane drifting, losing altitude. It was smoking badly. It rotated into a flat spin when he lost sight of it. Land was forced to divert his attention to his most immediate problem—leaking hydraulic fluid. He quickly set his landing gear while he still had some hydraulic capability. His plane was further disabled by damage sustained to the right fuel pump and two cylinders of his right engine. Land's crippled plane, flying at a reduced speed, fell out of formation, but made it back to Wethersfield. He used his emergency air brakes upon landing and brought his plane down to one side of the landing strip in direct violation of orders. The tower didn't want a pile-up on the runway. In October, Land completed his required sixty-five missions and headed home.

I cajoled and prodded him to divulge some personal details about Andy. He had none to offer. I tried again, months later, in a letter to Land, pleading for more. He made a few personal comments in a letter that followed. Andy was "very pleasant and likable," he noted, and a "good pilot as shown by his August 26th mission. We made local English pubs together—enjoyed their mild and bitters draught beer... Andy enjoyed good tales and stories. I furnished many Texan tales. We all played Black Jack at the Officer's Club, twenty-five cents a game. ... I believe he was one of our Bicycle Club (only transportation to pubs and cinema etc.)"

Land's letter gave me some degree of satisfaction, but still, I felt restless. His account only served to whet my appetite. I wanted more. Understandably, he had little to tell me about Andy's ship going down, because the safety of his crew depended upon his full attention, quick thinking, and immediate action as they faced their own set of dire circumstances. Surely there were others that remembered Andy or his final mission. Frustrated by scant feedback, I decided to draft a questionnaire. I enlisted the help of veteran Bob Basnett, a former bombardier navigator, who had volunteered to assemble and distribute the annual newsletter for the 416th. It would be mailed out in December. Bob agreed to enclose a copy of my questionnaire.

I was hopeful that I might make contact with some vets who had not made it to the reunion in North Carolina. Maybe one of my questions would jog their memory. While I was at it, I decided to include some questions of a general nature. I was curious about the mindset of the 416th airman, putting his life on the line. Besides questions relating to Andre Vleghels and his last two missions, I posed the following: "Were you drafted into military service or did you enlist? How did you deal with losses of your comrades? What was the best thing about your war experience? What was the worst thing about your war experience? Were you a POW? Did you expect the Allied forces to be victorious? Why or why not? How did you maintain mental toughness? How were your families supportive? Did this make a difference?"

In the meantime, I found a website for the Bomber Command Association in the Netherlands. I e-mailed an inquiry to them requesting information about Andy, his crew, and their last mission. The documentation Ger and Christel Boogmans sent back, via snail mail, was a compilation of reports from three separate sources provided by a two Dutch researchers and substantiated by records from three Dutch communities.

The first section was a U.S. Air Force Casualty Report identifying the date, 16 September 1944; the aircraft, A-20G 43-21767; the time, 1815 h.; the base, Wethersfield; the Bomb Group, 416 BG; the Squadron, 669BS; the target, road and railway junctions south of Bergen op Zoom. The details of loss: "In MACR [Missing Air Crew Report] 9103 is reported that this aircraft was observed going down in flames in the SE corner of the Oosterschelde Bay; two chutes were drifting towards the mainland near Bergen op Zoom, Holland. The aircraft crashed into the water about ¼ mile off shore."

Then "according to German reports, (17) provided by Mr. W. de Meester Alphen a/d Rijn, Holland, three 88 mm Flak guns located SE of the northern sluice of the Beveland Canal fired at three sections of 6 aircraft [first box], flying from NW to SE at 1806/1807 h. The sections kept their course in spite of the Flak, one aircraft was seen flaming at the tail end, peeled off immediately to the left and went down vertically. Crash site was 1 km SE of the sluice." They list the dead and their place of interment. Following that, there were notes:

a. Lt. Vleghels washed up on 25.09.44 along the sea-dike of the Community Scherpenisse, that had been evacuated at the time. He was buried in the General Cemetery of Scherpenisse. A report of the Community to the Dutch Red Cross in the Hague states that he landed after bail-out in the waters of the Oosterschelde and drowned.

b. Sgt. Rice may have been recovered from the wreckage when Canadian troops liberated that area at the end of October 1944. He was buried in the General Cemetery at Goes between British servicemen who were killed on the 3rd and 8th November 1944. After the war reinterred in Lorraine.

c. Sgt. Young was buried in the Military Cemetery at Bergen op Zoom, Grave 99. Reinterred in Ardennes.

The precise nature of the reports impressed me. Considering that I had no information that contradicted their findings regarding Andy, I had to assume that the assessment of Roger and Clay was fairly accurate. The "Dead List A/Z" was the third source cited. The details were collected by J.A. Hey of Holland. What a find! I was pleased to learn the German perspective, congruent with the U.S. report, and the new details that went along with it. Both reported that Andy's plane was on fire which directly contradicted Andy's mortuary record and the testimony of de Graaf of Scherpenisse.

In a subsequent e-mail, I asked the Boogmans if there was any record of the wreckage ever being recovered, because I had learned that the Dutch, in their continual pursuit of draining and reclaiming land (polders), had found many corpses of planes after the war. They responded, informing me that, in the 1950s, the wreckage was recovered by gypsies and sold for scrap. I felt quite relieved that Andy had come to a better end than his plane.

I learned rather quickly throughout my investigation that, like a detective, it is vital to gather as much documentation and testimony as possible and discern where there is agreement and where there are inconsistencies. Then, each viable piece of the puzzle must be laid out and evaluated for accuracy. And lastly, in the final analysis, it must be decided what most likely happened based upon all of the data available.

I had to remind myself, over and over again, not to assume, as Mom had, that just because the plane crashed a quarter mile from the mainland, did not mean that the two chutes carrying Andy and Clay landed near the shore. Also, depending upon when the two men extricated themselves from their disintegrating plane, would determine where they landed, which theoretically, could have been miles apart. The three were each buried in a different city. Scherpenisse is located directly across the Oosterschelde from the site of the Flak guns at Wemeldinga. Andy's body was carried by the current to Strijenham between Scherpenisse and Poortvliet where he eventually washed ashore. Clay, on the other hand, the turret gunner, was found closer to the target site at Rilland-Bath according to his mortuary record. Bergen op Zoom, the location of his interment, is eight miles north of Rilland-Bath.

I made many failed attempts to locate the families of Roger and Clay. Roger's hometown was Somerville near Boston, Massachusetts, but he was single and bore a common surname. I focused on his lone brother because, unlike Roger's three sisters, his name would remain intact. (Mom had saved a family photograph from Roger's mother, Mildred.) I spoke with numerous Walter Rice's, but, ultimately, came up empty.

Clay left a widow, but no children. Again, he had a common surname. With that door closed behind me, I decided to try to open another by writing to Washington, D.C., once again. Under the Freedom of Information Act, I was able to procure the mortuary records for S/Sgt. Roger W. Rice and S/Sgt. Clay E. Young. They were revealing.

As with Andy's record, I had to bear in mind that the information documented in the Individual Deceased Personnel File (IDPF) was not necessarily entirely accurate. However, being able to compare and contrast the three files gave me a better chance of aligning the pieces of the puzzle to create as exact and as complete a picture as possible.

According to Roger's file, his body was not found in the wreckage of his plane. Elaborating further, it states, "The Germans picked the remains up presumably from the seashore near Goes and buried them in the civilian cemetery of Goes leaving no information as to the nationality of the deceased or how and where he had been killed." He was buried between two Brits who were killed on November 3rd and 8th. Roger's re-interment form reports the condition of his remains: "Head crushed—all major bones fractured with parts missing." His hands were missing. Remnants of a fleece-lined jacket and a summer flying suit were present.

In Roger's "report of death" document from the Adjutant General's Office of the War Department, 26 January 1945, it states that Roger's missing in action status was terminated on 18 January 45, when "evidence considered sufficient to establish the fact of death was received by the Secretary of War from a commander in the European area." (I now knew why the Rice family was the first to receive a Killed in Action telegram.) It is no stretch to assume that this commander was Canadian and helped oversee Roger's burial at Goes in early November of 1944. It appears that Roger was in the water for a month and a half. When unearthed, it was discovered that his remains had not been placed in a coffin; his dog tag was buried with him; a cross marked his grave. Considering the condition of his remains, I have deduced that Roger slammed into the sea without benefit of an open chute. It would explain why only two chutes were seen and why all his bones were broken. Eyewitnesses later reported that the plane was burning at the tail end where Roger would have been positioned. It is very likely that he had no chance for escape, but rather, fell out of a burning, disintegrating plane. This scenario would also be congruent with the location of Roger's grave. Goes is just west of the northern sluice of the Beveland Canal, where the anti-aircraft guns were positioned, and the crash site was a mere kilometer south east of the sluice and a quarter mile from shore. Roger's body was never far from the crash site.

On April 17, 1946, Roger's remains were reinterred in Bergen op Zoom in a British military cemetery, an apparent mistake due to his first burial between two Brits. Ultimately, S/Sgt. Roger W. Rice was sent to Lorraine, the site of The United States Military Cemetery outside St. Avold, France where he was reinterred on October 31, 1946.

Mrs. L.N. Huismans, a Dutch citizen, provided witness to the U.S. Army during their post-war investigation in an ongoing effort to locate the remains of deceased American soldiers, in this case, S/Sgt. Clay E. Young. She testifies:

"On Saturday, 16 September 1944 at about 6 to 7 o'clock in the evening, about four groups of an ample eighteen planes came across. Among the second group of planes, one plane was hit. The plane crashed burning into the Schelde River. I suppose that the plane crashed between Rilland-Bath and Tholen. Nobody in this town saw parachutes. The concerned plane was a two-motor plane. I do not know anything about the crew of the plane."

Captured German records stated that Clay Young died in Rilland-Bath, Holland, the target area of the Bergen op Zoom mission, just eight miles down the road and south of Bergen op Zoom. Furnishing a wooden casket, the German Military buried Clay on September 30, 1944, in their POW cemetery at Bergen op Zoom, grave #99.

In a letter to Mrs. Fannie Young, Clay's mother, dated 5 June 1947, the Adjutant General of the Army informs her that "Sergeant Young remained in a missing status until an official report was received from the German Government through the International Red Cross that he was killed in action on 16 September 1944. No additional details were given." Elaborating further, he states: ... "several volumes of captured German records have been translated" confirming Clay's interment at Bergen op Zoom. Despite these reports, Clay's remains had not yet been found.

It was not until December 16, 1947 that they were finally located. Apparently, inaccurate records at the Bergen op Zoom Town Hall had caused confusion and subsequent delay. According to their record, J. Ball of the Royal Irish Fuseliers, killed 3 June 45 during liberation of the area by the British, had received the same grave designation as Clay. The U.S. Army's identification technician checked with the English Military Cemetery and learned that J. Ball had been moved to their cemetery in Bergen op Zoom.

When Clay was disinterred, it was annotated that "decomposition was only partial and bones were only partially disarticulated. Dressed in AAF fleece-lined flying jacket. Shoes were removed before burial by the German Military, OD socks. Identification Tag was found on a chain around his neck."

Finally, on January 15, 1948, the United States Military laid S/Sgt. Clay E. Young to rest at the Ardennes Cemetery near Neuville-en-Condroz, Belgium.

Both Roger and Clay were originally buried among other war dead. Andy was not. He was in a churchyard of Dutch citizens. I have deduced that this was the reason the Vleghels' family was the last of the three to receive notice that Andy was declared Killed in Action.

It should be noted that these initial burials of U.S. servicemen on foreign soil were temporary. The next of kin were contacted and their permission sought for permanent disposition of their loved ones. It was not until 1947 that the Secretary of the Army, in concert with the American Battle Monuments Commission, selected fourteen sites in foreign countries and designated them as permanent burial sites. Extensive beautification of the cemeteries necessitated yet another reburial and new grave designation upon the completion of construction. It appears that the task of providing the American war dead an honorable burial was a monumental undertaking.

Come December, completed questionnaires began to find their way to my mailbox. Twenty-six veterans responded in all. Each time I opened a mailing from a vet, I did so filled with the expectation and the hope that some new bit of information about Andy was waiting to be discovered. But, for the most part, my pointed questions about Andy and his missions yielded similar results as my phone survey had—no, they were sorry, but they did not know Andy, or they were merely acquainted with him. No, they did not take part in the mission to Bergen op Zoom. They were on their way to France.

I did happen upon one coincidence. Joseph Connor, a pilot for the 669th, had flown both missions on August 26th. (Andy had flown the afternoon mission to Rouen, France.) He had logged the serial numbers of the planes he flew that day. I cross-checked his numbers against the numbers documented on Andy's Missing Air Crew Report (MACR). Ironically, the plane Joseph flew on the morning mission, targeting a fuel dump in Compiegne, France, was the very same ship that Andy had piloted on his final mission to Bergen op Zoom, Holland. The numbers matched.

It was nearly Christmas when John Geyer's questionnaire arrived. A gunner with 668th, he was unsure if the mission he flew one late afternoon in September of 1944 was the same I cited. But he did recall that it was the "day before we dropped the 82nd and 101st Airborne Divisions at Arnhem (called later *The Bridge Too Far* in a book). Voilá! That was it! I wasted no time sending off an e-mail to John, December 23, 1999.

John and I exchanged several e-mails over the next six months. I posed many detailed questions, but I learned the most pertinent information with his first e-mail. Despite having participated in forty-nine missions, John had a clear memory of the raid over Bergen op Zoom. When his crew saw Andy's plane faltering, they "pulled out of formation and followed it part way down. He was burning." From his position as a tunnel gunner, on his belly in the dorsal end of his ship, he had a bird's eye view of Andy's plane, floundering. He caught sight of only one chute, but that did not mean that there was not a second.

It confounds me, but John's testimony gave me reassurance. As an eyewitness, he could account for the last minutes of Andy's life. Knowing that John's crew tagged Andy's ship as it spiraled downward touched me to the quick. One of "their own" was in imminent danger of being lost. Maybe it was the airmen's way of saying, "We're with you, buddy."

About a month later, I received a call from Vincent Fair. It turned out that Vincent was Willard (Pappy) Land's tunnel gunner. At the time he completed his questionnaire, he could not recall any details about the mission to Bergen op Zoom, though he knew he flew that day. But now he seemed anxious to tell me all he remembered. He reiterated what Willard and John had stated—that Andy's ship took a direct hit as they circled to return to England. He said the plane blew up before it hit the water. Like John, Vincent was a tail gunner. From his vantage point, looking out the rear openings of the plane to the back and to the side, he observed Andy's plane falling behind and losing altitude. Red-orange flames consumed the plane. He saw a chute.

These eye-witness accounts stood in contradiction to the testimony de Graaf had given to the U.S. investigators. I think it is possible the plane de Graaf saw hit the water was not Andy's ship. He had claimed that it had four engines and that there was no explosion. Clearly, the testimony of fellow airmen, closer to the action, would trump de Graaf's account.

Vincent had some disturbing news to share. He said there was a rumor that circulated among the enlisted men (the gunners) that the Germans went out in boats and machine-gunned airmen as they attempted to parachute to safety. I had not really considered this possibility. It became another loose end that I would have to address.

Vincent explained that it would be easiest for the tunnel gunner to escape a disabled ship, because he was already lying on the floor of the plane in close proximity to the escape hatch. It was simply a matter of falling through it. The turret gunner, on the other hand, would have to unbuckle his belt and crawl down from his turret to reach the same escape hatch.

Vincent Fair was only eighteen when he was drafted into the service. After the 416th moved their base of operations to France, he met Jeanne who later became his wife. She was the best thing that happened to him during the war.

The 2000 reunion was held in Hot Spring, Arkansas. That's where I met Claude Brown (Brownie) and his disarming wife, Dottie. Some of the vets rounded him up and brought him over to my table during our riverboat excursion. They were sure he was on the mission to Bergen op Zoom. Brownie had made a career of the Air Force and survived three wars. Dottie was a good sport all those years raising their boys and "just kept praying her rosary." She had lost her sight, but her sense of humor remained firmly intact. She was a cut-up; Brownie was her straight man. They were George and Gracie Allen, reincarnated. It was a joy to be in their company.

Following the reunion, Brownie wrote, explaining that he was not part of the 416th at that juncture of the war, but his group took part in the raid on Bergen op Zoom from Great Dunmow, another airbase not far from Wethersfield. He piloted an A-26. (In October, Brownie helped instruct 416th pilots when they transitioned to the A-26, a slightly larger and faster version of the A-20 that only required a single gunner.) He did not keep a log at that time, but was pretty clear about the mission, because it was the first time he encountered heavy flak. "As we approached Holland our landfall was an estuary which we were to fly up to avoid heavy flak, but the Germans outfoxed us by mounting their anti-aircraft batteries on barges in the waterway (the Oosterschelde)… Our plane was shot up good—over 100 flak holes and the right engine shot out. I hung on and managed to hobble home on one engine. Years later, I was cited and awarded the Distinguished Flying Cross for that mission."

*The search for the truth
is more precious than its possession.*

Albert Einstein

Chapter Five
An Ocean Away

As my search pressed on, I began to contemplate whether or not it would be possible to find those responsible for Andy's recovery and burial. Considering that fifty-five years had elapsed since Andy perished, realistically, I only expected to locate their descendants, if I was successful in locating anyone at all. I decided to give Dick Schmitt a call. Dick had worked for an American company with an office in Brussels where he had lived for four years. I was hoping he might have an educated opinion as to the soundness of my idea. Was I completely daft, or did I stand a chance of finding what I was looking for? To my delight, Dick thought the idea had merit for two reasons: typically, he said, Europeans do not stray too far from their roots and they keep meticulous records. Dick's affirmation was the encouragement I needed to add yet another dimension to my ever-expanding investigation.

I began by calling the local government for Scherpenisse on the island of Tholen in the province of Zeeland, which I learned fell under the jurisdiction at the seat of government located in St. Maartens-Dijk. The Netherlands is six hours ahead of Eastern Standard Time, so I needed to call early in my day and before the end of their business day. Knowing that the person on the other end would naturally be speaking Dutch, I felt awkward and self-conscious, but brimming with excitement and anticipation. I prayed they would understand my English. The phone was ringing! A pleasant-sounding woman spoke words unintelligible to me. Humbly, I apologized that I could not understand Dutch and that I was calling from America. Without skipping a beat, she slipped into English. I was so impressed, and very thankful. Explaining the reason for my call, I asked if she could give me an address to which I could forward my questions. She happily obliged. Another door had opened.

Each small success raised my resolve to take the next step. I would only stop when all attempts to locate the families had been exhausted. My passion was growing. I needed to feed the fire. On December 22, 1999 I sent off a detailed letter of inquiry to Mr. Quist, the burgomeester (mayor) of Tholen requesting copies of any records that may pertain to the recovery of LT Andre J. Vleghels, U.S.A.A.F. I enumerated all I knew of Andy's last mission and named the four individuals who gave statements to Investigator Pfc Robert E. Lawson, the Army representative of the United States government in 1946. These were the individuals I was trying to locate. Eager to personify the faceless soldier they had buried, I went on to elucidate, "Andre and my mother were very devoted to each other, writing every day. Though my mother eventually remarried, she was deeply wounded; her wounds lasted a lifetime." I assumed that confidentiality laws would preclude the government from supplying addresses. I fully expected that he would forward my letter to the citizens or families of the citizens identified.

A month later I received a mailing from the gemeente (government) in Tholen. For me, it was proof that my endeavor held promise. Mr. Zuurdeeg, the keeper of the records, stated, in part, "The whole island Tholen is in February 1944 inundated by the Germans. The greatest part of the inhabitants were evacuated. Only the residents of the little town Tholen should stay. In the villages like Scherpenisse were living about ten persons like a policeman and some workers of the polder with their family." He included maps of the Oosterschelde and shoreline of the Dutch lowlands--situation 1940, 1988, the third, more recent marking locations. A ledger documented the cost of Andy's recovery (f 20) as well as his coffin (f 35). The customary recording was an indication that Andy's burial was official, not impromptu. Everything came at a price. Burying a soldier was not exempt.

Most importantly, came the information I was seeking—the last known addresses for B. Suurland (born in 1904) and D. van't Hof (born in 1899). Actually, both addresses were for the locales as the U.S. Army record had indicated. However, the street number had changed for Suurland; I was told the home of the watermill worker, van't Hof, had been demolished, leaving the building of the watermill which was being used as a summer house. Although not stated, it seemed plausible that the two men were deceased. The Suurland number was for builder, J. Suurland, probably the son of Bernardus, Mr. Zuurdeeg theorized.

I wasted no time in composing a letter to the Suurland family. I began, "You may be wondering why someone from the United

Sates is writing to you. Well you see, fifty-five years ago, World War II made Holland part of my family's history. ..." I sketched the basic facts of Andy's last mission as I knew them, and thanked them for "their kindness performed so many years ago." I asked if they would be willing to speak with van't Hof and van Doorn family members, comparing their oral histories, so I might learn as much as possible about Andy's death, recovery, and burial. Further, I wanted to impress upon them that this was not a frivolous lark on my part, so I added, "I am very dedicated to my task, and I plan to visit your town and the place where André's body was found and the churchyard where he was first buried. Perhaps I will be able to accomplish this next year."

At the last moment, I debated whether or not to include my e-mail address. Would they have a home computer? I was not sure. It made me realize how ignorant I was about contemporary life in the Netherlands. I added my e-mail address.

I calculated that it should take about a week for the Suurland family to receive my letter and another week, minimum, for me to receive a response. But the following Saturday morning, a week after I sent my "message in a bottle", I flicked on my computer to check incoming e-mail. A return address grabbed my attention—jsuurland. I was incredulous. I burst into tears and then worked furiously to wipe them away in my effort to read their message. It was brief and to the point.

With this E-Mail we want to let you know that your letter has arrived. We were surprised and we can tell you that there is information available. We hope that we can be at your service. But first we want to collect this information and then we will send it to you..."

My world brightened. I printed off the message and ran to share it with Jeff. I spent some time, unabashedly, wallowing in my euphoria. I needed to savor the moment; it felt so good. I had made contact with the past and the contact held promise. The thread that bound us together was still intact. Gratitude filled me. I wanted to thank Jan as soon as possible. Better yet, now I had the convenience of an e-mail link, so our correspondence could be far more efficient. Determined to "follow my star", the next day I typed out a confirmation. I divulged more details about my mother's sequestered survival of Andy's death. I explained my motives for my search: "I'm delving into all of this history now, because I want to know who Andy was and how he died. Without this knowledge, it leaves me feeling like he didn't matter. I want to make him real, not just a story my mother once told me."

On Tuesday, February 8th, I followed up again to give them the serial numbers for Andy, Clay, and Roger. It was the surest and most efficient means to identify them. I had neglected to tell them that J. de Graaf, the policeman who was called by D. van't Hof upon discovering Andy's body, had also given a statement. I also mailed a letter to the van't Hof family. Even though Jan informed me that the van't Hof family no longer occupied the summerhouse in Poortvliet, I decided to write to the Schelphoekseweg address anyway. Making contact with the Suurlands bolstered my faith. It gave me confidence that my letter would find its way to the van 't Hof family, one way or another--their towns were small, their communities, close-knit.

Februrary 9, 2000: I heard back from the Suurlands. The son of Bernardus Suurland, Jan was sixty-six years old, a husband

and a father of four daughters. He was eleven at the time of André's burial. He remembered André's body being found and buried next to the church. Dies van 't Hof had died, but Jan spoke to his daughter. She did not remember much. "The summerhouse on Poortvliet is occupied bij other people... So far I haven't been able to talk to somebody who know the stat of his body, however my father told us that he was complete but harmed from the water. (This statement was in response to one of my questions; had Andy been shot?) My father does not live anymore, but he did not told us much about this. My mother is 92 years old and she has a picture of his casket with flowers on them that we as her children put on this casket from André. If you would be interested in this picture, we could sent it to you."

What good fortune, I thought. Jan's mother, an eyewitness, an adult in 1944, was still living. News that the Suurlands actually had a picture of Andy's casket staggered me. First, that they had photographed it, and second, that they had the film to photograph it. I had read numerous times about the scarcity of film in Andy's letters, so the idea that film was even available, surprised me. (Later, I realized that rationing in support of the war effort by free nations had created shortages. Holland was an occupied nation.) Knowing that the children placed flowers on Andy's coffin gave me great solace. It showed sensitivity, solidarity, and all the kindness of a family. An actual picture of Andy's casket--of course, I wanted it!

On the Thursday evening of February 24th, I received an e-mail from Dies Oosdijk. He wanted me to know that the family had received my letter with the "cooperation of several people". He explained that he was grandson and namesake to Dingenus (Dies) van 't Hof. He gave the dates of his grandparent's births and deaths. I calculated that Dies van't Hof lived to be eighty-four in 1982, while his wife, Jans, died at ninety-one in 1993 (van 't Hof would have been forty-six when he discovered Andy's body). Together, they had a son and two daughters. Tragically, the boy drowned at age three. The younger daughter, Jo, was Dies' mother and the only surviving family member. Dies addresses some of my questions:

About your question if my grandfather did ever speak about André (we did not know his name) I can tell you that we heard about a pilot that he had found during the war. He did not speak much about it. According to our information my grandfather has not seen the "accident". But it was as good as certain that André drowned. At that time the Oosterschelde was openly connected with the North Sea. It was not easy to swim in the Oosterschelde because every 12 hours the water went up and down. I don't know the English word for this. (In Dutch we call this high and low water, free translated). I hope you are a little satisfied with this e-mail.

I had no word from Dies again until March 24th when he sent an e-mail apologizing for the delay of information and photographs that he promised. His mother had just had surgery and was in intensive care. He thanked me for the photographs I had sent of Andy and Ginny and Andy's crew. Dies followed up with another e-mail on April 29th, alerting me that he sent out his mailing to me. In addition to any specifics about Andy, I was curious about the daily lives of the van' t Hof family during the German occupation.

March 15, 2000: The photograph and map, promised by the Suurlands arrived. It was a moment of truth waiting to be unleashed. I relished it and abhorred it at the same time. The simple wooden casket lay on a bier in tall grass. I could see the dog tag nailed in the upper right-hand corner just as the mortuary record had described it. But the large beautiful blossoms that adorned the coffin lifted my spirit. The contrast was as glaring as it was mind-numbing. Quite succinctly, the photograph captured the evil that took Andre's life and the goodness that honored it. I asked Maurine and Sharon if they wanted a copy. I did not want to be insensitive or make any rash assumptions. I sent them each a copy. Maurine e-mailed me that she could only stand to look at the photograph, a few seconds at a time.

May 11, 2000: Dies' long letter arrives. He shares the following:

My grandfather (Dies, pronounced as the sound of the word these) lived and worked with his family outside the villages at the sea dike between Poortvliet and Scherpenisse... The profession of Dies was (I will try to explain to you in English) engine driver of the sluice and controlled the water level at the inside of the dike; at first with engines on steam, later on, mechanistic. As the land of the island of Tholen is below sea level, he had to make sure that when the level of the water at the inside of the dike became too high, he had to pump it out of the land into the Oosterschelde. You probably know that the Dutch always had trouble with the water!

As Dies was engine driver of the sluice, he was forced by the Germans to open the doors of the sluice so the water from the Oosterschelde flooded the land. At that time the people who did not live in the villages, like farmers and the family of Dies, only could transport themselves by selfmade "boats"--most of the time only wooden boxes made of some planks... With that kind of boat Dies and Mr. de Graaf transported André along the inside of the dike to Scherpenisse

At the time the Germans occupied Holland they also sent troops to the island of Tholen. The German soldiers who came there, and probably saw the sea for the first time, thought that the land at the other side of the Oosterschelde was England, so I have been told often. But the land they saw was another island of Zeeland!

As Dies lived at the dike there was at the inside of the dike normally some kind of lakes to collect the water from the land and so he already had that kind of boat. He usually fished with that as extra income, and during the war when there was just a little food for everyone, he could trade the fish for other food products or something else they need. From the German soldiers the village people became a kind of tickets for food...

Sometimes it happened that the water level which flooded the land was going down. Then the Germans went to Dies because they thought that he had secretly opened the sluice to let the water go into the Oosterschelde. They did not understand that the water level went down by itself. They got angry at him and they forced him to open the sluice at high tide so the water from the Oosterschelde flooded the land again. You understand that Dies and the German soldiers were no friends, although not all the German soldiers were bad.

My Sister's Father

The reason that the Germans flooded the land was that they wanted to make sure that it would not be easy for their enemy to capture them. They also sabotaged the bridge which connected the island of Tholen with the mainland of Bergen op Zoom (Brabant).

My mother told me that during the war a lot of planes flew over their house at the dike. She said that several planes went down in the Oosterschelde...

As he did every day, Dies walked on the dike to see everything was alright. At the 25th of September, 1944 he did his round and saw the body of André drifted on the stones of the dike. I do not know exactly what he did when he discovered the body, but my mother told me as he came home that night he was in a kind of shock. My grandmother asked what was happened and he told the story, but my mother does not know all the details.

We think as Dies discovered the body he made a decision not to tell the Germans what he had found, so he went to get help, probably after he camouflaged the body. As they had no phone, he went to Poortvliet or Scherpenisse to get help. He probably knew the policeman, J. de Graaf and we think that he decided not to tell the Germans so they could give Andre a proper burial. They took the body of Andre and placed it in the boat of Dies which I mentioned earlier and covered him. Now it was an advantage that the land was flooded. As Dies was often fishing, it must have looked like he was fishing as he went with his boat along the inside of the dike to Scherpenisse. We are almost certain that this is the story how Dies and J. de Graaf brought over the body to the Suurland family. If the Germans had found out what Dies, J. de Graaf and the Suurland family had done, they would have been punished very hard. What they did was illegal. Let's not think about what could have happened if the Germans had discovered it. I expect it must have been very scary to all the families.

I hope you understand the story because sometimes it is hard to write in English

Dies wanted to know if Vleghels was Dutch or Belgian, "because his name sounds Dutch." This was understandable. Veghel is a city in the Netherlands, and briefly, during the mid-nineteenth century, Holland and Belgium shared the same ruler. He also wanted to know more about my family. He explained that his parents had met after the war at a "liberation party". Once Holland fell to Germany in 1940, his father, Piet, became part of the "Arbeiteinsatz", a system whereby all young males, eighteen or older, were forced to labor in work camps in Germany. Piet and Jo had two sons and two daughters, Dies being the youngest. As it turned out, Dies and his wife, Niekie, had the same gender combination with their four children—daughters, Inge and Iris, were the eldest succeeded by two sons, Pieter-Niek and Dirk-Jan. They ranged in age from six to eleven.

I shared information with Maurine and Sharon as I received it. Maurine wrote an e-mail to Dies to express her gratitude. In part, she wrote:

Andre was my big brother; it was just the two of us. He was shot down when I was in high school, and the year that passed with his being listed as "missing in action" was very hard on my parents and of course, his wife, who was expecting their child, Sharon. I think both my parents died of a broken heart. André was tall and handsome with a quick smile and a very concerned and loving nature. My own son is named after him.

I wondered just how accurate Dies' suppositions were regarding the details of Andy's burial, since his grandfather's statement to the U.S. Army after the war never indicated that he took such action. I wrote to Jan in hopes of clarifying just how Andre's body was transferred and by whom. Basically, Jan's account mirrored J. de Graaf's testimony. Bernardus Suurland was informed about André and made a casket. Then Suurland, along with several other men, rowed to the dike where they lifted André's body into the casket and returned to Scherpenisse and the cemetery. They were not sure from where van't Hof called the police, because, in those days, the only phone service was at the local post office and they were closed since the time of the occupation. All these details held importance for me. I wanted to know, as precisely as I could discover, what happened and how it happened. I wanted to understand the circumstances that the villagers faced when André's body was discovered. It seems a very natural curiosity to me for a family member, who is unable to be there for their loved one at the time of their death and burial, to learn all they can from those who were present. Mom had received much of the basic information through the International Tracing Bureau and the Red Cross in the Netherlands. I wanted more. I wanted to see it in writing. I wanted to touch it and be touched. And so, my pursuit pressed on, unabated.

May 18-21, 2000: I attended my second Bomb Group Reunion held in Hot Springs, Arkansas. I felt more at ease this time, since I had met several of the vets and their wives before, and maintained correspondence with several of them. They were always cordial and considerate of me.

May 25, 2000: I decided to request more information from Mr. Zuurdeeg's office. Primarily, I wanted to know if there were any other official records available. My hope was to clear up some of the conflicting reports I had from Jan and Dies. I realized they were doing their best, but their information was rooted in oral tradition and compensated by conjecture.

September 18, 2000: Before long, the Keeper of the Records, sent me more official papers that documented Andy's burial. However, they were all in Dutch, of course. But I remembered reading an article in *The Star*, the newsletter for the American War Orphans Network. They ran a story about a Dutch-American, Nico van Vliet, who gave a gift to a war orphan. (Her father's name appeared on the Wall of Remembrance at Margraaten, the Netherlands, the location of an American Military Cemetery, so Nico put together a collage for her.) I recalled that it gave the name of his town. I was able to trace Nico with a phone call to Information. Although I felt forward about calling him, I decided that a man as generous as him probably would not mind. My instincts held true. I told him of my dilemma and he agreed to translate the records for me.

Naturally, I wanted to hear a bit about his life and what his experience of the war was in Holland. He was in high school then. His family hid a Jewish girlfriend of his sister's, until they no longer could. She was eventually discovered by the Germans. In 1943, their circumstances became more dangerous and their family of five made the decision to split up. They took off in different directions and camped out for a few months, though it was strictly forbidden. When they felt it was safe, they returned to their home in Utrecht. Curfews were imposed and school was outlawed. During the winter of 1944 there was no food; they subsisted on tulip bulbs. Despite their hardships, Nico testified, "It was not as bad as others might think because of the close bond that was formed among family members." He said the Dutch had "incredible admiration" for the Allied soldiers and that they would help them however they could, without question.

Seventy-three now, Nico explained that he had a career in television and radio. He had traveled back and forth to America over the past thirty years. At one point, he was neighbors with Cornelius Ryan, renowned American author of *The Longest Day* and *A Bridge Too Far*. (Ironically, *A Bridge Too Far*, is the story of Operation Market-Garden, the offensive that launched in Holland the day after Andy's final mission.)

About a month later, Nico's translation arrived along with a note to let me know that he took special care in his translation to maintain the "bureaucratic flavor".

His translation revealed a new character in André's recovery--Jan Wondergem, sergeant-major of the Military Police. In the report that follows, Wondergem documents the chronology of events, the day Andre's body washed up.

Royal Military Police
Section: Tholen
Nr: 274
Post: Scherpenisse

Reporting the discovery of a dead body.

Monday September 25, 1900 and forty four at approximately 9:00 A.M. it was reported to me, Jan Wondergem, sergeant-major of the Military Police, honorary constable in Scherpenisse, member of above-mentioned Section, that a dead body had been washed ashore on the sea dike along the Oosterschelde in Scherpenisse.

I made my way to the site and found the remains of an English pilot in a state of decomposition and according to the identity tag, bearing the name of
ANDRE . J VLEGHELS Nr. 0-750488. T.42- 3 B. T. 44.

I remained on the site and thereupon informed the acting Mayor of Scherpenisse on Tholen and the Section Commander of the Military Police on Tholen.

Approximately at 3:00 P.M., the Section Commander of the Military Police in Tholen and Jan de Graaf, the gravedigger in the town of Scherpenisse arrived. The latter informed me as instructed by the acting Mayor of Scherpenisse, that the remains were to be buried in the General Cemetery in Scherpenisse.

J. de Graaf removed in our presence the name tag, five silver and eight bronze coins, a whistle, a nail file, a handkerchief, a key and a rosary from the dead body.

On September 26, 1944, in my presence, the dead body was laid in a coffin and buried in the General Cemetery at Scherpenisse on Tholen.

The coins that were found on the body, together with the other objects were handed over to the acting Mayor of the town of Scherpenisse on Tholen.

On the basis of the above I drafted this report whilst under oath of office and delivered it to my Section Commander in order that it be sent to the Honourable Mayor of the town of Scherpenisse on Tholen.

Scherpenisse, September 28, 1944

Endorsed by the Section Commander of the Military Police in Tholen

The report references the "acting" Mayor of Scherpenisse. The lower country, soon to be liberated by Canadian forces in October, fell under the jurisdiction of the Reich on September 26, 1944. And the Reich made an exception when it came to the local governments in the Netherlands. Rather than subjugate the Dutch following an Axis victory, Hitler had plans to annex them, deciding that they were part of the Arian race and therefore worthy. In an attempt to placate them, he allowed local and regional governments to be headed by Dutch leaders, though substitutions were made at the time of occupation-- hence the apposition, acting mayor, was assigned.

Two years later, the Mayor and alderman of Scherpenisse submits a statement of expenses for Andre's recovery and burial. He was seeking reimbursement of five and fifty guilders (f. 55) from The Hague.

Subject:

Costs transfer and burial Allied Flyer

STATEMENT OF EXPENSES

to the account of the Ministery of War in The Hague.

Due to expenses by the municipality of Scherpenisse for the transfer and burial of the body of an Allied Pilot As will appear from the herewith submitted evidence this town is owed the amount of:

FIVE AND FIFTY GUILDERS

Mayor and aldermen of Scherpenisse declare this statement of Expenses well-founded and valid to the amount of:

FIVE AND FIFTY GUILDERS
Scherpenisse, October 8, 1946
Mayor and aldermen above-mentioned
Mayor
Secretary

On January 24, 1946, an inquiry initiated by the Information Bureau of the Dutch Red Cross in The Hague, was the first of a string of correspondence that ensued between their office and the Bueregmeister of Scherpenisse requesting documentation that they had, indeed, transferred and buried LT. Andre J. Vleghels and were, therefore, due a reimbursement in the amount of FIVE

AND FIFTY GUILDERS. It took eight months to resolve the issue. Just as Nico had assessed in a note to me, the hard numbers testified to the bureaucracy of government. But the action of the Scherpenisse brethren, who cut flowers from their gardens and adorned Andre's bier, was lost in translation.

*Between people or nations,
there is no greater symbol of love,
no finer declaration of hope,
than the sincere expression of gratitude.*

Andrew Jackson

Chapter Six
In Our Stead

Benita gave me precise directions to our meeting point in Vlissingen, the Netherlands. I called her from our hotel room in Bruges the evening before our scheduled rendezvous. It was thrilling to hear her voice for the first time. She had some unexpected news to share. Andy's story was causing quite a stir, locally. She was interviewed by a radio station, while her father, Jan, had been interviewed by a provincial television station. They filmed him walking along the sea dike where Andy's body had been recovered. There were plans to cover the presentation of our plaque to Bueregmeister Nuis as well. It was a wonderful surprise.

We were instructed to arrive for the 10 AM ferry from Breskens, Belgium. I should position our vehicle in the right lane and follow the sign to England, exiting to my far right. They would be waiting at the nearest corner on the left. No, there were no geographical markers, just an open space where truckers stop to rest. I told Benita to look for our navy Ford Focus and our American flag. Benita, her boyfriend, Ko, her parents, Jan and Paulien, and Dies Oosdijk would be waiting for us. She promised that we would not be able to miss them. They would be holding a big banner.

Taking every precaution to arrive at our destination on time, Sharon and I started out early morning. We checked with the hotel desk clerk to confirm our route to Breskens, and allowed extra time in case of confusion or delays. I was nervous. I did not want to miss our connection or keep our hosts waiting. And then there was the fear of getting horribly lost, stranded, with no clue as to where we were and how to correct our mistake. GPS was non-existent in 2001. Driving through Europe was proving to be stressful and tedious. Fighting the lethargy of jet-lag, attempting to meander our car through a maze of narrow one-way city streets whose signs were posted on buildings, securing a parking space, tugging our too-heavy suitcases over cobblestones for blocks, exchanging currency, poring over maps every night, and now, we had the added stress of finding an intersection at a specific time in a foreign country. God be with us! I was beginning to feel like a pilot on a mission and I was beginning to swear like one too. Granted, I did not have to dodge flak, only bicycles.

But the rewards were magical, so far. Andy had a cousin, Bob Mere and wife, Karine, who lived in Ghent. We met up with them at a rest stop along E-40. They were most gracious hosts and treated us to a twelve-hour tour. As we strolled the streets of Ghent, surrounded by century-old buildings, it was as if I had boarded a time machine and been transported to another place in another century. The shift played tricks with my mind. My life in the States seemed far-removed. I felt like a character lifted from the pages of a nineteenth century novel. It left me awestruck.

Next we soaked up the beauty of Bruges seated in a boat traversing her pristine canals, utterly entertained by our flamboyant guide. Andy flew at least one of his missions over Bruges. If he could see her now! The weather was perfect—mild and sunny. Everywhere we looked was like a picture postcard, the clouds painted upon the azure sky. We investigated quaint shops and viewed priceless works of art. The clip-clop of horse-drawn carriages was ever-present as visitors toured the city. Shopkeepers splashed water over their walkways, scrubbing the stones with push brooms, sweeping the overflow into the gutter. We imbibed on leisurely lunches at tables lining the streets, covered in fine, colorful linens. The sampling of sumptuous Belgian chocolate quickly became our afternoon ritual. It was my maiden voyage to Europe and it was magnificent!

On our way to Breskens, the magic continued in spite of the trials of negotiating traffic and construction. Frantically, we searched out the signs that would point the way. There was little time to deliberate. Construction barrels squeezed the traffic. We turned right. I felt tentative. My internal compass was proving to be unreliable. Suddenly, we found ourselves on a lovely country road. However, I could see the highway off in the distance to my left, so I felt reasonably assured that we were headed in the right direction. It appeared that I had turned too soon, but for the moment I did not care. I slipped, helplessly, into a complete state of euphoria. Splendor surrounded us. Everything was enveloped in a golden hue. Majestic columns of

My Sister's Father

deciduous trees, newly-awakened, flanked the road. Sunlight danced on their leaves and flickered between their branches. It felt as if we were most surely on the road to heaven.

Once my ecstasy subsided, my anxiety returned with our race against time. Another snafu presented itself; the very large bank in Bruges had refused to exchange our traveler's checks for Dutch currency. At the time, I considered confronting the teller to let him know that his customer's father not only defended his freedoms in 1944, he was native-born. But my frustration never left my lips. It meant that we would have to make a stop near the ferry to make the exchange for our fare. Fortunately, we made it to the crossing with only minutes to spare. What a relief.

The skies had surreptitiously turned gray and foreboding. Clouds hung heavy with humidity. Any moment, we would make the same three-mile crossing as the Fifteenth Army had under the command of Nazi General Von Zangen, beginning September 6, 1944. Our location was not far from the site of Andy's final mission. My spirit tugged at my conscience to get out of the car and trudge to the ferry's lookout. But the cars were jammed in like sardines. It left little room to maneuver. To exit the car, I would have to hurdle the stick shift, constricted by my long, slender skirt and escape on the passenger side. After our tenuous trip, my flesh balked. I could not marshal the fortitude necessary to fight the driving wind and drizzle. Reluctantly, Sharon followed suit. We rested for the twenty-minute crossing, shoring up our strength for the next challenge—locating our Dutch friends at Vlissingen.

The fine mist continued, unabated. As we cleared the exit ramp, we spotted our friends almost immediately--our friends we had yet to meet. We could see a car with its trunk open and several people gathered around it. A semi was parked behind them. We saw no sign of a banner. Nevertheless, I cranked down my window, furiously waving my flag, and began honking my horn. Hands waved in response. Elation!

Here we were, three families separated by an ocean and decades, connected by one American pilot, making acquaintances. My anticipation rivaled an out-of-body experience, and yet, there was the awkwardness of unfamiliarity. Benita explained that they had only just arrived themselves as we greeted each other for the first time. She and Ko were having a disagreement about whether or not to hold up their sign. They had painted, "Welkom Debby and Sharon", onto a white bedsheet. It must have taken them hours and lots of patience. The greeting was sandwiched between an American flag and a Dutch flag, dated 4-5 May 2001, and signed, Benita and Ko, Jan and Paulien, Dies and Niekie. Benita did not want the rain to spoil it. Ko thought it was more important to hold it up. The banner remained in the trunk. We looked to Benita to introduce her parents, since we did not speak Dutch and they did not speak English. English was not part of the Dutch curriculum when Jan and Paulien were educated. For their children, however, it was required.

Sharon and I made the rounds giving and receiving the traditional European greeting—left cheek, right cheek, left cheek as we kissed the air. Dies squeezed into the back seat of our car next to the overflow of luggage. Jan volunteered to lead the way to a restaurant for some coffee and conversation. Some customs are universal.

An inherent organizer, Benita took charge and served as our unofficial translator. I felt weary for her as she patiently related her parents' questions, our responses, and vice versa. Ko and Dies could speak for themselves. Benita, Jan, and Dies had met months before to prepare for our visit and work out an itinerary. We would only be there for two nights with much activity to pack in.

Right from the start, I sensed Paulien's motherly compassion for Sharon. She maintained a protective closeness, and her expression was one of sympathy. Feelings, the common denominator, trumped the spoken word.

We were due shortly at city hall in Sint Maartens-Dijk where Perry Bakx, their PR man, wished to meet with us. He and others wanted to visually inspect the plaque so they could prepare it for mounting in time for the ceremony that afternoon. A wall inside the tower of the Dutch Reformed Church had been designated. A smattering of villagers had laid Andy to rest nearly fifty-seven years before in the shadow of the church. I was pleased with their choice. It made sense. For decades to come, churchgoers would be reminded of their kindness and our gratitude. In this little corner of the Netherlands, insignificant to most, would remain a lasting testament of good will between families and nations.

As we entered, Ko quickly disappeared into a large room off to the left. Standing tall behind a lectern, he teased, "Oh look, Benita, today we can marry!" Civil marriages were performed here.

Benita grew a bit stern and retorted, "Oh no, no, not today, but perhaps one day."

Ko went a few more rounds before he acquiesced, and the seven of us moved on. Mr. Bakx, tall and gracious, extended a warm handshake. There was little time before the ceremony would begin in a few hours, at three o'clock in the afternoon.

Mr. Zuurdeeg, the keeper of the records, joined us. I was especially excited to meet him and to thank him personally for his support. The records, maps, and addresses disseminated by his office were pivotal to finding the families and bringing us to this momentous day in our family's history. Of average height, his white hair brushed back, Mr. Zuurdeeg maintained a quiet reserve. I think my exuberance might have scared him a little.

Everyone was anxious to inspect the plaque. I apologized for its English words, explaining that I did not want to make a mistake in Dutch, cast in bronze. With good humor, all seemed to appreciate my dilemma. Mr. Bakx followed with his own story. When they evaluated the walls of the church tower in preparation for the ceremony, it was agreed that they "did not look too good," so they went to the trouble of applying a fresh coat of paint. Time was short and it proved to be a tall order, quite literally. Sharon and I were surprised and touched by their considerate attention to detail.

Intent on the plaque, they seemed impressed that it came complete with mounting screws, and after some consternation, it was decided that it would be best to install the plaque at a later date. They just did not have sufficient time to install it properly now.

We decided to ignore the fine drizzle that persisted and stepped out into the courtyard for some picture-taking. I could not let this moment pass, without a photo to document it. Ko, big and strong, held onto the plaque, sheltering it from the raindrops beneath his leather jacket. My dream was beginning to unfold.

Jan and Paulien invited us back to their home for some refreshment and to meet Granny, Jan's mother and the most senior member of the Suurland clan. It was thrilling to have an opportunity to meet her. After all, Marie Suurland was the only family member still living who was an adult at the time of Andy's death. She superseded my expectations simply because she was still alive and lucid. Granny was a sturdy woman who bore a gentle smile. At ninety-three, her strength astounded Sharon and me.

We sat on leather furniture gathered around a generous coffee table. The Suurlands were hospitable and very anxious for us to sample one of Zeeland's specialties—bolus, a sweet confection smothered in sugar and cinnamon. It was accompanied by a thick brew of coffee, dark as chocolate syrup, to wash it down.

Sharon and I used the occasion to present our new friends with some keepsakes of our visit. Jan and Paulien, Benita and Ko, and Granny each received a Pewabic tile handcrafted in Detroit.(18) The image of a dove, embossed in clay, represented the peace that was won in 1945 along with the hope that peace would continue to prevail. There were smiles and nods of affirmation. Next, we presented them with two photographs; one depicted Roger, Andre, and Clay clad in their Army Air Corps uniforms alongside an A-20. It was taken stateside just before their deployment. The other photo was the last known picture taken of Andy in London weeks before he perished. He was sporting the silly, sparse mustache that he had razzed Ginny about. The hatless pose revealed Andy's legendary locks, neatly trimmed. Andre had gone to his grave unrecognizable and faceless, so I was eager to restore the countenance of the flyer they had buried. The sight of the photos drew them in, noticeably stirring their emotions. They studied them. Granny, especially, seemed in awe. All agreed with Sharon that Andy looked conspicuously older in his London photograph than he had in his pre-combat snapshot.

Paulie and Ko served up soup and sandwiches. As we enjoyed their hospitality visited, I observed a church tower just beyond the Suurland's garage. I stood up and pointed. I was jaw-dropping incredulous. Benita had mentioned in past correspondence that the church was located behind her parent's house. I imagined that it would be several blocks away. But it was, quite literally, in their backyard. This meant that Andy's original grave site was only steps away from the Suurland homestead.

Recently retired, Jan had joined forces with his brother in his earlier days to form a contracting business. Most impressively, he renovated his childhood home, doubling its living space. The original was built in 1770. I was bowled over at the idea that Jan's home was older than America by six years!

Ko and Benita surprised us with snaps of themselves taken by the sea. How fitting. The sea is an integral part of the Netherlands. It can be friend or foe. The Dutch have fought the sea, labored to contain the sea, and romped in the sea for centuries. And it was the sea that had delivered Andy to this place.

Jan proudly presented Sharon and me each with a package. For one who appeared to keep emotion in check, Jan surrendered his reserve and looked eager for us to open them. I could not think what the wrappings might hold. As we tore at the paper, Benita explained that it was the flag of their local authority. The flag bore seven stripes of alternating royal and white, curved, mimicking the motion of the sea. At its center was a coat of arms--a red lion figure rearing up out of the sea-stripes. Jan asked Benita to explain its symbolism. The motto of the coat of arms, "luctor et emergo", I wrestle and emerge, was the legacy of their ancestors. Regret tugged at my heart. Andy had wrestled with the sea and lost. He had succumbed to the power of the sea.

Jan's desire to please us touched me. He was proud to be a Dutchman, proud of his heritage. I was beginning to feel a part of them.

Granny pulled her granddaughter aside and spoke in muffled tones. In turn, Benita relayed to Sharon and me that Granny wanted us to know that she had sewn the mattress, pillow, and coverlet for Andre's coffin. Sharon and I looked into each other's eyes and burst into tears, simultaneously. Benita worried that they upset us right before the ceremony. "It's OK," I assured her. I was in search of the truth. Truth is what mattered. Once again, my suppositions were set straight. I had imagined that Andy's body was laid into an empty wooden casket, never dreaming that, instead, his body rested upon Marie's handiwork. The Suurlands were surprised as well. This was the first time they had ever heard the story. Perhaps Marie's part in Andy's burial was a memory she had tucked safely away, decades past, together with the ravages of war. But today, this fourth day of May, the day that the Dutch set aside to remember the war dead, Marie could retrieve it, bring it out into the light without fear of Nazi reprisal, and share it with her family and the family of the pilot she honored.

Marie was quick to point out that, as Ben's spouse, it was simply her job to prepare the burial cloths for each casket crafted by her husband, the town carpenter. Her humble admission did not diminish my gratitude. Care had been taken to procure a proper burial for 1Lt. Andre Vleghels, while his family back in America, unaware, began to wonder why they were not receiving his daily missives. Acting in our stead, the Dutch had supplied, in resource and talent, what Andy's own kin could not. Andre had been treated as one of their own. That was good enough for me.

The time had arrived to walk over to the church meeting hall where the ceremony was to take place. As we stepped across the cobblestones to the church, we were overjoyed at a marvelous sight. In honor of our visit, two flags flanked an iron gate that framed the stone church—the red, white, and blue stripes of the Netherlands to the left and Old Glory to the right. A stiff wind whipped at the flags, unfurling their colors. It was a grand display of Dutch goodwill. Our hearts were gladdened as we feverishly took turns swapping cameras and taking pictures.

The hall buzzed with the chatter of villagers arriving. Invited guests included the Suurland and van't Hof families, members of the city council, and representatives from the Dutch Reformed Church. The ceremony was hosted by Mayor Nuis. Television cameramen were clamoring for our attention. Dies came up to us in the midst of it, eager to introduce his family to us. I felt rude excusing ourselves because the T.V. news wanted to get their footage to meet their deadline. Frankly, I wanted them to get the story, so we cooperated.

In a remarkable demonstration of family unity and support, Dies had assembled a table of relatives. His parents, Pieter and Jo, his siblings, Gerrit, Janny, and Addy together with his wife, Niekie, and their four children, Inge, Iris, Pieter-Niek, and Dirk-Jan. The boys clowned for my camera lens. Of the children, only twelve-year-old Inge, the eldest, knew some English. But it did not seem to matter much. Everyone was enthusiastic and seemed happy to be there.

I held the matriarch and patriarch of the Oosdijk clan in great esteem. It was Jo's father, Dies van't Hof, who had happened upon André's body, half-submerged, along the sea dike during his morning rounds. Jo remained the lone survivor of Dies and Jans van't Hof's three children. She was battling cancer. Jo had undergone surgery and chemotherapy, but the cancer in her belly was terminal. Pieter was seated in a wheelchair. He had suffered a stroke five years before that left him paralyzed on one side. But here they both were, in spite of their infirmities, to represent Dies van't Hof and the part he played in the recovery of 1Lt. Andre J. Vleghels. They were an inspiration.

Considerate of his audience, Major Nuis preempted his remarks by explaining that, in deference to his American guests, he would begin in English for a time, followed by Dutch throughout his speech. He touched upon my letter to the mayor's office, Andre's final mission, and …

Then it was my turn. I felt humbled and privileged to address these representative citizens of Scherpenisse. I was living a dream, and yet it all seemed so impossible. Mayor Nuis had already given much of the history of the mission that claimed Andy, but I wanted the townspeople to know that our pilgrimage to Scherpenisse, Sharon's and mine, was no coincidence. Clearly, it was meant to be. I needed to tell them that their single act of human kindness, burying Andy with dignity, might seem like a small act, even insignificant. It was wartime, after all. Airmen falling from the sky had become usual. "But to Andre's family, an ocean away, anxiously awaiting word of his fate, it was a great act of compassion." I called out the name of each family member that Andy had left behind. It was at that point that I began to falter. Emotion choked off my words. Precariously, I continued. "Today, it consoles our hearts to know that the people of Scherpenisse were there, in our stead, to bury 1Lt Andre J. Vleghels with dignity. May God bless you and keep you in His care."

Then Sharon, Andre's very own, approached the podium to speak. She stood before the villagers, so overcome by a rush of emotion that she was unable to utter a word. My instinctive reaction was to go to her side, but I thought better of it. I decided it was important for her to face this hurdle on her own. I remained seated. At least a minute passed before Mayor Nuis joined her. It was enough; Sharon quelled her sobs. Once she got rolling, she offered some much-appreciated comic relief. She spoke of how her father had hoped for a boy, and her mother had hoped for Andy's wavy hair. As it turned out, neither got their wish.

On behalf of the people of Tholen (the island where Scherpenisse is located), Mayor Nuis presented each of us with a gift--a framed etching of Scherpenisse with the church being the most prominent structure, and all things Dutch—the fields, the dikes, and the windmills. In the foreground was the Oosterschelde, the body of water that had delivered Andy to them, our representatives in kind, the generous people who took on the role of a family.

Suddenly, the most difficult duty was upon us. It was time for Sharon and I to pay our respects at the site of Andy's first resting place, the very spot where his simple wooden coffin had been lowered into the ground so close to his birthplace nearly sixty years before. His plot was marked with a full-sized American flag staked across it. Like a knee-jerk response, a small shock surged through me at the sight of it. Though their action flew in the face of American decorum, I knew their intentions were pure. They were simply identifying the place where they had lain a soldier, and honored it with the flag of his country. It was a thoughtful gesture of recognition and distinction. Nothing more, nothing less.

Demonstrating great respect for our privacy, the crowd did not follow us. But I encouraged them to come out into the open. They humored me, but stopped at the top of the path. I turned and snapped their picture.

There was no escaping it; Sharon and I walked the path to Andy's abandoned grave site, just the two of us. I was avoiding it like ill-tasting medicine. But first, solemnity aside, I snapped a photo of Andy's former grave as our friends had marked it. Picture taken, I settled down and slipped my arm under Sharon's. We stood in silence and wept. I wondered what our parents, Andy's parents, thought of all this. Surely they were with us. God was in this place. Sharon whispered, "One day, we would all be together again."

Jan told us about the day the American military arrived to claim Andre. Just a pre-teen, he was stung with a bit of morbid curiosity. He, along with his dad, led the Army representatives to the site. However, they were not permitted to stay. The military representatives insisted upon carrying out their duties "by the book". But Ben outfoxed them, crept inside the church, and watched from a window. He later reported that, after they exhumed the body, they broke apart the wooden casket along with the cross, and tossed everything into the vacated tomb. I had the impression that the brusque actions of the military hurt Jan's sensibilities.

One task remained. The time had come to "hand over" the plaque. The colloquialism, "hand over", was foreign to me. It felt less than friendly. The people meant no disrespect, but every time I heard the phrase, I pictured a bandit, back in the days of the Old West, holding the stagecoach driver at gunpoint and demanding the payroll.

A few curious male locals with their bicycles stood in the shadows, taking in the festivities. I noticed them when we first arrived. They were still there as we posed for the cameras with the mayor. Several photo-journalists were giving us direction and clicking away. They fought the glare of the sunlight, maneuvering to get just the right angle as Sharon and I struggled to regain our composure. Poking fun, I teased, "This is like the paparazzi." Everyone roared. I guess that explains why, in the finished product, Sharon is smiling through her tears, and I am all teeth.

We moved inside the church tower where the formal presentation to the mayor was to take place. The only problem was that no one had explained the game plan to Sharon and me. We were caught unaware. People were chattering away in Dutch, their voices echoing and rising up the silo walls. Then, before we knew it, the chatter subsided, an awkward hesitation, and someone instructed me to hand over the plaque to the mayor. I am not sure if I saved the moment, but I did my inept best.

Once the hoopla was over, Mr. Bakx related to us that the church alderman wondered if we would like to see the lamp inside the church proper that President Roosevelt had given to their congregation to commemorate the occasion of his visit.

Surprises seemed perpetual. Though we were growing weary, we cordially accepted his gracious invitation. The alderman scrambled to locate the key and unlocked the massive interior door. I had the impression that keys held great significance for them if judging only by their size. They were big. We followed the alderman's lead down the center aisle, when he stopped, abruptly, and pointed, excitedly, toward the rafters. Roosevelt's gift was actually a brass chandelier that bore an inscription. Though many have claimed him, we were told, Roosevelt's roots were in Tholen. The surname itself means "from the rose fields". It was another example of Dutch hospitality, and we, its fortunate recipients.

At this point, Sharon and I had yet to check into our hotel, The Draak, located in nearby Bergen op Zoom. Niekie worked evenings in the kitchen there. She enjoyed the change of pace from the demands of family life, and welcomed the chance to socialize. In keeping with the prescribed itinerary, the Oosdijk family accompanied us. Everything they did, they did with a sense of joy. The children were clamoring to help. We apologized and laughed about our excessive baggage. Each child accepted a suitcase with no complaint.

Proud papa, Dies, encouraged his youngest, Dirk-Jan, to sing for us. He was known for his good singing voice. Dirk-Jan had the countenance of a cherub and an apple-cheeked smile. It took a little coaxing, but he honored his papa's request and entertained us with *America* from *West Side Story*. It was pretty remarkable to witness this Dutch boy singing a song about America with a Puerto Rican accent!

We had one hour to situate ourselves in our room and catch our breath before Dies would return to drive us back to St. Maartens-Dijk, the seat of government for the island of Tholen. Sharon and I were to be guests of the mayor for the open-air ceremony held to honor the dead of the Second World War. Unlike Americans, the Dutch had lost thousands of ordinary citizens at the hands of the Nazis. Ceremonies to commemorate the Dutch Day of Remembrance were repeated simultaneously at eight o'clock in the evening in cities throughout the Netherlands to observe this solemn day. Within steps of our hotel entrance at the edge of the Town Square, stood a memorial, roped-off, a wreath at the foot of a faux monument surrounded by flowers in remembrance. It would be the site of Bergen op Zoom's commemoration of the war dead.

Dusk had fallen, the sun resting at the horizon, when we reached our destination. The wind intensified the chill of the rapidly-falling temperature. It felt like thirty degrees.

We met up with the Suurlands in the parking lot. Benita handed Sharon and me each a large, colorful blossom to place at the monument at the appropriate time. Another consideration—we did not expect to be part of the ceremony. The cordial Perry Bakx was there to greet us and to make introductions. We all crowded in, three rows deep, at the bottom of the path leading up to the monument.

The monument, itself, was surprisingly understated by American standards--a large slab of steely-gray granite cut into the shape of Tholen engraved with the words, "Gedenk Allen Die Voor Onze Vrliheid Vielen". The flag on the pole behind it was at half-staff amidst a garden of exquisite apricot tulips. A garrison of seven soldiers stood at attention, three on each side, and one in the center.

I shoved my hands deep into my pockets and continually shifted my weight in a futile attempt to stave off the cold. As it grew closer to eight o'clock, more and more people began to arrive, slowly filling up the sizeable path that encircled the monument. Each person represented a personal and national history brought forth in a spirit of comradery until the circle closed. The citizens, of course, could not have realized it, but for me, it felt as though *they* were embracing us—this circle of humanity who had come together to honor and to remember. It was a beautiful, peaceful experience.

The pre-ceremony activity touched me so deeply, that it rendered the actual ceremony a bit anticlimactic. But precisely at eight o'clock, two minutes of silence were observed. No words were spoken, no speeches given. A choral group sang accompanied by a band of musicians, Dies' brother, Gerrit, among them, playing bass, added to the air of respect and solemnity. Mayor Nuis and his wife, Johanna, were the first to pay homage with the placing of a wreath at the monument. Sharon and I were very privileged to follow, in turn, then Benita and Ko, and Paulien and Granny, as well as several children. A military man himself, the Mayor remarked to us that he always insists upon children taking part in the ceremony of remembrance so that they will come to appreciate the consequences of war. We concurred. The grandparents of these young ones paid a ransom for the peace they enjoy today. Their freedoms, arrested by the Nazis, had to be won, exacting great sacrifice from the occupied and their liberators. We dispersed in silence.

The ever-accommodating Dies shuttled Sharon and me back to The Draak. Like beleaguered runners at the end of a marathon, our bodies were spent. The non-stop, emotionally-charged events of this fortuitous day brought us to our knees. We could barely put one foot in front of the other. We needed rest. We needed food. We needed drink. Dies left us in the care of one of Nieki's co-workers at the hotel restaurant and asked her to take good care of us. We collapsed into a booth—happy to be off of our feet. That night we dined on ravioli and salad, and shared a carafe of wine. I never enjoyed a meal more.

The next morning, Sharon and I shuffled through the breakfast buffet, still reeling from the avalanche of emotion of the previous day. I observed a few of the hotel guests, turning heads and staring. I shrugged it off, chalking it up to my imagination. In my morning fog, making food choices seemed beyond my ability. I nudged my tray past the clean dishes and flatware, when a stack of complimentary newspapers on a shelf above the fare caught my attention. I pulled one down. My jaw dropped open. There, on the front page of BN De Stem (The Voice), was a color photograph of Sharon, Mayor Nuis, myself, and the plaque! In disbelief and wide-eyed, I rushed over to show Sharon, already seated. I was flabbergasted, figuring that any coverage would be buried in the back pages. We agreed that the picture was good of the Mayor and the plaque.

Again Dies, fast becoming our personal chauffer, picked us up to bring us to his parents' home where most of his extended family members were gathered. I had mentioned to Dies that I would like to interview his father, Pieter. Americans made countless personal sacrifices for the war effort to be sure, but we did not know what it was like to live day-to-day in an occupied nation. I was eager to learn about Pieter's war experience. Dies had explained in one of his letters that Pieter was among the young men, eighteen and older, who was "recruited" to labor in a work camp in Germany on behalf of the Fuhrer.

Daughters, sons, and in-laws took time out of their day just to meet us. I had a sneaking suspicion that they had been gently coerced by the affable Addy, one of Dies' sisters. Everyone was welcoming. Hurried introductions were made before they excused themselves and scurried off to their day's work. Once again, we found ourselves gathered around a large table. This one was situated at one end of the main living area. Pieter's hospital bed was situated in a cozy corner at the opposite end of the room. Addy helped to care for him.

Addy could hardly contain her exuberance. If it was not for my persistent state of exhaustion, her enthusiasm would have been infectious. We were served the famous, and now familiar, *bolus* and coffee. The room hummed with hospitality and anticipation. We felt most welcome and comfortable. They quickly observed that Sharon and I were not "lighting up" like many of them, and apologized for the cigarette smoke that began to hang in the air. We assured them to go ahead, that we just were not used to it, especially with public smoking summarily discouraged in the States.

"We really shouldn't smoke, Dies interjected. It's a filthy habit."

Jo had a gift for each of us. Her eyes danced, reflecting her eagerness. It seemed she wanted to please us. We were forever opening gifts from these generous people. They would all serve as mementos of our special time together. Under the tissue paper and inside a cardboard tube was an etching of the villages on the isle of Tholen along with a message. I suspect that one of Jo's children prepared it on the computer. In part, it read: "We like to thank our liberators, in particular Andre J. Vleghels. The sacrifice he and his family made is unpayable. Thanks to heroes like him we can live in freedom now." More tears.

Dies took on the translating duties. He explained that Pieter had a tendency to show his emotions much more since he suffered his stroke. I did not want my interview to be too upsetting for Pieter, but Dies gave me the nod to go ahead.

Trying to be as gentle as possible, I posed my first question. "What was it like for you in Germany during the war?" Pieter responded with tears. I was sorry, and hesitant to continue, but again, Dies encouraged me to go on.

During the war, Pieter worked constructing high-powered electrical towers and stringing cable. Much of the time, they lived within the natural shelter of caves. Food was scarce. Pieter and his fellow prisoners routinely were ordered to forage the countryside in search of anything edible. Their captors were fed first. They were lucky if there was anything left for them. Mushrooms that sprouted from cave walls helped to abate their constant hunger. At one point, a knee injury turned into a reprieve for Pieter. He underwent surgery in a German hospital where he remained, recovering for eight weeks. The nursing staff was kind and treated him well. Pieter dreaded the day his injury healed.

The Americans arrived on the scene in early April of 1945. Pieter was free to go, but his liberators prevailed upon him and others to stay a while longer. The captors-turned-prisoners presented a dilemma for the Americans and they were in desperate need of guards. Naturally, Pieter wanted to return home more than anything, but he succumbed to their pleas and stayed on. He helped out for one month, when the war in Europe ended. I asked Pieter how it felt to have the tables turned. He replied, "It felt good to be the ones with the weapons."

As weary Nazi slaves streamed back to their beloved homelands, Pieter's father, Gerardus, pregnant with hope, went to the railway station every night and waited for his son. But, night after night, he returned home, dejected and alone. There was no trace of Pieter. After many weeks of nocturnal trips, Gerardus surrendered his evening ritual.

When Pieter finally left Germany he said, "It felt like victory." At last, counted among the liberated, he hitched rides on trains and wagons with a fraternity of ex-captives through France and Belgium. But once he reached his home, he found it abandoned. Pieter soon learned that his family was living with relatives in neighboring Bergen op Zoom. Gerardus must have thought he was seeing a ghost when he finally laid eyes on his son.

Celebratory parties sprang up throughout Holland, a coming together of the liberated Dutch. They popped the cork of national sublimation and released a great energy. It was at one of these gatherings that Pieter first met Jo. They married soon after. They were two among millions more world-wide who must have been anxious to replace the misery of war with memories of their own creation. Was it possible to inoculate future generations from man's obsession to control nations and strip them of their identities? One could only hope and pray.

Dies checked the time. We were due to meet the Suurlands at Strijenham, the sea-dike where Andy's body had washed up. Again, I was impressed that Pieter and Jo continued on our pilgrimage with us. We stood in front of the engineer house for the sluice repurposed as a summer house. Its current owners greeted us, cheerfully, and invited us to come in for a tour. We thanked them, but declined. Time was precious and I was growing anxious to climb the stairs of the dike. We were within steps of the spot where Dies van't Hof had pulled Andy's battered body to safety. I could wait no longer. The only thing that stood between me and sacred ground was a towering, grass-covered dike. As I stamped up its cement slabs wedged into its side, the dike sheltered me from the ever-present winds that slammed toward us from the west and the North Sea. When I reached the top, the brilliance of the sky and sun greeted me as if to say, "Welcome. You finally made it." In my own way, I realized Pieter's sentiment. It felt like victory.

When I looked to my right, I saw a sandy area that fanned out around the easterly corner known as Schelphoek (shell corner), Bank 25. Shells, driven from the sea, accumulated there forming piles. Dies' children scampered over the beach, bathed in sunlight, eager to collect them. Although some reports identified this as the location where Andy's body was recovered, Jo wanted us to know, most assuredly, that the precise location was further to the west, four barrels down. The barrels must have served as markers of some sort. They were equally spaced, so I assumed they measured distance. I walked along the ridge of the dike until I reached the fourth barrel. All of the adults stood in a line, looking out over the Oosterschelde. No one made a move to go any further. They were content to remain where they stood. I was not. The incline down to the water grew more precarious with my descent. I held out my arms from my sides, teetering on the mosaic of volcanic basalt, working to keep my balance. Dies followed me down, not knowing if he should try to steady me or let me be. There simply was no question that I could come all this way without immersing my hand into the waters of the Oosterschelde. And so I did.

The thing that amazed me more than anything was my emotional reaction. It took me completely by surprise. I expected to be tearful, but not a single tear did I shed. The experience lifted my spirit. I had accomplished what I had set out to do. The disturbing doubts of the past were washed away. The same waters that delivered Andy, delivered me. Serenity reigned.

Before moving on, I snapped off a sequence of pictures of the shoreline, adjusting the distance with my lens from far to near. Again, documentation was important. In addition, I wanted to take something back with me from this place as a keepsake, so I began searching for a few shells—one for Maurine. The children had already picked the sands clean of the larger shells. Pieter-Niek, grinning, proudly displayed his stash he held cradled in his jacket. Caught up in the moment, forgetting that Pieter did not understand English, I asked him if I could have a couple of the shells for Maurine as I reached out my hand. He understood and happily obliged.

Before we continued on our tour, we bade farewell to Pieter and Jo. I would never forget their great generosity. I knew it was unlikely that I would ever see them again.

Next we were headed for Wemeldinge, a town across the Oosterschelde from Scherpenisse. German soldiers had set up their antiaircraft guns there—the fire power that took aim at American fly boys on the evening of September 16, 1944.

We were out in the open, exposed to the elements, forever bracing ourselves against the relentless wind. As we surveyed our surroundings, Jan pointed out four locations where the guns had been strategically positioned. He had spoken at length with a man who lived at this location all of his life. In one case, he informed Jan, the Germans razed one of the homes to set up shop. They had a clear line of fire. They could pluck the bombers from the sky at will, like so many sitting ducks. However, an element of luck also existed. It was not an exact science. Planes were moving targets.

When we returned to the Suurlands, Jan was anxious to show us the nightly news that he recorded on the Day of Remembrance. Shock! Elation! I gasped and covered my gaping mouth when a likeness of Andy and Ginny appeared on the television screen, a copy of one of the photographs I had sent to Jan the year before. Sharon was on camera explaining the purpose of our trip and they showed the Mayor receiving the plaque. This was just too perfect. Unbelievable! I thought I would burst. Jan gave us a copy to take home. He also packaged up our gifts from Mayor Nuis for safe travel. It seemed like I was constantly saying, "Danku, danku. I was left reeling, trying to absorb it all.

It was time to drive over to Granny's. She was expecting us. Filing into her living room, Granny's home was neat and inviting. Sharon and I were amazed that she was able to maintain her own home so well at her advanced age. As so many others had, Granny also wanted to give us a little gift. We each received a silver spoon; mine was adorned with a windmill on the spoon and Amsterdam City Hall at the top of the handle. We thanked Granny for her thoughtfulness. "Danku."

Before I left home, I had decided that I would like to video tape an interview with Marie and Jan Suurland if they were willing. I wanted to garner as much information as possible from two people that witnessed Andy's burial and record it for our family. I asked Ko to help me set up my equipment. He had videotaped the ceremony, so I trusted his know-how. I tried my utmost to leave nothing to chance. I had prepared myself with a cursory lesson, charged the batteries, brought extra batteries, but still I worried that, somehow, I would overlook something important, and this once-in-a-lifetime opportunity would slip through my fingers. Ko served as my second head in the "two heads are better than one" theory. He also agreed to be my test subject. A good-natured man-child, Ko, entertained me with his rendition of Woody Woodpecker—"Aah-ha-ha, aah-ha-ha, ah-ah-ah-ah-ah! Ko's antics allayed my paranoia, slightly.

Granny and I sat across from each other at a round table covered with a beautiful cloth. She wanted Benita to let us know that she had made it. The open cut work was hand-stitched, intricate. We praised her ability. It was quite remarkable.

Yet again, I prevailed upon Benita to serve as translator for my questions and Granny's responses. It was a tedious process. I felt uneasy. I had no time to prepare a list of questions, but I did have a fairly intimate knowledge of my subject matter, having spent more than two years doing research. I had no choice but to pose my questions "off the cuff". My brain was mush. I wondered how to begin. But I persisted.

Marie Braal-Suurland explained that it was her husband, Ben, who taught her how to make the mattress for a casket and how to fill the blanket with cur lies to make it puff up.

I asked what kind of day it was, the day that Andre was buried. Who was present? Granny remembered it being a sunny day. She and Jan were there along with a few others. But when it came time to lower the casket into the ground, they were told to leave by the military police. Jan Wondergem took over from there.

Daily life during the occupation was busy for Marie. She was mother to five young children, the youngest about two years-old. It was a scary time because of the flying bombs (V-1 rockets). They made a lot of noise and some came down in a neighboring village. When they heard them overhead, Marie would gather up her children and find shelter. It was a sad time.

Jan had mentioned earlier that there were Armenians in the area during the occupation, so I asked about them. The Armenians were a conquered Russian people who were enlisted by the Germans to help them maintain order. They were friendly enough and never gave them any trouble. A man from a nearby town assisted Ben with his carpentry work. Each day he would travel to Scherpenisse, and frequently, he would bring along some Armenians for company. Jan, who was able to follow my line of questioning, chimed in, "They were the kind of people you could have a drink with."

The few families that lived in Scherpenisse were self-sustaining. They had cows for milk, but they rode their bicycles to St. Maartens-Dijk for food. It was impossible to plant crops on their land due to the continuous state of flooding.

I wanted to hear about the day when liberation finally came. Their section of Holland, the low country, was the first to be liberated in October of 1944, about six weeks after Andy's final mission. They felt a "lot of happiness," but there was no money to host a proper celebration. About a year later, they held a festival.

My Sister's Father

Ben Suurland did not like to talk about his brief stint in the Dutch Army before Holland surrendered. He had served in communications. One day, as he was riding in a horse-drawn wagon, he was shot at when the Germans strafed the area. Ben escaped physical injury, but he feared the German soldiers after that.

I asked about the rebuilding after the war. For Ben, the opening of the sluices and subsequent flooding of the land transformed austerity into prosperity. He experienced a business boom due to the many homes and other buildings in need of restoration.

Jan suggested that we move into the kitchen for his interview. I quickly agreed because others were conversing in the living room, which made it difficult to focus. Jan seemed intent. I sensed that he wanted to do a good job. He folded his large hands in front of him on the kitchen table.

I began by asking what the war was like for Jan as a child. For the most part, he testified, "It was not too bad." But at first, when the townspeople were evacuated from Scherpenisse, they were housed in the town of Gorichem about 100 km away, across from a German outpost for seven weeks. The children felt frightened during this time, because they sensed their parents' fear. No one had any idea what would happen to them.

As it turned out, the Suurland family was permitted to return to Scherpenisse solely because Ben, a constructor, as Benita translated, could perform a service. Only a smattering of villagers returned--fewer than six families. Most of the others operated the sluices. The rest were relocated; the men sent off to Germany as prisoners, forced to toil in labor camps.

Since Andy was the only soldier to be interred in Scherpenisse, Jan explained that his recovery and burial in their churchyard had "a big impact on the villagers and caused quite a stir." They understood why Andy was there, but out of fear of reprisals, they kept very quiet about it. Their mayor had ordered Ben Suurland to build a casket for Andre. However, the mayor had been handpicked by the Germans, so they had no way of knowing, for sure, if the order was an independent decision on the part of the mayor, or if he was acting upon a direct command from their occupiers. Furthermore, it was not clear to them if the mayor was sympathetic to the Nazi cause. In light of the tenuous situation, they decided that prudence demanded silence.

Due to the flooded countryside, he believed the recovery team--Ben Suurland, along with de Graaf, a reserve policeman and gravedigger, Wondergem of the military police, and Bollier, the owner of the boat, traveled to the sea-dike where Andre's body lay. They would need the strength of several men to lift Andre into the boat. He had been in the water for nine days. His body was swollen and heavy with salt water. A larger than average casket would be required. Ben would have to take this into account.

My brain went stagnant. No more questions came to mind, so I ended my interview with Jan by asking him if there was anything that he would like to add about the story of Andre. Jan became restless in his chair, shifting. He said that the townspeople have never forgotten Andre, though they did not know him by name. From time to time, they would remark, "Remember the English pilot." (At the time that Andy's body was recovered, there was some confusion as to whether he was an Englishman or an American.) Jan's feelings began to surface. He stalled to subdue them. He took a gulp of water from the glass next to him. He began to talk about the day he received my letter. "It was a big surprise for him, a big experience for him," Benita translated. For the first time Jan learned the name of the American pilot and he read about the family who mourned him. "It made a world of difference for me." Jan's expression underscored his words.

I managed a faint thank you, my voice faltering. They had not forgotten Andre. What he had done mattered to them, still. Jan nodded in kind.

The culmination of our stay came in the form of a celebratory dinner at a restaurant a few blocks away. Life felt easy here in Schrepenisse… church, home, eatery so close-by. No need to drive and fight the traffic.

We learned from Benita that Jan had renovated the restaurant in recent years. Jan did not seek out the positive comments that followed, but he seemed proud of his work just the same. The nine of us were ushered to a sizable back room. It felt like our own private party. I welcomed the opportunity to just kick back and enjoy each other's company. There were some questions about America and our families. Naturally, many of their impressions of Americans came from our exported television shows and films. Were city streets like those depicted on *Hill Street Blues*? I moaned when I heard they had seen *Jerry Springer*! Ugh!

Marie, the matriarch, watched over us from the head of the table. I wish I could have read her mind. She looked content and happy over the past couple of days. I could tell by her little smile and the gleam in her eyes. Earlier, when we paused in front of her husband Ben's grave, she grew pensive and said she wished Ben could have joined in the commemorations. It gave me great pleasure that Sharon and I were able to personally thank her for her part and Ben's part in Andy's burial. In all of her wildest dreams, I am certain that Marie could never have anticipated this day. It truly was a blessing, a little miracle, for all of us to cherish.

At the end of a very satisfying meal, Ko wanted to know, "Is there ice cream for the children?" We laughed in unison.

The time had come to part with the Suurlands; next morning, Dies and family planned to escort us to the highway in the direction of Amsterdam. I insisted on one last photo before we parted. We never had a chance to take a picture of the beautiful banner that Benita and Ko had so painstakingly made. So, in the spirit of fun and friendship, Jan, Pauli, Ko, Benita, Dies and Niekie lined up, and held up the bed sheet WELKOM to their chins. It seemed a fitting close to an unbelievable two days.

Come morning, the Oosdijk family arrived at our hotel, on time, as promised. I reviewed our route to Amsterdam with Dies. Everyone helped load up our car with our bulging, gift-laden baggage. Our time together was running out, quicker than we wished. It was hard to say good-bye. Pieter-Niek and Dies exchanged some words in Dutch. Then Pieter-Niek's face became contorted and I saw his tears. He buried his face in his dad's jacket. I was very surprised that an eight-year-old could feel so strongly, so quickly. I melted. Then I remembered that I still had a couple of American flags, the kind stapled to sticks. I dug them out from my suitcase and handed them to the boys. Their faces broke into grins. We could see two American flags dancing in the back window as we followed the Oosdijk family to a gas station by the highway. Our hearts were aching, but as the driver, I had to keep my wits about me. We pulled into the station to top off our tank. Dies made sure I was pumping auto diesel, not truck diesel, and cautioned me not to mix them up, or I would ruin the engine. Sharon was in tears and Dies gave her one last hug. We departed with the hope that, one day, we would meet again.

All who shall hereafter live in freedom will be here reminded
that to these men and their comrades
we owe a debt to be paid with grateful remembrance of their sacrifice
and with the high resolve that
the cause for which they died shall live eternally.

American Military Cemetery Hamm, Luxembourg
General Dwight D. Eisenhower

Chapter Seven
Hamm, Luxembourg

May 10, 2001

Pulling into the nearly empty parking lot at the American Military Cemetery in Luxembourg felt surreal. Cognitively, I knew I was there, but my brain had not yet convinced the rest of my body. So many springs had come and gone since Andre's remains were first laid to rest in Hamm's glade. I should be crying, I thought. But the tears were not ready to come. I had to find my bearings, force myself to be present. I could barely feel the ground beneath my feet.

Sharon and I had been anxious about where we would find flowers for Andy's grave. How could we pay our respects for the first time in our lives, empty-handed? We had spent the night in the tiny provincial town of Durbuy in the middle of Belgium--the Walloon half of the small bilingual country. It really was the first stop where we had a chance to take a breath, and I razzed Sharon about it. By nature, she never wants to miss a thing—a trait, I am convinced, marks her as a true Vleghels. Somehow, I had agreed to cover nine cities in fourteen days! I decided to christen Sharon "Little Patton", marching through Europe at breakneck speed. Though a lovely respite, Durbuy did not have a single shop that sold fresh flowers; I had learned that the cemetery did not sell flowers either. Nonetheless, I held this notion, a premonition, that we would find a market attached to a modern fuel stop on our way to Hamm, the section of Luxembourg City where the cemetery is situated. I could even picture it in my mind. Was I going daft? Was I being intuitive or delusional? I wondered. It turned out to be a small miracle, because, just as our gas gauge tipped toward empty, we spotted a fuel oasis along the highway, still under construction. Sure enough, there was a mini-mart attached to it that sold flowers! I was astounded. It made a bona fide believer out of me.

Renée Schloesser, a member of US Veterans Friends Luxembourg, had generously offered to let Sharon and I board in her "American Room" for our two-night stay. We arranged to meet her, along with her fellow members and the assistant superintendent of the cemetery, about 11:30 AM. (I had made several frantic calls to contact her the night before in order to make a final confirmation.) Renée calculated that our trip should take about two hours. She had forgotten about the road construction en route, however. We did not arrive until after noon. I felt guilty that we had kept our hosts waiting. They had gone to so much trouble for us. I reverted back to my wave and beep of my horn to reassure them that Andre's family had arrived. Sharon, bouquet in hand, stopped in her steps. The stark reality of approaching the cemetery where her father was buried began to crack her stoic façade. My hope was that the experience would be liberating. Today, once and for all, we were confronting decades of secrecy and all the shadows it cast.

I could see our welcoming party between the bars of the stately wrought iron entrance gate, opened wide. Opposing gilded bronze eagles stood atop pillar-perches that anchored it as if they served as a look-out, standing guard for the fallen. Gilded laurel wreaths, the ancient award for valor, adorned each section of the gate. The representatives waited, in readiness, on the steps of the visitor's building like stalwarts—patient and reverent, as we, tentative, made our way toward them. I was eager to make Renée's acquaintance after our many precursory e-mails, but it paled in comparison to the daunting purpose of our visit. The president of USVF, Constant Goergen, Philippe, and Josée rounded out the rest of the delegation. Constant stepped forward and read some prepared remarks about André… something about his bravery and their gratitude. Assistant Superintendent, Gerard Flambert, explained that they had marked Andre's grave with an American flag and the flag of Luxembourg. Also, for the sake of picture-taking, they filled-in the engraving on Andre's marble cross with sands from the beaches of Normandy mixed with gold coloring. He led the solemn procession. I fell in behind Sharon. When we reached Plot E, Row 7, Grave 65, Andy's child, now fifty-six, bent at her father's cross and placed her floral bouquet at its foot. Constant followed in kind with a spray of lilies.

Renée asked if she could say a prayer.

"Yes, please."

She recited the 23rd Psalm, *The Good Shepherd*.

"In meadows of green grass he lets me lie" was salve to my aching soul. I kept imagining Andy's spirit there, standing above his own grave, between us, shoulder to shoulder.

Then, sweet Renée played a tape recording of a poem, *Do We Remember?* recited by a young girl with a voice as fresh as Springtime. A choir sang angelic backup. "They were ordinary people like us," she lamented, "but we call them great heroes. When we think of all they did for us--now they rest far from home in our fields. Do we remember them?" That finished us.

Despite my sorrow, the opportunity to pray for Andy at his final resting place brought serenity. It may have taken more than half a century, but we finally made it to Andy's graveside, Sharon and me. It felt right. We had come a long way from the two young sisters rummaging through our mother's treasure trove of memories. At long last, our old reality was morphing into a new one; I embraced it, wholeheartedly. It all seemed so impossible, and yet, here we were, standing on hallowed ground dedicated to over five thousand American soldiers like Andy. As if on cue, the carillon filled the cemetery with the sound of taps. *"Day is done, gone the sun... God is nigh."* I thanked Him for this unimaginable blessing. It was as if everything and everyone came together at precisely the right moment. It reaffirmed my faith in God and man.

Before we knew it, Mr. Flambert had us posing for pictures for his Polaroid, on our knees, behind Andy's cross. Choked with grief, we certainly were not ready for it. It seemed like a lot to expect just then--no time to savor the moment or recover from it, but we did our best to oblige our very gracious hosts.

With ceremony concluded, we headed for the chapel. Some time to reflect was most welcome. Above the chapel entrance was written: HERE IS ENSHRINED THE MEMORY OF VALOR AND SACRIFICE. Above it stood a magnificent sculpture of the Angel of Peace, twenty-three feet tall, wrought from Swedish Orchid Red granite. The angel's left hand was raised in blessing. His right hand held a laurel wreath. The sun, super-imposed by a dove, hovered above the tip of the angel's wings. Inside, the altar, flanked by two American flags, bore the prayer from St. John X, 28: I GIVE UNTO THEM ETERNAL LIFE AND THEY SHALL NEVER PERISH. It represented a bit of Andy's native country--its marble was Bleu Belg mined in southern Belgium. On the mosaic floor in front of the altar laid a generous wreath of red Gerber daisies in memoriam.

The exterior theme of an angel, God's messenger, extended to the interior. I threw back my head, straining to take in a sublime mosaic, high above us on the ceiling. It depicted four angels, arms outstretched against a golden sun, holding up a dove at its center. Their message followed the perimeter of the circle:

IN PROUD AND GRATEFUL MEMORY OF THOSE MEN OF THE ARMED SERVICES OF THE UNITED STATES OF AMERICA WHO IN THIS REGION AND IN THE SKIES ABOVE IT ENDURED ALL AND GAVE ALL THAT JUSTICE AMONG NATIONS MIGHT PREVAIL AND THAT MANKIND MIGHT ENJOY FREEDOM AND INHERIT PEACE.

Lastly, we stopped at the Visitor's Office where Mr. Flambert presented each of us with a notebook of information about the cemetery, including the photos he had just taken of Sharon and me. We decided that we would return the following day, to spend some leisurely time amongst the crosses and Stars of David. Who knew if we would ever return?

Everyone was remarking about the mild weather we were all enjoying. April had been cold and rainy, and only the week before, a little snow fell. It was just another stunning example of our good fortune. It seemed that everything fell into place and every occasion was fortuitous.

We followed Renée to Josée's house where we deposited our car. She wanted to taxi us around Luxembourg to see various memorials dedicated to American freedom fighters. It was only then that we learned of Renée's surreptitious identity. She was a reporter, it turned out, for a small Catholic paper, the *Letzeburger Sonndesblad*. Sharon and I piled into the back seat. Renée handed us a tape recorder and a microphone, and asked us to "tell our story" while she drove. Sharon and I exchanged dumbfounded glances. Renée said Luxembourgers loved to read the personal accounts of their liberators, especially if the patrons, themselves, were survivors of the Second World War. By the time we reached the first of several stops, climbing out of the car was like stepping off a raucous amusement park ride. Renée's speedy driving, coupled with the winding roads and our gut-wrenching testimony left my stomach in my throat and my head, whirling.

Despite a half century plus since the Armistice, Luxembourg remains a grateful nation and continues to express her gratitude at every turn. Her citizens were more than willing to erect numerous memorials to honor the American G.I. and welcome their families with open arms. In fact, there is a memorial entitled, The American G.I.--an American soldier, standing in fatigues atop a pedestal of rock, opposite women and children gathered at a window, waving a flag in celebration of their liberation. They have not forgotten how close they had come to falling to Nazi tyranny.

As we prepared to retire for the night on Friday, Renée asked if we would be interested in attending a Mass for the Military to be held the following morning at the Cathedral of Our Lady of Luxembourg. It would be one of a series of masses offered over a fortnight, each Mass with a particular intention. (19) Sharon and I were pleased that we had the opportunity to attend.

Renée showed kindness and consideration towards us with little niceties—a snack of bottled water and an apple, left on the dresser, some booklets about Luxembourg and a covered ceramic dish as a keepsake. We presented her with our signature Pewabic tile. She was thrilled. She had a collection of tiles.

Saturday morning over breakfast, Renée told us of her uncle who was executed by the Nazis for refusing to join their ranks. I had noticed a framed article about him hanging on a wall in her "American Room". She also had one letter written by him that she treasured. I was left to wonder what I would have done in like circumstances.

We chattered in the car on the way to the cathedral as Renée highlighted points of interest. Every so often, a brightly painted cow would catch our eye, each, part of an exhibit. Renée, forever congenial and enthusiastic, led the way to the terrace of the cathedral. We entered through the less elaborate western portal dedicated to Our Lady. Renée arranged for us to be seated in the choir loft, a wonderful vantage point from which to observe all the festivities and to take photographs as well. We squeezed by the band members, making our way to the front pew. Though I could not understand her words, I had the impression that Renée let everyone know that she was entertaining American guests. Whenever we passed by, people seemed to nod in acknowledgement.

Military personnel flanked the altar. Assuming it would be a Mass of Remembrance, I was preparing myself to be met with mournful, somber hymns. But, with the stroke of the choirmaster's baton, it became abundantly clear that we were in for a treat. The tempo was quick, the voices, cheerful, rising strong, up the vast cathedral walls. The choirmaster bobbed and weaved with all the skill of a prize fighter. His enthusiasm was catching. I could not take my eyes off of him.

It is confounding to describe my mood, because so many emotions flooded me, all at once. I felt as though I was halfway to heaven. It all seemed so perfect. It was like I had been waiting for this moment all of my life. Here, today, at this glorious cathedral in Luxembourg, I could pray for the souls of Andy, Ginny, and Egon, at the same concelebrated Mass. It really was a dream that I had never dared to dream.

At Communion time, Renée signaled to us to move out. We filed out to a thundering rendition of *Amen*. I wished we could have stayed longer, but Renee had plans to take us on a tour of the infamous rock fortifications of Old Luxembourg City. Afterwards, however, we returned to the cathedral's vestibule to light vigils for Andy and Ginny and Egon, in their memory.

Later in the afternoon, we stopped in at the Alfa for a drink. The hotel bore historical significance. General Patton and his cohorts spent Christmas of 1944 at the Alfa. It served as their headquarters during the Battle of the Bulge campaign, the Third

Reich's last stand, the final blow that sent them collapsing like dominoes and brought victory to the Allied Forces in Europe.

Renée explained that the hotel had in its possession a large photograph of their revered Christmas guests which frequently hung on a wall in the restaurant area. But when she could not locate it, she approached a server to inquire, explaining about her American visitors. Immediately, the gentleman disappeared and returned with the sizable framed photograph in question. He even went to the trouble of setting it on an easel and placing it, just right, so the light would not cast a glare. I was beginning to feel embarrassed by the extremes he entertained simply to please us. But, yet again, it was testament to the deep-seated regard Luxembourgers hold for their liberators, and, that, was touching.

That evening, Renée and Sharon and I enjoyed a relaxing meal, just the three of us. It gave Sharon and myself a chance to decompress, as though we had been aboard a time machine these last couple of weeks, a whirlwind journey to the past. As we left the restaurant, Renée stopped to introduce us to one of the servers that she knew. He did not speak English, but he nodded, knowingly, kindness in his eyes and a little grin on his face. I swear his grin was like Andy's.

Come morning, we bid Renée and Luxembourg farewell. As a final courtesy, Renee agreed to assume her familiar role. One last time, she led the way and pointed us in the right direction. We followed her through her tidy neighborhood of pastel stucco to the highway, feeling blessed that our lives had crossed.

Men of the 416th Bomb Group-(L-R) Ed Renth, Debby and others, Kinston, North Carolina, 1999.

The boat used to transport Andre's body from Poortvliet to Scherpenisse, the Netherlands. (L-R) Sgt.-Major MP Jan Wondergem, son, Jackie, and others during the occupation.

Andre's coffin and bier made by Benjamin Suurland, adorned with flowers by the townspeople, September 26, 1944.

(L-R) Maurine and Debby with the memorial plaque of thanksgiving, Spring, 2001.

Welkom banner made by Benita and Ko- (L-R) Ko Berkhout, Jan Suurland, Dies Oosdijk, Niekie Oosdijk, Pauli Suurland, Benita Suurland, May 5, 2001.

The Dies van't Hof family at the site of their home and pumping station, WW II.

The pumping station, (L-R) Sharon, Jo, daughter of Dies van't Hof, Pieter Oosdijk, Debby, Poortvliet.

Gathered around Marie's table for an interview, (L-R) Debby, Benita, and Marie Suurland, May 4, 2001.

Schelphoek (Shellcorner), the location of Andre's recovery.

At last—Debby touches the waters that delivered Andre.

Finally, Sharon places flowers at her father's grave, Hamm, Luxembourg, May 2001, fifty-seven years after Andre perished.

Jan and Pauli Suurland honored Andre by visiting his grave, August 2001.

NOTATION

*On April 22, 2002, Ko and Benita became the happy parents
of a baby girl.
They baptized her, Andrea Benita, in honor of
1LT Andre J. Vleghels USAAF.*

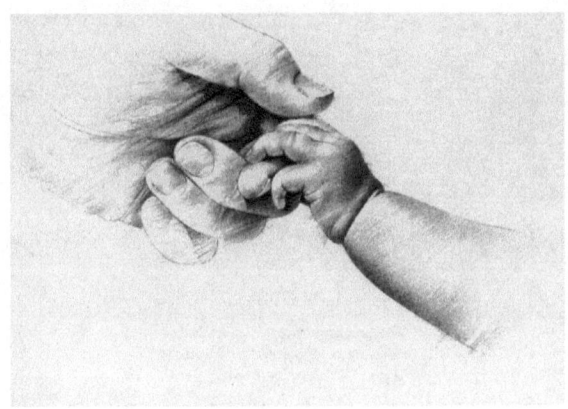

My Sister's Father

EPILOGUE

John Gray, author of the book, <u>Men are from Mars, Women are from Venus</u>, once said that when a parent is unable to express pain, their child will absorb it. I can attest that Gray's hypothesis held true for me. Numerous times during the writing of this memoir, I experienced my mother's pain on a very intense, intimate level. No matter how many times I have related the story, dissected the story, it has continually moved me to tears.

The gift I attempted to give to my mother was the permission to grieve, to deal with her feelings, honestly. Like all of us, she was influenced, controlled, by the social mores of her generation when emotions were more often squelched than expressed, and privacy was staunchly protected. Ironically, however, the attempt to subjugate her feelings only inflicted further pain.

And although mom kept her comments to a minimum where Andy was concerned, I think I realized a measure of success in my endeavor. In a phone conversation just prior to her death, I told mom of a friend's response when I related the story of Andy and Ginny. My friend had said, "They would just have to put me away." Mom laughed. I was the one stifling sobs.

Ginny's faith had sustained her. Her family had sustained her. Andy's daughter had sustained her. Egon had sustained her. And in the twilight of her life, through Andy's written legacy, she revisited the turbulent, sweet days of her past as a *soldier's wife. Before too long in the early hours of July 23, 1998, God called her back to Him, to Andy, and to Egon. I suspect it seemed like only yesterday when she was frying eggs for her groom in their one-room cottage on those dreaded hotplates.*

This time, it was my mother who left the bedside letter at her parting. It became her gift to us that inspired my search. I have come to believe that in some way I am carrying out a portion of God's plan for me. This realization has been confirmed, again and again, as events began to unfold before me and one discovery spawned another.

Of course, it was not a case of natural combustion. My search required consistent effort and diligence, but once it was set in motion, I never really encountered any major roadblocks. The timing of it seemed right. I am convinced that it was all meant to be and that I acted in concert with God in bringing the life and death of Andre Joseph Vleghels full circle. If it was not so, I believe my journey would never have materialized. As it is, I am left in a state of peace, joy, wonder, and always, gratitude. Our family is whole. It is finished.

BIBLIOGRAPHY

Alton Glenn Miller "n.d." Retrieved from http://glennmiller.org.

Childers, Thomas (1995) *Wings of Morning*, Reading, Massachusetts Addison-Wesley Publishing Company.

Conte, Ralph (2001) *Attack Bombers--We Need You!* Nashville, Tennessee: JM Press.

Encyclopedia of Detroit, Pewabic Pottery "n.d." Retrieved from httpp://detroithistorical.org.

Forgy, Jack (2003), Mail and Soldier Morale, *The Star,* #29, pp. 10-11.

Gottsegen, Ted "n.d." Benny Goodman (1909-1986). Retrieved from http://redhotjazz.com.

Island Ikaria—The Online Guide "n.d." The Myth of Daedalus & Icarus, Retrieved from http://island-ikaria.com.

Mesko, Jim (1994) *A-20 Havoc in action*, Carrollton, Texas: Squadron/Signal Publications, Inc.

North American B-25B "Mitchell" "n.d." Retrieved from http://wpafb.af.mil.

Ryan, Cornelius (1974) *A Bridge Too Far*. New York, New York: Simon & Schuster.

Severo, Richard "n.d." Dorothy Lamour: 1914-1996. Retrieved from http://kcmetro.cc.mo.us.

USAF Museum History—Cessna UC-78B "Bobcat" "n.d." Retrieved from htpp://wpafb.af.mil.

USAF Museum History—WWII History AAF Report, Women's Army Corps. "n.d." Retrieved from http://wpafb.af.mil.

Van Schaack, "n.d." Drawings of Famous Hollywood Landmarks, Retrieved from http://historichollywood.biz.

World War II Training, Primary Flying School "n.d." Retrieved from http://wpafb.af.mil.

WWII Combat Europe V-1 "Buzz Bomb", "n.d." Retrieved from http://wpafb.af.mil.

CITATIONS

1. Established in 1939, the primary flying schools pre-empted the attack on Pearl Harbor and bolstered America's preparedness to enter the war in 1941. The schools were operated by civilian companies under contract with the Army Air Corps. Each cadet received sixty hours of flight training over the course of nine weeks by civilian instructors. p.26

2. The USO, United Service Organization, was chartered by congress as a non-profit charitable corporation whose mission was to provide morale, welfare, and recreational services to uniformed military personnel. As Andy testifies, they sponsored dances for soldiers across America. Entertainers often toured with the USO to cheer the troops and give them a respite from intense training exercise in the United Sates or the stress of combat overseas. p.29

3. You could "dance-til-dawn" at the Macambo, a Mexican themed hot-spot on Sunset Strip. Frequented by stars like Frank Sinatra and Judy Garland, it featured big bands and big birds. p.31

4. Known for its elaborate stage productions, the Earl Carroll Theater was unique and extravagant to any other standard. They boasted a main stage with a sixty-foot-wide double revolving turntable along with three swings could be lowered

from the ceiling, a rain-making machine, revolving staircase, and elevator. p.31

5. Film star Dorothy Lamour, a favorite American GI pin-up girl, was best known for her "road" pictures with Bing Crosby and Bob Hope. She popularized the sarong, her trademark. p. 33

6. Glenn Miller, the world-renowned trombonist and band leader, began his rise to fame in the thirties after he moved to New York City and began to work with several bands. He helped the Dorsey brothers as well as Ray Noble form Big Bands before venturing out to form his own orchestra in 1939. His unique blend of jazz, swing, and improvisation coupled with frequent radio broadcasts gave rise to his popularity. But in 1942, at age 38 and at the height of his career, he made the decision to contribute to the war effort by becoming part of the Army Specialist Corps. His mission was twofold: to boost troop morale through his live performances and to modernize military music. Along with his fifty-member dance band, they followed the troops overseas to England, touring bases and performing radio broadcasts. p.38

7. WAAC stood for Women's Army Auxiliary Corps. In anticipation of enemy attacks on the United States, women were enlisted to operate listening posts and other aircraft services. The first six thousand women were so successful that by the summer of 1943, auxiliary was dropped from the name and the organization was assigned to the Army, becoming the Women's Army Corps (WAC). Once the Air Force was permitted to do their own recruiting, the organization evolved

into the Women's Air Force Service Pilots (WASP). WASP pilot graduates ferried aircraft, towed targets for gunnery, and served as instrument instructors. By replacing men in these various capacities, more men were made available for combat. p.42

8. The Cessna "Bobcat", designated AT-17, was a fabric-covered craft made of wood and tubular steel. It proved to be a reliable trainer and easy to fly. Cessna produced 4,600 of them by war's end for the Air Corps. Pilots dubbed it the "Bamboo Bomber". p.47

9. The B-25B or Mitchell was a medium bomber, the type flown by General Doolittle in the Tokyo Raid of 1942. It was slightly larger than an A-20 Havoc and widely used during World War II. p.56

10. Selfridge Field is a military airfield about twenty miles north of Detroit. p.61

11. The Link Trainer, the first flight simulator, was used as a training device to teach instrument flying or to aid a pilot in transitioning to a different plane. The trainer, a generic mockup of an airplane cockpit with working controls and instruments, responded to the trainee's actions as if it were in flight. The use of the link trainer saved the Air Corps time and money in personnel and aircraft, making it a highly efficient and economical aspect of pilot training. p.62

12. Pinks were the lighter-colored trousers that were worn with the winter uniform along with a green blouse and khaki shirt. p.70

13. Wasserman was a pre-nuptial test for syphilis, required by law. p.86

14. Credited with being the driving force that gave birth to the "Swing Era", it was apparent from the age of twelve when Benny Goodman first picked up a clarinet, that he was exceptional. Discovered by bandleader, Ben Pollack, Goodman made his first recordings with him in 1926 at age seventeen. Goodman later became a popular freelancer in New York City which was fast becoming a musical Mecca. He corroborated with the Dorsey brothers and in 1934 formed his first big band. p.136

15. "Swoonatra" was coined in the early forties when Frank Sinatra became all the rage, especially among the "bobby-soxers". He had previously sung with the Tommy Dorsey Orchestra before going solo in 1942. He was classified 4-F due to a punctured eardrum. *Life The Way We Were, Life Books, Time*, Inc. p.208

16. Von Zangen was ordered to evacuate his troops from northern Belgium via the Breskens-to-Flushing (Vlissigan) crossing and march east until they reached the mainland north of Antwerp, a vital port. (A Bridge Too Far, pp. 58-59). p. 226

17. The German report, asserting that three 88 mm Flak guns were employed, contradicted what Willard Land had logged, namely, that 105 mm shells were fired at them on the Bergen op Zoom mission. p.355

18. Pewabic Pottery, a Detroit invention, was begun in 1903 by Mary Chase Perry and partner, Horace Caulkins, at the height of the Arts and Crafts movement in America. Their colorful tiles and vessels adorn private homes as well as public buildings across America. It is Michigan's only historical pottery. p.391

19. The Octave is a religious observance held each year beginning the third Sunday after Easter, calling the faithful to venerate the miraculous image of the Consolation of the Afflicted. p.422

My Sister's Father

ABOUT THE AUTHOR

A Michigan native, Debby Fricke Smith was born post Second World War, when families wanted to put the war of the century behind them and get on with living. She grew up in a suburb of Detroit, part of the post-war building furor, where she remained, married, and raised two children. In 2008, she and her husband joined their family in Charlottesville, Virginia where they enjoy family celebrations and two grandchildren.

It is her enduring faithfulness to family that led her to set out on a personal journey of discovery and resolution, culminating in a pilgrimage to Europe and *My Sister's Father*.

www.ingramcontent.com/pod-product-compliance
Lightning Source LLC
Chambersburg PA
CBHW030333230426
43661CB00032B/1395/J